Praise for *Revolution of Jew. How to Revive* Ruakh *in Your Spiritual Life, Transform Your Synagogue & Inspire Your Jewish Community*

"Rabbi B and Ellen Frankel have opened their hearts, directed their minds, and shared their soulfulness so that a path long covered is again revealed! We are invited to dance our liberation, and the ancient incense of Torah ascends through their wondrous insights."

—**Rabbi Bradley Shavit Artson**, dean, Ziegler School of Rabbinic Studies; vice president, American Jewish University; author, *Passing Life's Tests: Spiritual Reflections on The Trial of Abraham, the Binding of Isaac*

"From radical hospitality, to synaguides, to under-constructionists, this book made me think about the language we use in Jewish life today and the way it can revive or dilute human spirit.... An intimate portrait of synagogue life ... to help readers discover and re-discover the wonder of Judaism."

—**Dr. Erica Brown**, author, *Inspired Jewish Leadership: Practical Approaches to Building Strong Communities* and *Spiritual Boredom: Rediscovering the Wonder of Judaism*

"Read this extremely interesting and impressive book.... It offers hope, courage and inspiration to all who long to find or renew a congregation with spirit, learning, art, sustainability and radical hospitality."

—**Rabbi Rachel Cowan**, senior fellow, Institute for Jewish Spirituality

"Every religious leader, clergy and lay, will find something of value for the managing and guiding of religious institutions to become centers of spirit and community. An important addition to the happily widening bookshelf for all interested in synagogue transformation."

—**Rabbi Mordecai Finley**, spiritual leader, Ohr HaTorah Synagogue, Mar Vista, California; professor of liturgy, mysticism, and Jewish ethics, Academy for Jewish Religion

"An inspiring and insightful manifesto to breathe life into the American synagogue in this age of choice and change. Filled with candid advice and specific examples of purpose and strategy, it's valuable reading for clergy and lay synagogue leaders."

—**Rabbi Sheila Peltz Weinberg**, Institute for Jewish Spirituality

"For those who have lost faith in our people and institutions.... Provides important ideas to help us improve our own synagogues and communities. *Ruakh* might also be the most important missing ingredient of Federation life. *Revolution of Jewish Spirit* can help us there as well."

—**Barry Shrage**, president, Combined Jewish Philanthropies

"Inspiring! Refreshing! Visionary and pragmatic, traditional and innovative, personal and institutional, spiritual and authentic! A must read for anyone interested in the reimagining and revitalizing of contemporary Jewish life."

—**Rabbi Irwin Kula**, co-editor, *The Book of Jewish Sacred Practices: CLAL's Guide to Everyday & Holiday Rituals & Blessings*; president, CLAL—The National Jewish Center for Learning and Leadership

REVOLUTION of JEWISH SPIRIT

How to REVIVE *Ruakh* in Your Spiritual Life, TRANSFORM Your Synagogue & INSPIRE Your Jewish Community

Rabbi Baruch HaLevi & Ellen Frankel

Foreword by Dr. Ron Wolfson

For People of All Faiths, All Backgrounds

JEWISH LIGHTS Publishing

Woodstock, Vermont

Revolution of Jewish Spirit;
How to Revive Ruakh in Your Spiritual Life, Transform Your Synagogue &
Inspire Your Jewish Community

© 2012 by Baruch HaLevi and Ellen Frankel
Foreword © 2012 by Ron Wolfson

All rights reserved. No part of this book may be reproduced or transmitted in any form or by any means electronic or mechanical, including photocopying, recording, or by any information storage and retrieval system, without permission in writing from the publisher.

For information regarding permission to reprint material from this book, please mail or fax your request in writing to Jewish Lights Publishing, Permissions Department, at the address / fax number listed below, or e-mail your request to permissions@jewishlights.com

Library of Congress Cataloging-in-Publication Data
HaLevi, Baruch.
    Revolution of Jewish spirit : how to revive ruakh in your spiritual life, transform your synagogue & inspire your Jewish community / Baruch HaLevi, Ellen Frankel; foreword by Ron Wolfson.
        p. cm.
    Includes bibliographical references.
    ISBN 978-1-58023-625-6
    1. Spiritual life—Judaism. 2. Jewish way of life. 3. Synagogues—United States. 4. Synagogues—United States—Organization and administration. 5. Judaism—21st century. 6. Leadership—Religious aspects—Judaism. 7. HaLevi, Baruch. 8. Frankel, Ellen. I. Frankel, Ellen. II. Title.
    BM723.H3147 2012
    296.7'1—dc23
                                                                    2012026165

10 9   8   7   6   5   4   3   2   1

Manufactured in the United States of America
Cover Design: Jenny Buono
Cover Art: ©iStockphoto.com/Qweek

Published by Jewish Lights Publishing
A Division of Longhill partners, Inc.
Sunset Farm Offices, Route 4, P.O. Box 237
Woodstock, VT 05091
Tel: (802) 457-4000 Fax: (802) 457-4004
www.jewishlights.com

To my wife, my partner, my soulmate, Ariela.
Your *Ruakh* has given me life, light, and love.
—Baruch

To my husband Steve, and children, Allison and Matt,
who continually shine their spirit and light in the world
and inspire me every day.
—Ellen

Contents

Foreword ix

Introduction: Revolution of Jewish Spirit xiii

Part 1: Journey Forth

And the Divine called to Abram: *Journey forth....*

—Genesis 12:1

1. *Lech Lecha*: Individual Call to Journey 3

2. *Na'aseh*: Communal Call to Journey 21

3. Choose Life: Choosing to Journey 33

Part II: From the Known to the Unknown

And the Divine called to Abram: Journey forth, *from the known* [from your land, from your birthplace, from your father's house] *to the unknown* [the land that I will show you]....

—Genesis 12:1

4. The "When" of *Ruakh*: Erotic Shabbat 51

5. The "What" of *Ruakh*: The Synaplex Experience 65

6. The "Who" of *Ruakh*: Re-Membering the Tribe 95

Part III: And You Shall Be a Blessing

> And the Divine called to Abram: Journey forth, from the known [from your land, from your birthplace, from your father's house] to the unknown [the land that I will show you]. And I will make you into a great nation, and I will bless you, and I will increase your name, *and you shall be a blessing.*
>
> —GENESIS 12:1–2

7. **Vision and Visionaries**   115

8. **Future Shul**   135

9. **Revenue Revolution**   151

Conclusion: And You Shall Be a Blessing   171

Acknowledgments   177

Notes   184

Suggestions for Further Reading   187

Foreword

When I was the regional president of EMTZA United Synagogue Youth during my high school days in Omaha, Nebraska, the most thrilling and memorable experience was leading hundreds of teenagers in a rousing singing session we called *Ruakh* (spirit). On a typical Shabbat weekend at a regional conference, raising our voices in joyous song was perhaps the single most important moment in building a sense of community. The melodies and lyrics connected us to Shabbat, to Israel, and with God. Punctuated with hand motions ("*David, Melekh Yisrael*"), whoops, hollers, and dance, an energetic *Ruakh* session would transform us from individuals into a pulsating, sweaty *chevra*—a sacred community—giving voice to the cherished relationships we were creating with each other and with Judaism.

In this provocative, challenging, and inspiring book, Rabbi Baruch HaLevi and Ellen Frankel have correctly identified *Ruakh* as a key missing ingredient in Jewish institutional life, especially in the synagogue. Their call is for a revolution of spirit and a rejuvenation of our purpose, our worship, even our sacred spaces. It is recognition that the craving for community can bring people back to our institutions if we welcome, engage, and inspire them.

The penultimate expression of this *Ruakh* revolution is the weekly *Ruakh* Rally that culminates the weekly Shabbat morning experience at Congregation Shirat Hayam in Swampscott, Massachusetts. As a number of alternative worship and study sessions for young and old alike conclude, hundreds of people gather together in the main sanctuary for a fifteen-minute rollicking song session. Instead of the decidedly boring, dreary, anticlimactic recitation of announcements at the end of the formal worship, this congregation revels in their diversity of expression by physically coming together in an explosion of song and movement, a celebration of sacred community that caps a morning, indeed, a week, of learning, praying, healing, and repairing the world.

Lest you, dear reader, think this is some sort of happy-clappy West Coast "New Age" flaky idiosyncratic never-can-be-replicated anomaly, I hasten to point out that Congregation Shirat Hayam is, in fact, located in a suburb of Boston, a recent merger of two Conservative synagogues that were literally across the street from each other, populated by a fair share of small "c" conservative folk initially resistant to the out-of-the-box ideas of a young rabbi whom they hired to steer a potentially rocky marriage of congregations, each with its own history, ideology, and set of "but we've always done it that way" principles and policies. May I also underline the fact that Rabbi HaLevi, ordained by the Ziegler School of Rabbinic Studies at American Jewish University, was born and raised in that radical midwestern city of my youth—Omaha, Nebraska—and Ellen Frankel hails from Chicago. If you read this book with a "we can't do that" attitude, you will be missing the opportunity to explore a veritable feast of innovative ideas for transforming synagogue (and other) communities into places of meaning, purpose, and blessing, attractive to both longtime members and those unaffiliated, under-affiliated, and disengaged people everyone is hoping to reach.

Revolution of Jewish Spirit is a compelling case study of synagogue transformation. Granted, it is a first-person account from the key professional and a leading lay leader of the congregation, but the number of self-reflective, "thick" ethnographic descriptions of synagogue life can be counted on one hand. It is a welcome addition to a small, but growing literature in the field of synagogue studies. For clergy, synagogue leadership, and community professionals, it is a must-read—a page-turner—filled with good ideas and intriguing responses to the well-known challenges facing those committed to creating new expressions of sacred community in the twenty-first century.

In our Synagogue 3000 work, we are always on the lookout for examples of congregations that are thinking differently, taking risks, and experimenting with ways to reinvigorate sacred communities. Yet, when reading or hearing about case studies or reports of best practices, we caution against the tendency to want to replicate and adopt, preferring to encourage an understanding of principles underlying the success. Thus, as you read this case study, don't think replication; think application. Don't think adoption; think adaptation. Resist the temptation to say, "There's no way that will work in our place." Rather, say, "The principle at work here is offering multiple opportunities for engagement," and then ask, "How might that look in our congregation or community?"

Rabbi HaLevi and Ms. Frankel have thought deeply about what they and their colleagues are accomplishing at Congregation Shirat Hayam. They skillfully weave Jewish texts within the narrative to illustrate the roots of their principles of institutional transformation: the imperative for radical hospitality, for welcoming the stranger—including a new and (I hasten to add) controversial category of membership called "spiritual friends"—the immediacy of being "called" to service, the importance of choice. They are unafraid to admit mistakes, to voice doubt, to hold themselves and their community accountable. They understand the allure of experiential programming, yet recognize that creating relationships with and among the people in the congregation is the ultimate goal. But, most important of all, they challenge virtually every assumption about the twentieth-century model of synagogue in their search to create the synagogue of the future.

Are some of their ideas out-of-the-box? Yes, indeed. Asking people to invest in specific purposes of the synagogue rather than dues? Wow. Instituting what might be called a policy of permission, a come-whenever-you-can-and-however-you're-dressed? Hmmm. Abandoning Sunday school in favor of the kids being in shul Shabbat morning? Interesting.

Yet, if we are to create the kind of inspiring Jewish communities necessary to sustain and grow the Jewish people, if we are to fashion what I have called a "relational Judaism" for the twenty-first century, we will be well-served to ask the right questions and then be bold enough to experiment in our search for good answers. *Revolution of Jewish Spirit* is an excellent step in that direction.

Dr. Ron Wolfson
Fingerhut Professor of Education, American Jewish University
Co-founder, Synagogue 3000

Introduction
Revolution of Jewish Spirit

Ellen's Journey Home

As I'm driving to synagogue one warm, sunny Shabbat morning, I'm thinking of all the things I could be doing instead. Going out on a kayak, going out for breakfast, even going to the grocery store, I imagine, would be better than attending services. Last year, I didn't even make it to the synagogue for the High Holy Days, so why I am following through on this plan, I'm not so sure. I've spent too much time moving away from Judaism toward the spiritual teachings of the East to be spending a perfectly good Saturday inside a temple. When I think of being in a synagogue, I think of long, dull services where I am an observer, not a participant. The cantor sings with a choir hidden away, there are the never-ending dictates to "please rise, please sit," and there's the sermon that feels long and boring. The truth is that, even as an adult, I have kept myself awake by counting how many pages were left in the service.

The problem is that for the past few years, some people in my community have asked me to try going to their synagogue. They claim the new rabbi is full of spirit, and the community is alive and vibrant. Mostly I would smile at them and try to change the subject. I've been in a lot of temples in my life, and *alive* and *vibrant* and *full of spirit* are not words and phrases that fit my experience of synagogue. When I think of entering a temple, I can almost smell the musty scent, feel the stagnant air that speaks of lack of movement. I would smile and tell them how glad I was that they found a place that was right for them. But I knew it wasn't for me. I had already figured out that my spiritual home was at least a forty-five-minute drive to a meditation center in the city, or a two-day flight from Boston to Nepal.

This Saturday morning would be my way of proving that, regardless of the claims people made to me, or how exciting the rabbi seemed, there was no place for me within the walls of a shul. I pull into the parking lot and am taken aback. You'd think this was Rosh Hashanah, the parking lot is so full. When I told a friend who is a member here that I was going to finally give it a try, she was thrilled but advised me to get there early. "You don't want to miss a thing," she had said. I wanted to tell her that she was wrong, that I actually wanted to miss everything, but that sounded like the antithesis of a spiritually minded person, which is how I wanted to think of myself. I'd get through this morning somehow.

As I close the car door, the action is already beginning. "Good morning, *Shabbat shalom*," a young man says to me. I don't know him and I wonder why he's talking to me, so I just nod and smile. I'm used to older people being at temple, but when I look around the parking lot, there are people of all ages—young and younger, old and older. And everyone is smiling and talking and laughing as if they're glad to be spending this Saturday morning here. I walk up to the temple doors and wonder why so many adults, teenagers, and children are giving up a perfectly good Saturday to be here and actually seem happy about it. I vow not to drink the proverbial Kool-Aid if it's offered at some schleppy *Oneg*.

Then I walk in to what I can only describe as controlled, happy, and friendly chaos with a whirl of activity and people headed in every direction. The moment my foot touches down on this strange and foreign land, a woman greets me at the entrance, saying, "Welcome, I'm Joyce, a synaguide here at Congregation Shirat Hayam."

"Okay, seriously," I think to myself, "what in the world is a synaguide?"

"We're delighted to have you with us today. Is this your first time? Can I help you find your way through our Synaplex?" she asks.

I watch dozens of people going this way or that while some are sitting on the couches sipping coffee and talking as plasma screens behind them broadcast various services. "I'm not a member" is the only thing I think to blurt out.

"Oh, that doesn't matter," she says nonchalantly. "You don't need to be a member to participate in our congregational family. You don't even have to be Jewish; we welcome people of all faiths. *Ruakh*—spirit—is what we cultivate and share with everyone here."

In the Beginning There Was *Ruakh*

What is *Ruakh*? *Ruakh* is the stuff of creation. Regardless of how we imagine God or don't imagine God, it is something bigger than ourselves. The Torah cites *Ruakh* as the vehicle by which God entered into and created the universe. Before *Ruakh*, there was darkness, chaos, and a void.

> When God began to create this reality there was first only immense formlessness and darkness. And a *Ruakh Elohim* [Divine Spirit, Energy, Vitality, Breath, Life Force, and Soul] hovered above the dark, formless, chaotic waters.
>
> —Genesis 1:1–2

Ruakh began to transform the chaos into order, the darkness into light, the waters into dry ground. *Ruakh* is the energy of God in this world; it is what vibrates throughout the universe. It is also what animates all things; it is what pulsates throughout each and every one of us.

After the universe was created, the Creator then moved on to human beings:

> And the Divine formed humans of the dust of the ground, and breathed into his nostrils the *nishmat chayim*—breath of life; and man became a living soul.
>
> —Genesis 2:7

This *nishmat chayim* is synonymous with *Ruakh*. Divine energy is the beginning of creation; it is the spark that ignites Judaism, the Jewish people, and Jewish community.

That spark is what keeps people coming back on their annual pilgrimage to the synagogue for the High Holy Days in spite of the boredom or lack of inspiration they might feel. It is what compels them to attend a Passover seder no matter how far they have traveled from their roots. It is what is awakened in them from time to time, in passing moments, when encountering another Jew, or when hearing of an Israeli achievement. *Ruakh* seems to be ignited communally every time there is anti-Semitism in our midst, or across the shores, or when Israel comes under attack. We feel it at a tribal level every now and again, particularly when we are scared. Now it is time to unleash it and harness it proactively, not through fear, but through vision and hope.

Ellen Continues Her Journey Home

I have never been greeted at a temple with words that speak of spirit, and I've gotta tell you the *Ruakh* within me begins to stir. Joyce watches me trying to take in the energy of the place and smiles at me as if she knows something that I haven't yet figured out.

"Here, let me show you around," she says as she takes my hand. I hesitate because I can't get my bearings, but Joyce is leading me to the smell of coffee, so I follow along.

"Over here we have our Boker Tov Café. Feel free to help yourself to the coffee bar, grab a nosh, and just hang out and schmooze," she tells me as I watch others eating and talking while babies toddle around with their toys. "Are you more of a traditional or alternative type?" she asks with a smile, and I am baffled to be asked such a question in a temple or to be given permission just to hang out and relax without feeling guilt and the stare of disapproving eyes.

"Alternative," I answer, thinking that if I'd been born a decade earlier I would definitely have gone to Woodstock.

"Great, well, if you change your mind, you can always check out the traditional service. However, for the alternative we have two more options for you. Yoga or chanting?" she asks. I think I'm going to *plotz* hearing such options in a temple.

"Chanting," I say because I'm wearing this cute little skirt. I mean really, who would have thought to bring yoga clothes?

"So come with me," Joyce says as she leads me down the hall into a space that looks like the Pottery Barn crashed into a Zen center. Nothing has prepared me for this sight. I see a room packed with people sitting on cushions and chairs, others swaying or dancing, with everybody chanting Hebrew phrases as the rabbi pounds away on his African drum.

I don't know what to make of this. How can this be happening in a synagogue? Maybe if this were a more informal group, like a *chavurah*, I might get it. But c'mon, in a large suburban Conservative New England synagogue? You've got to be kidding me. It's too interesting, too exotic, and too spirited, and before I know it I'm drawn in, but I still hold back. I don't feel ready to fully participate. I still have it in my head that I'm going to get through this morning so that I can reaffirm to myself and everyone else that despite growing up Jewish I don't belong in a synagogue, that I am not seeking a renewed connection with my Jewish heritage. But what's in my head is now fighting with my heart. I feel the vibrations of the chant as my foot begins to tap in rhythm, and I watch how, in the final round of the chant, there seems to be a collective breathing in and a collective breathing out. I breathe in and feel a sense of renewal beginning to take root.

Joyce invites me to see all my options. "There's more?" I think to myself as she introduces me to another synaguide, who is also nice. "Why is everyone so nice?" my old cynical mind asks. The synaguide takes me back down the hall, pointing out the kids and families in the Miniplex down the other corridor. But since I'm here solo, she takes me to the Torah study, where yet another big group is gathered, enthusiastically engaged in a lively debate. I decide to sit in for a while. When I finally get up, I wander down the hall and pass the Jewish yogis.

Joining the others in the main sanctuary, I'm unexpectedly moved by a healing service followed by the rabbi's sermon, which is relevant, engaging, and inspiring in ways I never imagined a sermon could be, and I actually can't wait to go home and get my husband to listen to it on the podcast. And since when have rabbis begun using podcasts anyway? I love how he refers to the cyber-Jews in their cyber-pews as he broadcasts on closed-circuit TV as well as live on the Internet. His words have inspired me, and I realize that I am actually enjoying this morning more than I care to admit.

But nothing, absolutely nothing prepares me for the grand finale of this pleasantly strange, refreshingly chaotic, wildly passionate morning. "It is time for the *Ruakh* Rally," the rabbi is yelling out as he and the few hundred other people are clapping and singing and dancing around the place. As the rabbi is explaining that *Ruakh* is about spirit, I see the room begin to expand. The few hundred swells into four, five hundred people flowing into the sanctuary, and I wonder, "When did they start making sanctuaries in the round, with no bimah and with so much light, creating such a calming space?" More adults pour in, followed by what feels like an endless stream of children who come in, dancing and singing their way to the front of the room, high-fiving the rabbi as they pass. They are guided in by the sounds not just of their parents and grandparents clapping along, but to the rocking rhythms of the *Ruakh* Rally Band singing modern Israeli rock songs, American reggae, hip-hop songs, and songs about peace in Hebrew, English, and Arabic, too! As the rabbi is shouting for everyone to stand up, hundreds of people of all ages and backgrounds, some in suits and dresses, some in soccer uniforms, some in yoga clothes, and others in jeans, put their arms around one another, swaying and singing "*Am Yisrael Chai*—The Jewish people are alive." And boy, are they ever! I sing with them as the people standing on either side of me put their arms around my back, and as I look around the room, I blink back the unexpected tears of joy. The rabbi is up on a chair crying out, "Peace to our Muslim brothers and sisters in the Gaza Strip, to our Christian brethren across the country, to our Jewish friends down the street—peace, *l'chayim*, and *Ruakh*—spirit unto you!" And before the *Ruakh* Rally is over, the rabbi yells out one more set of instructions. "Radical hospitality,"[1] he says before inviting everyone into a full, sit-down lunch. "Everyone is invited. We want you here," he says, and it feels like he's saying it to me. "Radical hospitality—introduce yourself to everyone and invite people to sit with you at lunch. Here we don't save seats, we save souls," he cries out. "So enjoy. Rejoice. *Shabbat shalom* and welcome home."

And I can't believe these words are coming out of my mouth, but as I am welcomed to sit down with a group of people for the *Kiddush* lunch, with a full plate and a full heart, I tell them how much I enjoyed this morning and that I'd like to come back next Saturday.

Rabbi B and Congregation Shirat Hayam

Serving as the rabbi at Congregation Shirat Hayam (CSH), just north of Boston in Swampscott, Massachusetts, I see this scenario play out again and again. Ours is the rare synagogue that offers the Shabbat morning Synaplex on a weekly basis, providing a variety of ways for people to celebrate Shabbat. CSH is a Jewish spiritual community that is blossoming in the twenty-first century. We are a dues-paying member of the United Synagogue of Conservative Judaism, and I am a Conservative ordained rabbi from the Ziegler School of Rabbinic Studies of American Jewish University and a member of the Rabbinical Assembly. Yet, like others in the midst of a Jewish Renaissance, we often find ourselves at the edge, pushing the boundaries of our movement, or as I like to think of it, initiating growth. Yes we are Conservative, but rather than limiting ourselves by the labels of Reform, Conservative, Orthodox, Renewal, or Reconstructionist, at Shirat Hayam we like to refer to ourselves with the enlightened term used by author and lecturer Dr. Alan Morinis: we are Under-constructionists; we are a work in progress.[2] Instead of a stagnant program and a dying congregation, this synagogue is a vibrant, creative expression of spirit, of *Ruakh*. The congregational doors are open to all: Jews, semi-Jews and non-Jews, members and nonmembers. Shabbat services are webcast, reaching nursing homes that tune in every week, families who are unable to physically join us for a Bar or Bat Mitzvah, along with Jews and non-Jews within the country and around the world who are homebound or just want to connect from the comfort of their homes. In an age where Judaism, synagogues, and Jewish institutions are seeing declining affiliation, membership, and involvement, this congregation has continued to flourish. This book is about shining that light, that *Ruakh*, into the darkness and reigniting Judaism with spirit at its core. It's about exploring a new path to reclaim and revive Judaism instead of schlepping along a crumbling road that is leading us toward a dead end, or inventing a new age Judaism that cuts us off from our roots. Like the Jews of the Exodus, wandering in the desert toward the Promised Land, it is crucial to examine how the Jewish community, Jewish institutions, and Jewish people have become enslaved by old ideas and practices that are no longer useful and how we must move forward toward a land flowing with milk and honey, one that is sustaining and sweet, for the sacred future of our Jewish heritage. *Revolution of Jewish Spirit* reflects the importance of partnership between rabbi and congregant in the practice of Judaism and Jewish life. Both I, as rabbi, and Ellen, as congregant, will speak from these pages about working together to breathe life into a Jewish practice with *Ruakh* at its core. Our voices will be both distinct and blended, reflecting both the individual and community. We offer a new message and model to reignite the spirit of Jews, Judaism, and Jewish community.

No matter who you are—rabbi, cantor, lay leader, layperson

No matter what label you place on your Judaism

No matter how you identify—born Jews or Jews by choice, interfaith families or no faith, same-religion couples, married or single, straight or gay, senior, empty-nester, young families, or youth

No matter where you sit: on the bimah, on the board, or in the pews

No matter how far away you have drifted or how engaged you might be

No matter if you are attempting to merge two synagogues, other Jewish institutions or just going it alone

No matter if you are trying to revitalize or reimagine a synagogue or Federation, a Jewish Community Center (JCC) or another Jewish organization or institution

This book is for you.

The *Ruakh*-less Mess: From Crisis to Hope

In so many areas, American Jews in the twenty-first century have succeeded. We are overwhelmingly and disproportionately educated, affluent, and professionally accomplished. If ever there was an ideal time or place to be born a Jew, that era is now and that place is undeniably here. But while we are flourishing as individuals, we are floundering as a Jewish community, people, and religion.

- The average Jewish person today doesn't belong to a synagogue, affiliate with the Jewish community, or engage in Jewish practice in any measurable way. In the 1990 National Jewish Population Survey, the Conservative movement was found to be the largest denomination with 43 percent of affiliated Jewish households, but that figure fell to 33 percent by the year 2000 and continues to decline. The United Synagogue of Conservative Judaism (USCJ) reported that it lost about 6 percent of its congregations, a drop from 693 in 2001 to 652 in 2010, and about 15 percent of its members, dropping from 241,300 members to 204,200.[3] It is estimated that overall, about 40 percent of Jews belong to synagogues, down from about 60 percent at midcentury.[4]
- Those who do belong to a synagogue attend infrequently. According to a 2010 survey by the Pew Forum on Religion and Public Life, 37 percent of Jews polled said that, aside from funerals and weddings, they attend religious services only a few times a year; 19 percent responded they seldom attend religious services; and 12 percent answered that they never

attend religious services. That translates to 68 percent of Jews who rarely, if ever, attend synagogue.

- Along with declining membership, American Jews are becoming an increasingly aging population. The number of elderly Jews, sixty-five years and older, more than doubled from 1957 to 2000, reaching more than a million people. Elderly Jews outnumber younger Jews in their affiliation within the Jewish community. For example, 29 percent of elderly households belong to a Jewish Community Center and 43 percent belong to another Jewish organization, such as B'nai B'rith or Hadassah, compared to 18 percent and 23 percent, respectively, of non-elderly households.[5]

- Jewish day schools are costly, and as a result, many families are priced out. It is estimated that approximately 200,000 students attend more than 700 Jewish day schools in the United States. Tuitions at the schools average about $14,000 and in the past five years have typically increased about 7 percent a year, outpacing wage increases for most families.[6]

- Many people think that most Hebrew schools have failed by almost every measurable standard, and nearly three out of four Jewish children quit religious school after their Bar or Bat Mitzvah.[7] Did you have a good experience in Hebrew school?

- Average Jewish Americans can't access their tradition even if they wanted to. They consider Torah, Talmud, and the siddur foreign and perceive them as irrelevant to daily life. Hebrew literacy in America has declined significantly over the past sixty years, and American Jews are far less fluent than Jews in most other Diaspora communities.[8]

- The average Jewish person has not been to Israel and is growing ever more likely not to care about the Jewish homeland. A 2007 study argues that American Jews' connection to Israel drops off with each subsequent generation.[9] In this study, a consistent increase in alienation from Israel was found in each younger generation, with middle-aged Jews less attached to Israel than older Jews, and younger Jews less attached than middle-aged Jews.

- People in the Jewish community donate or bequeath more money to non-Jewish institutions, such as colleges, hospitals, and the local symphony, than they do to Jewish institutions and Jewish causes. A 2003 report by the Institute for Jewish Community & Research in San Francisco found that of the $5.3 billion that major Jewish philanthropists gave, only $318 million went to Jewish institutions.[10]
- Young, committed, and accomplished Jewish lay leaders are more likely to volunteer their time to a non-Jewish institution than a synagogue, Jewish Federation, or Jewish cause, in part because they feel they are better-run organizations or more relevant to their lives. In a 2011 study, only a small portion of young Jewish adults preferred to or actually did volunteer with Jewish organizations.[11]
- Visionary, charismatic, inspirational professional leaders are too scarce. Many of those with such qualities tend to opt for other professions rather than becoming rabbis, cantors, Jewish educators, or Jewish professionals.
- Many synagogues are tired, crumbling, and empty, and congregations are uninspired, aging, and in dire financial straits. Often Jewish communities are apathetic, redundant, and fragmented, and Judaism is seen as uninteresting and inaccessible.
- Some synagogues and Jewish institutions are merging or contemplating mergers without a clear vision or inspired models of how to proceed, resulting in failed attempts to change the direction of their community or institutions.

Contrary to the outward success Jewish people are having, many Jewish institutions, Jewish communities, and Judaism itself are not enjoying similar success. Most Jewish leaders and institutions know this, but too many sit by helplessly, not knowing how to fix the problems. Others are facing these problems head on and searching for ways to reignite the *Ruakh* within Judaism. Rabbi Lawrence A. Hoffman and Ron Wolfson's Synagogue 3000 (S3K) was a ten-year project that shined a light upon synagogue transformation and what is possible when creativity, openness, and inspiration are front and center in tackling the problems we face.[12] They continue to follow synagogues in the process of change and offer up models of moving forward into the future. *Revolution of Jewish Spirit* is our proactive response to add to the conversation and to share both our experience and our vision.

The Blame Game

While the problems are clear, in my experience too many of today's Jewish leaders—both lay and professional—are not addressing the issues aggressively, not addressing them with vision, and all too often not addressing them at all. For many Jewish professionals and leaders who are mired in the problems, the answer seems obvious that the Jews in the pews, or not in the pews as the case may be, are to blame. Such leaders throw up their hands as they yell at the back of the heads of those walking out the door. They sit and stew in resentment, anger, and despair but do little to connect with the hearts, minds, or souls of those leaving the synagogues and simply validate what those leaving suspected all along—Judaism, Jewish institutions, and Jewish communities seem reactive, uninspired, and broken. But whose fault is it if Jews today are walking out the door? Does it make sense to blame people for being uninspired, unengaged, and unattached to something they perceive as irrelevant to their daily lives, that doesn't speak to their mind, body, heart, or soul?

Other "isms"

When one door closes, another opens, and today many Jews are walking through the doors of Buddhism, Hinduism, Sufism, and other "isms" of all types. Visit your typical urban Zen center and you are likely to find not only Jews meditating but Jewish-born Zen masters teaching at the center. Attend a local yoga studio and chances are you're more likely to find a minyan there than you will in your neighborhood shul. It isn't necessarily that these Jews are uninterested in religion; they are uninterested in the religion of their birth as it has been presented to them. It isn't that they aren't out there seeking spirituality; they just aren't seeking it within Judaism. Jews—young and old—are searching and seeking pathways of spirit in other religions, other ways of connecting to the Sacred.

And those not seeking out explicitly spiritual paths are getting their souls' needs met and finding *Ruakh* in other, more modern, quasi-religious ways. They are turning to social activism, environmentalism, feminism, political activism, multiculturalism, animal advocacy, politics, and a whole host of other areas that fall under the umbrella of *tikkun olam*. For many, these pursuits have filled the void of a *Ruakh*-less Judaism and taken the place of a synagogue.

Today Jews get behind, support, and sustain a whole host of secular nonprofits the way they did for their once beloved Jewish institutions. Jews are out in the world, passionately making a difference because, frankly, this is what they were taught and raised to do. "Our mission is *tikkun olam*," Jews were told time and again. "Get out there and fix the world and be a mensch."

And so they are out there "fixing the world," searching and sustaining, giving and creating, committing themselves to all kinds of important and worthy efforts and causes. But they learned they could be a mensch without joining a temple. While the walls of synagogues echoed with the important themes of social justice and repairing the world, they fell all too silent when it came to the themes of a spiritual and personally transformative Judaism. While many rabbis and Jewish leaders preached continuity for the sake of continuity, this uninspired mantra was heavy with coercion and guilt rather than *Ruakh* and joy. Obligation is important, but it is only a part of walking the spiritual path and is certainly not enough to encourage a commitment to Judaism. The incessant pressure to support dying Jewish institutions, to stay Jewish, marry Jewish, and raise Jewish children without discussing or embodying the beauty and spirit embedded within Jewish practice significantly contributed to the increasingly empty pews.

Restoring Hope through Restoring *Ruakh*

The most effective, motivating, and Jewish response is to move forward through painting a picture of possibility, inspiration, and hope. For two thousand years we were the people who were exiled from our homeland but sustained the vision of our return. *HaTikvah*, "The Hope," is not just modern Israel's national anthem. Rather it is the essential message of the Jewish people, not just in regard to Zionism, but in regard to Judaism and Jewish communities today.

Look around and see the many unengaged, uninspired, searching, seeking, directionless Jews and potential Jews. In the 2010 Pew Forum on Religion and Public Life, Jews were asked how important their religion was to them. Thirty-one percent of the respondents claimed their religion was very important, while 41 percent said their religion was somewhat important, compared to 28 percent who answered that their religion was of little or no importance in their lives. We have 72 percent of Jews who believe their religion plays a role in their lives, so where are they? They are out there, but they have voted with their feet. While their Judaism may be important in their lives, that is not translating into involvement within synagogues. They will follow something and someone only if it is meaningful, motivational, and inspirational. We need to inspire them back. Instead of more studies telling us what we already know, let's lead the call with renewed spirit, breathing in new life and reviving our Judaism. What is needed today—now more than ever—from our bimahs, within our Hebrew schools, from our Federations and elsewhere is literally to "inspire," to breathe into the Jewish enterprise, our Jewish institutions, and our people a breath of fresh hope, possibility, vision, and life. And that is why no amount of recruitment, solicitation, or guilt-laden arguments to return to Judaism or Jewish community will prevail except this: a call to revive an inspired Judaism and Jewish community.

Although the *Ruakh* has grown faint, even though the Jewish spark has grown dim, it still flickers. In both our experiences and research, we have seen many examples of *Ruakh*. There are tremendous organizations and think tanks that have begun to tackle our modern challenges and are reinspiring Jews and Judaism: the spearheading work of S3K; Clal—The National Jewish Center for Learning and Leadership; The Hartman Institute; and the Institute for Jewish Spirituality are a few of the shining examples. There are established synagogues as well that continue to grow not simply in terms of membership, but in terms of *Ruakh*: Valley

Beth Shalom, Encino, California; Temple Sinai, Westwood, California; Central Synagogue, New York City; and B'nai Jeshurun, New York City, are a few examples of courage and excellence in the pursuit of synagogue transformation. There are a handful of pioneering Jewish spiritual communities arising as well, such as the Kavana Cooperative, Seattle; Ikar, Los Angeles; Hadar, New York City; and Mishkan, Chicago, to name a few. These institutions, and others like them, exemplify models of courage, vision, and *Ruakh*. It is in this spirit that CSH set forth on our path to create a congregation embodied by *Ruakh*. And this *Ruakh* can be fanned into a flame, the flame into a fire, the fire into a creative force, and within that creative force, the breath of life is reignited.

"I Wish ...": The Response of Our Guests

Every single week at the end of Shabbat morning services, when the *Ruakh* Rally is over and everyone is literally wiping away their sweat, even their tears, I get the same set of responses, usually a dozen times or more, especially from visiting guests, clergy, or entire Ritual Committees sent as scouts to check us out:

- That was the most amazing service I have ever been to ...
- I have never seen anything like this before ...
- I wish my rabbi would do this in our synagogue ...
- I wish my cantor would be open to this type of experience ...
- I wish my congregants [spoken by fellow rabbis] would go for this ...
- I cried tears of joy for the first time in a synagogue ...
- If I lived here I would join ...
- I only wish I had this or could do this at my shul ...
- I'll be back next week and I'm bringing my friends ...

And every single week I say the same thing:

- You can do this too!
- You should do this if you want to survive!
- You must do this if you want to thrive!

It is all or nothing. You cannot kind of unleash your *Ruakh*. You cannot merely hope your *Ruakh* will come forth. And above all else you cannot simply "wish" that a *Ruakh*-less community will become *Ruakh*-full. The truth is that wishing is not Jewish; will is Jewish. As Theodore Herzl said, "*Im tirzu ayn zo agadah*—If you will it, it is no dream." Willing our needs, hopes, and dreams into reality is what Jews have always done. Our will, certainly our collective will, has always been inspired, guided, and sustained by divine will, by *Ruakh*.

Ruakh is real. *Ruakh* is here. *Ruakh* is our now and our future. If Judaism and Jewish communities are to survive, we are going to have to finally be honest that something is fundamentally broken in our religious practice, in our synagogues, Jewish institutions, communities, and priorities as American Jews. If Judaism is to be embraced and traveled as a meaningful spiritual path, we are going to have to change our focus, our message, and our tune. Most of all, if we are going to move beyond merely surviving, if we are going to thrive once again, we can only get there if we reclaim at our center this concept, this idea, this clarion call of *Ruakh*. Join us as we reengage, reignite, and reclaim Jews, Judaism, and Jewish community in the twenty-first century and beyond. Read on as we revive *Ruakh* and breathe life into our spiritual heritage. It's time for a revolution of Jewish spirit!

Part I

Journey Forth

And the Divine called to Abram: *Journey forth*, from the known [from your land, from your birthplace, from your father's house] to the unknown [the land that I will show you]. And I will make you into a great nation, and I will bless you, and I will increase your name, and you shall be a blessing.

—GENESIS 12:1–2

1

Lech Lecha

Individual Call to Journey

How Do We Hear the Call?

We get called all the time on our BlackBerries and iPhones; we receive messages through voice mail and texting. We hear ringing and beeping all day long as people try to get in touch with us. We seem to be living in a world where we're always on, open, and ready to make contact; but thank God for caller ID. We need advance warning about who is on the other end. And when we don't know who's on the line, with the readout saying, "private caller," we find ourselves momentarily unsure how to proceed. Is it an important call or is it someone we'd rather avoid? Is it someone who wants something from us or someone who is calling to offer us something we might need? Are we ready for whatever presents itself or do we let those calls go to voice mail as a way of closing our ears to that ringing, thereby missing the call and potentially a whole lot more?

Missed cell phone calls are one thing. However, there is another type of calling that has the potential to change the course of our lives. Unfortunately, we often avoid those calls instead of answering them as well. There are so many things pulling at us that we are at risk of ignoring the deep ringing that is calling for our attention. We're obsessed with having all four bars at the ready on our cell, while our spirit's

3

reception often goes unattended and, more often than not, is spotty. We're multitasking, phone in one hand, coffee in the other, while we're watching the headline news, checking the stock quotes in the corner of the TV, and rushing out the door to get the children to school. We wonder why we feel frazzled and depleted, as if there's something deeper missing from our lives. We wonder about greater meaning, about how we can find some peace. We wonder if somewhere along the way we missed our true purpose, that all-important call.

So what does it *really* mean to be called? What does that sound like? You might experience that call as an inspiration, an inner knowing, a gut feeling, a pull. You might hear the words or feel them within. The call might come from a person or people in your life or it may feel divinely inspired. Perhaps some sort of sign appears repeatedly, and it moves you to pay attention to its meaning. Or maybe the call comes in more challenging, perhaps tragic ways, as calls so often do. The call is simply something bigger than ourselves, our daily lives, our earthly routines. It is ultimate purpose, a purpose that is offered to each and every one of us as individuals, as families, communities, and nations. It is offered to us if we are able to listen and if we are willing to respond.

Rabbi B's Story: Early Ringings

When I was fifteen years old, my paternal grandmother took my grandfather's gun and proceeded down to her basement. There she methodically laid out a sheet, stood on it, and took her own life. While her years of suffering with depression had come to an end, my family's sorrow, particularly that of my dad, was only just beginning. Over the next decade I would watch my beloved father unravel. The suffering, guilt, grief, confusion, and anger over his mother's suicide proved too much for him to bear. It was the catalyst that led to his demise.

And yet, one man's end is another man's beginning. In the days and years that followed my grandmother's death, while my father began to descend, I began to ascend—ascend in my life, in my calling, and in my journey. Out of the depths of that tragedy, compounded by watching my father's world slowly and tragically come apart, I heard one calling and he another. Whereas I heard the call and moved forward because of it, he heard the call and spent his life trying to drown out the ringing, hiding in the distraction of noise. For him, it was the beginning of the end; for me, it was the beginning of the journey.

Some calls come from tragedy, pain, and the darkness of life. Some calls, however, come in the simple moments, when all is fine and we are immersed in the seemingly trivial, daily routines of our lives. Sometimes we are moved by joy, by the happy moments as we celebrate life-cycle events, monumental achievements, or milestones along the path. There are callings of all types, in all places, and at all times. It doesn't matter where the call comes from. What is important is that we take that call when it comes and most of all that we respond.

Ayeka: **Where Are You?**

The first call recorded in the Torah comes from God after Adam and Eve fail their first and only set of instructions. Life in the Garden is so simple. Adam and Eve have everything provided for them. There are no bills to pay, no mortgages to deal with, no children to feed. They can rest and play, make love, and eat as much and as often as they like. They can have whatever they desire, except for the forbidden fruit from the forbidden Tree of Knowledge of Good and Evil. That is God's only prohibition, and, of course, that is the one thing they have to have.

Like children, Adam and Eve want the forbidden fruit more than anything else. And so, like children, they disobey God and they eat the apple. However, God doesn't respond with anger, with lightning bolts, or with guilt. Instead, God comes calling, asking one question, offering one word. It's not a question of accusation or judgment. Rather, it's an open-ended question offering them an opportunity to respond. "*Ayeka?*" God asks. "Where are you?" (Genesis 3:9). Where are you in your life? Where are you in your relationship? Where are you now that you've stumbled and fallen? Have you learned from it? Have you grown from it? And, if not, are you ready to hear this call and begin your journey toward deeper understanding? Perhaps Adam and Eve's eating from the tree is exactly what God wanted. Maybe it is all a ploy to get them to open up and see their life as a journey. Maybe it is all a setup to get them to respond to the call.

In the end, Adam and Eve's failure stems not from eating the forbidden fruit, but from not answering the call. Instead of standing their ground, owning up to their actions, and facing themselves and their Maker, they run and hide. Adam and Eve are passed over for the opportunity to become the first Jews for one reason. Judaism begins not with obedience, not with perfection, not with refraining from eating from the forbidden fruit of life. Rather, Judaism begins through hearing and responding to God's call wherever we are, whatever we have done, whenever it comes.

And that brings us to Noah, the famous ark builder. He may have been a *tzaddik b'dorotav*, a righteous man in his generation (Genesis 6:9). However, as many Torah commentators point out, it was only in his generation that he was deemed righteous. In another generation he would have been passed over for the job, but as the story goes, the civilization of Noah's time is not so civilized. In fact, things have gotten so bad that God feels it necessary to start over by destroying the earth and all that is on it through a flood. But Noah is singled out for salvation because he is the most righteous of an unrighteous bunch. God calls out to Noah to build that infamous ark, to stock it two by two with all the earth's creatures. God calls out and Noah hears that call. And yet, Noah is not chosen to be the captain of Judaism.

If he hears the call, then why isn't he the patriarch of Judaism? Because while Judaism is predicated on hearing a call, hearing is not enough. One must hear not only with one's ears but also intuit the deeper meaning of that call with one's heart. Hearing is not listening. Noah fails to truly listen to what God is asking. He hears God's instructions: *build a boat, yay high and so tall*, but, unfortunately, that's all he hears. Later in the Torah, when God first tells Abraham and then Moses God's plans to destroy various groups of people, both these individuals have the chutzpah (audacity) to stand up to God, argue with God, and fight for the lives of the innocent and not so innocent. God responds to Abraham and Moses, welcoming their arguments as holy chutzpah.

Noah is seemingly interested in one person alone—Noah. He doesn't speak to others and try to help them or invite them onboard.

He doesn't hear the real call to reach out to his wife, family, neighbors, friends, and community. Unlike Adam and Eve, Noah is dutiful and obedient and yet is still passed over for the job. By saying *Ayeka*, God isn't calling for us to blindly obey and follow along. Rather, as it says in the Talmud, *Rachmana liba bayei*[1]—God wants the heart. Noah builds a boat, providing a physical refuge, but he fails to offer *Ruakh*, the spirit to fill his fellow companions' sails, helping them to journey into the unknown. Therefore, Noah, too, is passed over for the job of becoming the first Jew.

So who finally gets the job? Not Adam and Eve, who run and hide. Not Noah, who blindly and silently follows instructions without listening to what is really being asked. The position is filled years later by a man named Abram (later to become Abraham) and a woman named Sarai (later to become Sarah). They not only hear the call and respond to God, but respond through one word that embodies Judaism and ultimately *Ruakh*: *Hineni*—Here I am!

The call of *Ayeka*—Where are you?—is more than a physical question of location; it is a spiritual question. Where are you on your life's journey? Are you ready to answer this call? The response of *Hineni*—Here I am—is more than a physical accounting of where we are on the path. It is a mental, emotional, and spiritual response. I am here, ready to begin. I am here, ready to set forth. I am here, ready to do my part, to be in relationship and partnership with God. To answer *Hineni* is to have heard the ringing and answered completely: I am ready to begin.

The call of God is not about religious observance. The call of God is not about moral piety. The call of God is not about blind obedience. God does not want us to spend our lives frozen in fear of violating God's will or making mistakes. God does not call on one religion, one denomination, or one person alone. The divine calling is a family plan, including everyone, available to anyone willing to hear it, willing to listen, and willing to respond. Like Abraham and Sarah, our task is to answer the call of *Ayeka*—Where are you?—and to respond *Hineni*—Here I am. This four-thousand-year-old call was ringing then and is ringing now—for you, for me, for us.

Fear of the Unknown

Of course, hearing and answering a call with *Hineni* is not so easy. While the call holds the possibility for spiritual growth, it often involves moving out of our comfort zone and making sacrifices. Think of Moses and the burning bush. While he answers God's call with *Hineni*, he proceeds to tell God all the reasons that he doesn't feel up to the task, why he isn't the person to talk to Pharaoh, and why he isn't worthy or ready for such a huge undertaking. There exists a Moses in each and every one of us. No matter how great our calling, regardless of how definite our *Hineni* response may be, doubt is real. Uncertainty is human.

When Abraham finally declares *Hineni*, in what is often referred to as the *Akeidah*, the Binding of Isaac, we feel incredible trepidation in his response. For what is he being asked to do? He is being asked to sacrifice what is most important to him—his son. These calls aren't casual checking-in, catching-up calls. When Moses, Abraham, and other truly great men and women of the Torah have responded with *Hineni*, life-changing events occur, and with them necessary struggles ensue.

While answering the call holds the power to move us forward, fear, distraction, and complacency hold the potential to pull us back. After all, we can get pretty comfortable in our lives and routines. We aren't necessarily looking to shake things up. Sometimes we just want to press the mute button and keep plugging along. Maybe you're busy with carpool and the demands of running a household. Maybe you are sailing along comfortably in your job and are eager to try out your new golf clubs with your favorite foursome. Maybe you are part of a community, a Jewish community or a synagogue that is okay, it's adequate, it's fine; it's good but not great. Perhaps you feel settled in a relationship, but without much passion; feel comfortable in your job, but without inspiration. Or maybe things are not good. Maybe they are bad. Really bad. Possibly you feel trapped in a loveless or abusive relationship. Perhaps you are battling an illness or living with chronic pain, suffering in ways that others simply can't understand. Maybe you've lost a loved one and feel hopeless, wondering how you will ever live again, love again, unsure of how you will go on. Or maybe you are depressed and feel that you have lost your way. Whether your call is a faint but incessant ringing or a loud, shrill alarm, calls are there to wake us up and propel us forward.

Maybe the fact that you're reading this book right now is your response to a call you've heard. Perhaps you've been searching for a Judaism that speaks to you, that feels like a calling to your soul, as opposed to being an obligation or a response to guilt or pressure. Or maybe you just happened to pick it up at the bookstore or at a friend's house and, for some reason, you began reading these pages. Or maybe you are part of a Jewish community: a Federation, a Hillel house, a day school, or a synagogue that has heard a call and decided the status quo is no longer acceptable, that the community needs to forge a new path for the future. Calls come in a variety of ways, and it is up to each one of us to discover how we will hear and how we will respond. We need to be willing to open up to that challenge, even with all our reservations and apprehensions. To say *Hineni*—Here I am; I'm ready—is how we begin the journey. The Chinese philosopher Lao-tzu said, "A journey of a thousand miles begins with a single step." The Jewish people have been traveling thousands of miles together since the very beginning of our rich history. We are part of that history, both individually and collectively. It is time to add our own footprints to this fertile soil. It is time to answer our call.

Abraham Hears the Call

So often we imagine that we have a set plan for our lives in place, that we know just where we are going, how we are going to get there, and what we will experience once we arrive. But typically this is far from the case. What we thought was set and solid turns out to be variable and fluid. That's why we relate to the Yiddish proverb "Man plans, God laughs" on a visceral level. We all have many examples of how we thought we had it all down pat, with every base covered, and yet, things managed to turn out altogether differently. We might do better to adopt the Chinese proverb "The journey is the reward." That way we can answer the calls we hear with an openness that allows for continued growth, and also a lot less grief, as we allow our lives to unfold

in a spirit of journey, rather than a forced movement toward a preconceived destination.

While Judaism is virtually synonymous with a people, a community, and Israel, Judaism finds its origins in Abram as he begins
his journey in response to a call. Too often the "call" is imagined as a
verbal set of instructions, as if God gave Abram a GPS and an address
to punch in that would take him directly to Israel. However, nothing
about this man's experience is direct. The place he is going is not clear,
the path he is supposed to take in getting there is not defined, and
above all else, we're not even sure if God ever really spoke to him at all.
What we do know is there is a calling and a road map, in spite of the
absence of clear signs as to which way to proceed. We must be mind-
ful that the truth is rarely arrived at directly, the journey is hardly ever
without detours, and though we may experience God calling, we must
be open to vehicles other than words.

The Hebrew text does not say that God *spoke*. *Vayomer Adonai
el Avram* is best translated as "God *communicated* to Abram" (Genesis
12:1). Callings are most often felt, rather than literally heard. More
than coming from "on High" they come from deep within, from a
knowing, an intuition. Maybe God's *vayomer* came vis-à-vis a feeling,
an inclination, a hunch. Perhaps Abram had a dream, a vision, or a gut
feeling in response to some issue he was struggling with, in response to
some question from deep in his soul. Maybe this was how God communicated; what Abram "heard" was "*Lech lecha*—Go forth."

The interesting thing about Abram and Sarai is not that they
answered the call but why they answered it. How many others could
have heard it, responded, and been chosen for the job? Clearly
Abram and Sarai were different and sought something more than
the others around them. As visionaries, they were looking toward
the horizon, driven by a desire for the future. We don't know much
about this couple before they set forth on their grand journey, but
we do know this:

But Sarai was barren; she had no child.

—Genesis 11:30

The Rabbinic tradition points out that this sentence is redundant if read only about childbearing. In fact, Sarai and Abram were barren in other ways, and Abram understood this by his readiness and willingness to leave and set forth. For while the land in which they lived was both fertile and abundant, providing security and physical sustenance, spiritually it was barren. So they set forth into the unknown in hopes of bringing forth life literally, through Sarai carrying the sacred future, and spiritually, through living in partnership with God. This was their calling. This is why they made the journey. This is how Judaism was inspired. And so God spoke: "*Lech lecha*—Go forth" on a journey, a journey about many things, not the least of all about *Ruakh*, divine purpose, divine presence, divine spirit. Journey forth.

Rabbi B's Story: In Search of Spirit

The Judaism I and so many of my contemporaries were raised with was undoubtedly a calling:

- Be a mensch: Be a good person and an upstanding human being.
- *Tzedakah*: Give money to those in need.
- *Tikkun olam*: Go out into the world and make it a better place.
- Identify: Identify with the Jewish people.
- Join: Join Jewish institutions.
- Support: Support Jewish causes.
- Zionism: Defend Israel.
- Marry: Marry a Jew.
- *L'dor vador*: Have children—Jewish children, to be exact.
- Death: Mourn and die as a Jew.

Although this was perpetually ringing in our ears, it was far from being a calling that spoke to our hearts. So many of us chose to hit the road in search of something else, something compelling, something spirited.

My journey began during the winter of my sophomore year in college. I woke up to the fact that much of my life was on autopilot, and I began asking myself important questions that led me to explore the newly developing world of motivational psychology and the burgeoning interest in Eastern spirituality, particularly Buddhism.

As wonderful as these discoveries, teachers, and communities were, however, they were not mine, and I remember the moment this realization was crystallized. I was standing in the office of an admissions officer at the Naropa Institute, a Buddhist university in Boulder, Colorado, applying for a master's program in psychology. Talking to this wise, Buddhist sage was both inspiring and jarring, as I could not get past his name. We'll call him Sunshine Ginsburg. You get the point. This was a school founded by Buddhists, founded by Jews, founded by Jewish Buddhists, often referred to as JuBus, and though I loved the synthesis, I felt out of sync with it all and ultimately out of place. But the fact that so many Jews were following an Eastern spiritual path sparked within me a question that ultimately would change my journey: How is it that Judaism has survived for thousands of years if Jews were now practicing, even leading, other people's religions and communities? There had to be *Ruakh* somewhere within my Jewish heritage, and so I set off to find it in the religion of my birth, in my homeland. I moved to Eretz Yisrael.

In Israel, beyond ethnicity and culture, I discovered a vibrant Jewish religious and spiritual practice for the first time in my life. In Tzfat, on Friday night as the sun was setting behind the mountaintops, I was literally pulled into a circle of men ecstatically singing and dancing the hora, their souls ablaze as they davened (prayed) *Kabbalat Shabbat*. Preparation for the High Holy Days entailed hiking into the wadi (riverbed) at midnight, joining the Hasidim (mystics) literally screaming out to God, "*Abba, Abba, Abba*—Father, Father, Father," until I dropped from exhaustion in a state of revelry I had never before experienced. The Judaism I was experiencing was joyous, real, and defined by *Ruakh*. I knew in my heart I had come home.

Over the past ten years of being a rabbi, I have heeded my call to help educate and inspire American Jews to a fuller exploration of Judaism. And now, as the rabbi of CSH, I have begun to watch that response take root and flourish. Congregation Shirat Hayam is far from perfect and certainly not complete. It is a work in progress. However, it is a place, a space, a community where we have put *Ruakh* front and center, translating these ideas into reality. It is what I wish my grandmother and father would have had in their lives. It is what I wish my brother and sister, friends and fellow Jews would have been raised with to inspire them to remain Jews and feel inspired by their Judaism. But most of all it is what I believe will ensure that my children and future generations not only survive but thrive as Jews and as human beings. Congregation Shirat Hayam is a response of *Hineni*—Here I am, to that eternal call *Ayeka*—Where are you?

Transformation as Part of the Journey

Because of Abram's journey, he is the father not only of Judaism, but of Christianity and Islam, too. That is what each and every one of us is here to do as well: to face our "barrenness," to see where we hunger and thirst, and to heed our call to journey. Our individual journey is important, holy, and part of our Jewish legacy. Too often, Judaism is overcomplicated. To be a good Jew you must _____ (fill in the blank). You must keep kosher, observe Shabbat, join a synagogue, give to the Federation campaign, call your mother, and calling your mother after having given to the Federation is a double mitzvah, for sure. As important as each of these aspects of Judaism might be, however, they are a distant second to this simple yet profound notion of journeying.

Abram, after all, is called *ha'ivri*—the Hebrew. What is *ha'ivri*? As the famous Torah scholar Rabbi Shlomo ben Yitzchak (aka Rashi) tells us, it is one who crosses over the river, making a journey from one reality to another. Abram was a man who made a journey not merely across the geographical terrain, but rather, *lech*—go forth, *lecha*—to yourself. Abram makes a journey crossing over the mental, emotional, and spiritual landscape of his life. In the end *Abram* becomes *Abraham;* through his journey he grows and changes, and the letter *heh* is added to his name, symbolizing this transformation.

Heh is thought to be symbolic of God's presence in the Torah. Abram becomes AbraHam and Sarai becomes SaraH. Because of their willingness to journey into the unknown, each has become infused with divine spirit, with God. This isn't, however, to suggest that transformation is easy. It isn't. It is often painful, requiring much sac-rifice and some birth pains along the way. After all, although Abraham and Sarah discovered a new life and reality, receiving answers to their prayers as they realized their dreams, it wasn't without sacrifice. They had to leave behind life as they knew it. They had to say good-bye to their families, to their comfort zone, and they had to face challenges and tests along the way as they ventured into the unknown.

Later, as their grandson Jacob sets forth on a journey, he spends years responding to calls, answering his own *Ayeka*, and struggling every step of the way. Literally. One night during his journey, Jacob's struggle leads to his name change from *Jacob* to *Israel*, from a boy who "holds on to his brother's heel" to a man who "wrestles with God." Jacob spends the night wrestling, perhaps with his brother, an angel, or possibly his own ego. He wrestles with himself and all the ways he has failed to answer his call. At that moment, his name is changed to *Yisrael*: one who wrestles with God and other people and is able to stay engaged in the challenges. It doesn't mean that you always prevail or that you must achieve a preconceived outcome. Rather, the task is about being able to hear and respond to the call. It refers to being engaged in the struggles that lead to growth as you journey forward, even with the scars that you acquire along the way. From the night of Jacob's wrestling, he spends his life with a wounded thigh, with an injury, with a limp. He is able to move forward, but it is clear he will be forever changed as a result of his past struggles. These scars are sacred, as they attest to the journey that has been made, carrying the past while moving forward—wounds and all.

Ellen's Journey: From *Ayeka* to *Hineni*

I grew up on the North Shore of Chicago, where I learned to take pride in the fact that the public schools were closed on the High Holy Days and that Sandy Koufax refused to pitch game 1 in the 1965 World Series because it fell on Yom Kippur. But the forty-five-minute drive to our Reform temple in the city felt long and tiring, and the

High Holy Day service itself felt even longer and more exhausting. I understood that being Jewish was something to be celebrated, but I didn't see a door open to that joy. At home, while my parents spoke of the importance of Israel and kept track of who was Jewish and who wasn't, we never lit candles on Shabbat or went to services beyond Rosh Hashanah and Yom Kippur. But my spirit hungered, and by the time I was in sixth grade, I had saved my allowance and bought a copy of the New Testament to read. Maybe I would find joy there. Proud of my purchase, I showed my mother what I had bought. I remember how her face fell as she looked at me, shaking her head and saying, "Ellen, you bought the wrong one!" I explained that I didn't want a copy of the Old Testament, this was the one I wanted to read, the one that told the story of Jesus. I read the four Gospels and began to visit some of the nearby churches to hear how they prayed, how they talked to God.

Every week my mom drove the forty-five minutes to Sunday school, and one day in class I let it slip that I had read the New Testament. The teacher looked at me much as my mother had. The following week, the rabbi stopped in our class and said to me, "Christians believe that Jesus is the son of God, but Jews don't believe that. What do you believe?" My heart was pounding, but somehow I looked him in the eye and said, "I thought we were all the children of God." He did not look pleased with my response. I learned that my spiritual quest was not something to be brought into the temple.

A few years later, on a family vacation in upstate New York, we stopped in a gift store where I saw a little ivory Buddha statue. I picked the Buddha up and held him to my heart, feeling as if I couldn't let it go. At that point in my life, I clearly didn't understand nonattachment, one of the basic tenets of Buddhism. Not wanting to part with this statue, my parents relented and bought it for me; some forty years later, it still sits on my dresser.

The following year, I read Herman Hesse's *Siddhartha* and fell in love with the teachings of the Buddha and the idea of following a spiritual path. I imagined living in the forests in India, meditating by a river, traveling the road to enlightenment. Though I continued to go to temple for Sunday school, I never even considered that a spiritual path could take the form of a Jewish spiritual path.

I did, however, find great joy in my temple youth group, especially on the occasional weekend retreats in Oconomowoc, Wisconsin. Sitting around a fire on Shabbat with friends, singing the tunes of Debbie Friedman's versions of Jewish prayer, a spark was ignited in me, a vision of what could be transforming—both personally and in community—in connecting to something sacred.

But when I attempted to speak with the head rabbi about my interests or thoughts, about spirituality and spiritual paths and the teachings of Buddha and Jesus, I felt dismissed at best. And when I tried to follow along in services, my heart just froze. There was nothing within the synagogue walls that kindled my spirit, and the days of youth group retreats were ending. With no teacher or rabbi to validate or encourage my spiritual search or to present me with an inspirational Judaism, I decided that there was no place for me within the religion of my birth.

Eventually, I went on to find a spiritual home within Buddhism. At first I was surprised to find a lot of other Jews in the meditation and retreat centers, and even more surprised that so many of the Buddhist teachers were born Jewish. For me, it only validated what I'd suspected all along—that to find spirituality, you had to look beyond Judaism. Later, after I was married and had children, although I had given up on Judaism, there was a stubborn root that wouldn't give, which led my husband and me to join a Reform synagogue. While physically brighter than the temple of my youth, this synagogue, too, failed to inspire me. It was nice, the rabbi was nice, we talked about *tikkun olam* and social justice. But I did not experience anything close to spirit, except for when the rabbi, who played guitar and sang in ways reminiscent of the youth group retreats of my past, would sing and strum "*Lechi lach*, to a land that I will show you, *Lech lecha*, to a land you do not know ..." The tears would come, flowing down my cheeks then, and I'd try to hide them. My soul resonated with those words, and my heart understood that my spiritual journey was deeply connected to my Jewish heritage. But while the Ju part of me was welcomed into the temple, I felt the Bu part of my JuBu was not, and they were both part of my spiritual path. I continued to practice as a Buddhist, meditating at Buddhist centers and trekking through the Himalayas. Over the past thirteen years, I have also studied with Alan Ullman, an inspirational rabbi, unconnected to a pulpit, who teaches Torah as a spiritual path to various groups across the country.

When my husband and I became empty-nesters, like so many other Jews, we decided it was time to leave our synagogue. By that time my husband had already joined me in studying Torah, and we had no need of or plan to join any more synagogues. But there was God laughing as I walked through the doors of Congregation Shirat Hayam and my plans, thankfully, fell apart.

It felt like the door that I had looked for in my youth had now appeared and was fully open, both literally and figuratively. There was so much spirit and joy, so much welcoming and openness. I felt accepted fully for who I was, the JuBu and the seeker. I go to shul almost every Shabbat now; it's one of the highlights of my week. The mystic Renewal Minyan feeds my soul, the Torah Yoga feeds my mind and body, and the sermon and *Ruakh* Rally feed my spirit. Where once the rabbis of my youth discouraged my seeking and questioning, the rabbis of my adult life deeply encourage and respect my spiritual path and search, and we travel along together. Joining the temple was an unexpected joy.

After Rosh Hashanah services this year, a group of women at the synagogue were chatting in the parking lot about how inspired we were at this congregation. One by one we began discussing where our spiritual searches and journeys had taken us. We had all traveled far: some to India, throughout Europe, Nepal, and Bhutan. And we all started laughing because one woman said, "We've schlepped the world for spirit, and here we all are experiencing it so close to home in our own backyards!"

Making the Journey Our Own

Your journey is uniquely your own. No one can make your journey for you. To fail to make your unique journey is ultimately the only failure you can make in this life. There is a beautiful Hasidic tale that demonstrates this idea:

Each day Rabbi Zusya's students came to the house of study, called the *beit midrash*, eager to learn what they could from him. One day, Zusya did not appear at the usual hour. His students waited all morning and through the afternoon. But Zusya did not come. By evening his students realized that something terrible must have happened. So they all rushed to Zusya's house. The students knocked on the door. No one answered. They knocked more loudly and peered through the frost-covered windows. Finally, they heard a weak voice say, "*Shalom aleichem*, peace be with you. Come in." The students entered Rabbi Zusya's house. In the far corner of the room they saw the old rabbi lying huddled in bed, too ill to get up and greet them.

"Rabbi Zusya!" his students cried. "What has happened? How can we help you?"

"There is nothing you can do," answered Zusya. "I'm dying and I am very frightened."

"Why are you afraid?" the youngest student asked. "Didn't you teach us that all living things die?"

"Of course, every living thing must die some day," said the rabbi.

The young student tried to comfort Rabbi Zusya, saying, "Then why are you afraid? You have led such a good life. You have believed in God with a faith as strong as Abraham's. And you have followed the commandments as carefully as Moses."

"Thank you. But this is not why I am afraid," explained the rabbi. "For if God should ask me why I did not act like Abraham, I can say that I was not Abraham. And if God asks me why I did not act like Moses, I can also say that I was not Moses." Then the rabbi said, "But if God should ask me to account for the times when I did not act like Zusya, what shall I say then?"[2]

We must celebrate individuals for who they are and encourage them to offer their unique self to the world. For too long we have been told there is but one path to walk and one way to walk it. If the *Ruakh* of Judaism is to return, then the *Ruakh* of the individual and his or her path is going to have to be recognized. Forcing your spirit into a box has had deep, negative consequences for both Judaism and Jews. You should not be asked to check your unique spirit at the door. On the contrary, it is what you will someday be called on by the Creator to explain, account for, and defend. "Why weren't you more like yourself?" is what, according to Zusya, we will someday be asked.

In the Torah this is reflected through Abraham and Sarah's son, Isaac. Isaac, after all, is the only patriarch not to make a significant journey and the only patriarch whose name remains unchanged. At the end of his life he is blind, a blindness not only of physical sight but also of spiritual vision. This is in sharp contrast to his son, Jacob, whose journey is so profound that he has his name changed to Yisrael, for whom we are later named. Unlike his son Jacob, Isaac seems to be tethered to a particular time, a particular place. And what is that time and place that he has declared as authentic? His father's time, his father's place, his father's footsteps, his father's Judaism.

The only journey Isaac ever makes is to retrace his father's journey, to literally walk in those footsteps and never veer left or right, never go beyond the places where his father stopped. Ultimately, instead of breaking new ground, Isaac spends his life literally "redigging his father's wells." And though Isaac's efforts may be noble, clearly they are joyless, which is ironic, as his name means "laughter" and yet he has none. His journey is stunted. Isaac is a reminder of the consequences of failing to recognize our individual spark and unique call, the call of *Ruakh*.

We cannot allow our Jewish communities and synagogues to stomp out our individuality, to put roadblocks in our path, or to try to extinguish our unique sparks. Each of us has a *derekh*, a pathway, and each of us, like Abraham, needs to walk our unique pathway home. Judaism is a path made up of these individuals and their unique journeys walking forward together. The point is to keep moving. When we stop, when we think we have arrived and there is no more journey to make, we run the risk of becoming stagnant and frozen in both our practice and spirit.

That is what the Israelites did in the desert, what King David embodied in his Temple, what the Kabbalists did in medieval Spain, what the Hasidim did in Europe, and what the early Zionists did in modern Israel. It's what all uninspired Jews walking away are waiting for—their path to be recognized, their individuality to be validated, and their journey to be welcomed. This is an inspired Judaism and this is the "Jewish Movement" to which we should devote our energy. Rabbi Sharon Brous, spiritual leader of Ikar, reaffirms this sentiment when she states, "I have heard from so many people—especially young and unaffiliated—that they gave up on Jewish life altogether because they found it spiritually empty, intellectually dishonest, morally inconsistent, and socially unstimulating.... Ikar is part of a national trend toward revitalization of Jewish engagement and Jewish life."[3] As a progressive community that is reimagining what it means to be Jewish in today's world, Ikar, and other communities like it, are celebrating the diversity of community and reigniting sparks that create openings for invigorating Jewish life and fostering personal and social transformation. When individuals and their journeys are recognized, there is joy, life, and *Ruakh*. It is incumbent on each of us to step up and step out, forging new directions and leaving our unique footprints in the Jewish soil.

2

Na'aseh

Communal Call to Journey

Although most religions have at their origin a male mystic who set forth on a journey, only Judaism is founded by a husband-and-wife team, joined by a nephew and a community they gathered along the way.

> So Abram went forth, as the Lord had spoken to him; and Lot went with him; and Abram was seventy-five years old when he departed from Haran. And Abram took Sarai his wife, and Lot his brother's son, and all their possessions that they had gathered, and the souls they had acquired along the way; and they journeyed to go to the land of Canaan ...
>
> —Genesis 12:4–5

What began as one man's calling turned into one community's journey. And though Abraham's unique calling was still central to the journey, it was shaped by and ultimately made most meaningful through walking side by side with others. As a central tenet of Judaism proclaims, *kol Yisrael areivim zeh bazeh*—all Jews are responsible for one another.[1] The Jewish journey may begin with the individual but must culminate in the communal.

Rabbi B's Story: From Caveman to Community

I'm a caveman by nature. I would be quite happy spending most of my time writing, studying, contemplating, and living alone. In spite of the fact that I'm married, a father of four, and the rabbi of a large congregation, I'm still a caveman at heart. And so it made sense that, after college, having sold most of my worldly possessions and carrying everything I had left on my back, I set off for Israel, where I intended on journeying alone.

Though my journey began as a solo adventure, it quickly morphed into something else. Alone in a country where I had never been, in a place where I didn't know a soul, I felt not merely alone, but lonely. Months later, it dawned on me that without others my journey would be incomplete. What I needed—what all humans need—are other individuals in our lives to love us and for us to love. We need relationships to sustain us.

Abram could only become Abraham through the highs and the lows, the ups and the downs offered to him through his relationships not only with himself and with God, but vis-à-vis his wife, his nephew, his children, and his community. The people in his life and the individuals along his path were not simply encounters and experiences along the journey—they were the journey itself.

Thousands of years later, in places where Abraham himself literally placed his feet, I walked out of my cave and into community. What struck me about living in Israel was an ethnic, cultural, and tribe-like familiarity. My entry into Judaism was not explicitly through religious or spiritual pathways; rather, it was through community and these tribal awakenings taking place within me. I remember feeling a great sense of kinship with Jews of all types: garbage collectors and soldiers, black men wearing yarmulkes and women of Arab appearance shopping for Shabbat. One day I was getting out of a taxicab and saying good-bye to the driver, with whom I'd been speaking and had known for all of ten minutes. As I was preparing to part ways, he asked me if I had anywhere to go that night for Shabbat dinner. When I told him no, he invited me to his home to join him and his family. And it struck me—we were brothers. No, we were not from the same parents. No, we didn't speak the same language. No, we hardly knew each other from

Adam, but we were brothers nonetheless. And thus began my awakening to the centrality, significance, and necessity of community as part of my journey. In so many ways, from that moment onward, though never giving up my caveman, solo-adventurer tendencies, I began to place community and communal journeys at the center of my life.

Jewish Bachelors: The Origins of Our Great Patriarchs

The great heroes from our Torah didn't always look like such great catches. We might think of the important characters of the Torah, like Jacob, Joseph, and Moses, as grown men, but at first they act more like boys. Each of these figures begins as self-absorbed, shallow, and unattached. Quite literally, they were bachelors. They were not only unhitched, they were unwed to a purpose, a people, or a place.

Early in the story, Jacob seems to have few family loyalties. He is willing to finagle away the birthright from his brother and steal his father's blessing out from under his nose. Joseph may grow into a mighty provider, sustaining his family and his people when they fall on hard times. However, at first he is an arrogant dreamer with total disregard for his brothers' well-being or his father's peace of mind. Before Moses takes upon himself the monumental task of leading his people across the harsh desert, he's unwilling to commit himself to this community.

And yet, eventually, each one of these boys grows into manhood. Each settles down, gets married, raises children, and assumes the duties and responsibilities of being an adult. Leaving bachelorhood behind, they intertwine their path with others. Judaism necessitates relationships. In the words of Hillel, "If I am not for myself, who will be for me? If I am only for myself, what am I? And if not now, when?"[2]

From a Jewish perspective, although we may be perfectly content being alone, ultimately it does not offer us our greatest opportunity for growth. As we read in the Torah:

> And the Lord God said: It is not good that man should be *l'vado* [lonely]; I will make an *ezer kenegdo* [someone to help him, someone to challenge him].
>
> —GENESIS 2:18

Though initially Adam is fine on his own in the Garden, it is clear that he needs something more. We are here to create, to contribute, and to bring forth life, and for that we need others; we need a lover, a spouse, a partner. We need brothers and sisters, family, friends, and community. Without them we may be alive but we are far from fully living. Or, in the words of Albert Einstein:

> Strange is our situation here on Earth. Each of us comes for a short visit, not knowing why, yet sometimes seeming to divine a purpose. From the standpoint of daily life, however, there is one thing we do know: that man is here for the sake of other men—above all for those upon whose smiles and well-being our own happiness depends.[3]

So it was that Abraham set forth not alone, but with his wife, his nephew, his family and community. The Jewish heritage began first and foremost as a people. It was only centuries later, when they were established within the identity known as "the Israelites" that they formally became a religion. Even then when they organized themselves around religious principles and faith, still they entered into the *brit*, the covenant, as a community:

> And Moses came and told the people all the words of God and all the laws; and all the people answered with one voice and said, "All the words that God has said will we do!" ... And he took the Book of the Covenant and read for the people; and they said, "All that God has said *na'aseh v'nishma* [will we do, and we will listen/understand]."
>
> —Exodus 24:3, 24:7

Judaism is predicated not on individuality but on community. It is the only religion that entered and continues to enter into the covenant as such. *Na'aseh v'nishma*—we shall enter the covenant and we shall listen together—was how the Israelites responded thousands of years ago and continue to respond today. We are, by definition, part of something much larger than our individual selves. In a world that is growing increasingly fractured, where people are feeling rootless, alone, and cut off from one another, Jewish community is rife with possibility and potential.

While each of us must make a choice about our own commitment to travel a Jewish path, at its origin Judaism is about traveling that road in community and being in relationship with God, together. We are significant as individuals, unique souls making our way in this lifetime. We are even more significant, greater, and stronger when that way is bound up, as it inevitably is, with other travelers. In taking part in this communal journey, we are part of something ancient, enduring, and profound.

Rabbi B's Story: You Never Know

After my father died we held a memorial service in the town in which he was living. As we were in the midst of our service in one of his friend's homes, the door opened and in walked a young woman. She sat there for a while listening to the impromptu eulogies, the poetry being read, and the somber songs being sung. And then, as we were beginning to wrap up this fitting tribute, she asked if she could speak.

"You don't know me and I don't know you," she began. "I hardly knew Shelly [my father] and yet he saved my life." Needless to say, we were intrigued.

"Shelly used to frequent the café where I work as a barista. It's in a part of town caught up in the hustle and bustle of busy corporate life where the customers are frequently quite rude. When Shelly was there one day, I was particularly down and out. I have suffered from depression most of my adult life, and that particular stretch was really tough for me. My little brother had just died. I was a wreck. I was contemplating suicide. I felt so alone.

"And then Shelly walked into my life. Shelly was always so full of joy, so kind to me and the others in the café and always asked how I was doing, and he meant it, too. On that particular day, he not only asked the question but, seeing I was so sad, he pursued it and wouldn't take 'fine' for an answer.

"The café was empty that day, so we sat and talked and talked and talked. It was perhaps the most wonderful conversation I have had in my life. Here was a man who was practically a stranger to me, owed me nothing, and yet sat and listened and empathized and loved me for who I was and what I was going through.

"I never told Shelly this, but that was a turning point for me. It was also the moment I decided to stop contemplating suicide. He made me want to live. Shelly, I believe, was an angel of God put here at that very moment to save my life.

"When I heard he took his own life, I was heartbroken. I felt as if my own father had died. It seemed as if one of God's angels had fallen from the sky. I never told him how much it meant to me that our paths had crossed. I never told him how much he meant to me. I only wish I could have seen that maybe our paths had crossed so that I could have helped him the way he helped me. Maybe I was supposed to see him as he saw me."

Throughout the Hasidic tradition, there are stories of strangers and beggars wandering into and out of Jewish villages and into the lives of individuals. Although these beggars are always dressed in the garb of the "other," they are often more than what they appear. They are not beggars, strangers, or mere mortals. Rather, they are Eliyahu HaNavi, Elijah the Prophet, the holy angel, who, according to the tradition, reminds us of God's saving presence in our lives. He is a reminder that God is not up there, removed from this world. Rather, the Divine is made manifest at the crossroads of our respective paths and the inter-sections of our journeys, at the meeting places in our lives. You never know how your journey might be part of someone else's journey, you just never know.

Craving Community

What has become evident over the past decade or so is that even as communities are splintering, fragmenting, and breaking apart, that hasn't eliminated the human need to be in relationship. We are social beings in search of connection. In many ways, our changing society only makes community more necessary today than ever before.

Take, for example, Temple Valley Beth Shalom in Encino, California. Under the leadership of Rabbi Harold Schulweis, one of the greatest visionary rabbis of our time, this "mega-shul" has created an increased sense of community and intimacy by establishing over fifty *chavurot*, each of them unique and separate while still fostering a greater sense of connection between the groups and the membership as a whole. People are looking for ways to connect to community but on their terms and in ways that speak to them.

This has proved true at CSH. There are many portals of entry where individuals have found their way back not only through educational, religious, or spiritual avenues, per se, but through the sacredness of connecting through community. Time and again Jews confess, "Rabbi, I don't know if I believe in God. I'm not sure how I feel about spirituality. I can't say for sure that I care about the religious aspects of my tradition. However, Rabbi, I am a Jew. I feel a connection, a pull, a commitment to Israel, to community, to the tribe." And time and again I reassure them that their pathway into community is beautiful and noble. Judaism is about community. Our people are hungry for it, and it is our duty and privilege to provide nourishment for them, their journeys, and their souls.

Ellen's Sisters at the Sea

There is a group of women at CSH who call themselves the Spirited Sisters. They are committed to joining together in sacred community to share in the joys and challenges of life. This past summer, a healing service was held for a woman in the group who was scheduled to have surgery that afternoon. We met at the beach at six in the morning to watch the sunrise as we shared healing prayers, thoughts, and songs with our spirited sister in need. At one point, she was asked to express her fears and then, by picking up small rocks, she was invited to throw her fears into the ocean. We surrounded her as she carefully tossed these stones into the waves, letting go of the worries as we held her in our arms and our hearts. I remember watching the glow of peace spreading across her face as her body relaxed in the embrace of love by a community that held one another. After leaving the beach that morning, she set off for the hospital. I remember thinking about those I love who have had to face the medical unknown, leaving for treatments or surgery filled with fear, anxiety, and apprehensions, alone. This healing morning offered another way to move into that space. With the rising of the sun, the rhythms of the ocean, and the spirit of sisterhood, what dawned that morning was a rededication to ourselves, our loved ones, and the Sacred. I remember thinking that whatever I may face in the future, I want to face it this way, within the heart and soul of the Spirited Sisters, who recognize individuality while bonding together with the blessing of togetherness.

As the synagogue offers new ways for people to come together, the shul takes on new meaning. Not only is that sacred space available in bricks and mortar, but in numerous ways as it is carried in the hearts and souls of those who live together in spiritual community. It is like throwing that stone into the ocean and watching the concentric circles form. The innermost ring is like the synagogue, and the ripples of growing circles are the result of that center—the blessings that spread beyond the center out into the unknown waters.

Rabbi B's Scotch and Schmooze

The financial, educational, and business successes Jews have achieved in this country are staggering. Day in and day out I meet with many men and women who have wealth, achievements, and success by numerous outward standards. Yet so many of these individuals are dissatisfied or unhappy. Though this is true for both sexes, what has been striking to me in my work, and the direction I have gravitated to in my counseling, revolves around my experience with Jewish men.

So many Jewish men share similar journeys, varying only in detail and degree. They were afforded opportunities to pursue their dreams. They realized their personal and professional goals. They fell in love and married. They have the house, the kids, the dog, and the proverbial white picket fence. Yet they wonder why it isn't enough, why they don't feel happy or satisfied or spiritually nourished or complete. Worse yet, they feel duped. Where is the satisfaction? Where is the passion? Where is the purpose? And often, when they have looked to their religion, many have come up empty-handed, feeling an emptiness in their soul.

During my tenure I have focused much time on creating *chavurot*, groups with a shared interest or purpose. In particular, I have run numerous men's groups. Some have focused on Torah study, others on alternative prayer experiences like hiking, kayaking, and the like. But perhaps the most meaningful is what we at CSH call "Scotch and Schmooze."

"Scotch and Schmooze" is pretty much self-explanatory. A group of men, ranging from a minyan to a few dozen, of all ages, gather together to study or watch a movie or a video clip, to drink a little scotch, and most of all to talk. We always orient the conversation toward issues, topics, or ideas pertinent to the lives of twenty-first-century, modern Jewish men. And each and every time it is staggering to see successful men open up and share their feelings of struggle, loneliness, and isolation. Those outward personas are shed. The truth about marriages or illusions of financial success come tumbling down. And there, in the midst of community, many of these men who are impervious or impenetrable in the outside world open up and fully come to life.

I have watched men who normally would find their outlet on the golf course, at a sporting event, or at a bar with friends instead choose to attend a Scotch and Schmooze. Rarely are they disappointed with their choice. They confide in me that, for the first time in their adult life, they feel like they can speak honestly, be heard, and experience a sense of community. And to that I say, *L'chayim!*"

A Threefold Cord Is Not Easily Broken

During times of national struggle in America or Israel, it is often in community that people seek refuge. For instance, after Yitzhak Rabin was assassinated, many were drawn to the synagogue. Entering with sorrow, despair, and powerlessness, people found comfort with one another, emerging with the feeling that we were all in this together; we weren't alone groping in the dark. And after the tragedies that befell this country on 9/11, many American's sought out houses of worship to congregate in community. We intuited what the author of Ecclesiastes touched on:

> A person standing alone can be attacked and defeated, but two can stand back-to-back and conquer. Three are even better, for a threefold cord is not easily broken. (4:12)

Who could forget the pride we felt when Israel and world Jewry gathered around Soviet Jewry with rallies and marches, surrounded by fellow Jews shouting, "Let my people go," or the *naches* we experienced when Israel rescued Ethiopian Jews. We beamed with pride at the words of *New York Times* journalist William Safire: "For the first time in history thousands of black people are being brought into a country not in chains but in dignity, not as slaves but as citizens."[4] That is power. That is Judaism. That is what it means to be a part of this tribe. Individually we may be vulnerable, but collectively we are strong. In such moments we reverberate with the message emblazoned on each and every coin: *E pluribus unum,* "From the many [comes] one." We have our individual journeys, but when we come together to walk side by side, our journeys become one.

Planting Roots on the Journey

While the Israelites carried the *Mishkan* (Tabernacle) on their backs, setting it up and taking it down whenever it was time to move, eventually it was erected permanently in Israel, high up on the hill in Jerusalem that later became known as the Temple Mount. The Temple was more than a holy place. The *Beit Mikdash* was the center of the Jewish world. It was the center of religion, commerce, community, and Jewish identity throughout the land. But when it was destroyed and the Jewish people were scattered throughout the world, the Rabbinic tradition understood something profound: people need places to orient themselves toward, to congregate and to gather. And in that moment synagogues or Jewish congregations were born. Rather than one big Temple, wherever Jewish people were to be found, little temples were built. Instead of demanding that Jews journey toward the Temple Mount, now Jews would make a journey of a different kind.

All physical journeys must come to an end. We cannot stay on the move forever. Oftentimes, when the physical journey is prolonged, it can distract us from the real work of exercising our spirits, rather than our legs. At some point we simply need to stop wandering, pick a spot, and put down roots. And that place where we anchor ourselves collectively must be a dynamic and breathing home, able to both inspire and nourish our very souls. It must serve as a resting and reinvigorating spot that is able to water our roots and allow for individual and collective flourishing.

Although there are many important institutions and structures necessary for a Jewish community to survive and thrive, as Rabbi Lawrence A. Hoffman so eloquently argues in *Rethinking Synagogues: A New Vocabulary for Congregational Life* (Jewish Lights), nothing is as essential as a synagogue at the center. Synagogues are needed now more than ever. JCCs are at a crossroads. Many feel that their day has come and gone. In an era when Jews are no longer excluded from non-Jewish organizations, Jewish cultural centers and institutions are struggling to define themselves and stay afloat. Other Jewish institutions may or may not survive. Synagogues, however, have been central to Judaism for the past two thousand years. But they must adapt and change to fit the culture and needs of today. If we insist on staying frozen in time, if our shuls fail to become energetic gathering places for our journeys, embracing the spirit we bring forth, we will continue to see empty pews and fewer Jews. We will die. But if we move forward into the unknown with openness, fearlessness, and faith, we will inspire, and our synagogues can once again play a central role on the journey. We will live. It is up to us. It is our choice.

3

Choose Life

Choosing to Journey

This day I call heaven and earth as witnesses against you that
I have set before you life and death, blessings and curses.
Now choose life, so that you and your children may live.

—Deuteronomy 30:19

From Crisis to Birth: A Tale of Two Temples

I'm frequently asked how Congregation Shirat Hayam has succeeded when so many other synagogues have failed. It is a complex answer that encompasses the work of many who came before us along with the keen vision and inspired work of our lay and professional leaders today.

As we write this, CSH is a seven-year-old congregation. It is the by-product of a merger of two Conservative synagogues, which just happened to literally face one another from opposite sides of the street. Why they merged isn't half as interesting as why they split apart. As legend has it, someone with money was somehow slighted, or perhaps it was his wife—the details have been lost to history—but it's unfortunately an all-too-familiar story, and you know how it ends. Instead of working through the issue, he and his supporters had the financial means and the egos that led them to build another shul as a response to the conflict. For decades these two Conservative synagogues stood apart, competing for members and for money, but competition was not cutthroat; there were plenty of Conservative Jews to go around.

Of course, the party didn't last. Toward the end of the twentieth century, the writing, as in most communities, began to appear on the wall. There was too much infrastructure in Jewish communities, too many synagogues, and not enough Jews to go around. Although it was a process, a long, arduous, and often contentious process, ultimately, over a decade later, the merger was complete.

In Hebrew there is an important word that sums up not just this moment but much of Jewish history as well. That word is *mashber*. A *mashber* in modern Hebrew is a crisis, literally a "shattering." However, in ancient Hebrew it had another connotation as well. A *mashber* was a stool on which a woman would squat while she was giving birth. Childbirth then, and now, is an event fraught with anxiety, danger, and all too often, death. Yet through those birth pains, on the other side of those contractions, is life. A *mashber* is, indeed, a moment of peril. A *mashber*, however, also holds the power for the potential of life.

When former Temples Beth El and Israel were first diagnosed with a *mashber*, a crisis, needless to say there was panic, denial, resentment, and mudslinging within those walls and back and forth across the boulevard. Some members quit. Others jumped ship to join other shuls. However, there was a critical mass of leaders—men and women of vision—who were willing to step up and lead.

What those leaders committed to was one thing and one thing alone. They weren't committed to a label, a brand, or a building. They didn't know the specifics of the programming, the flavors of the experience, or exactly who would take the reins and run the place. But they knew they wanted a shul that was living, not dying. They wanted a synagogue that was breathing, not suffocating. They wanted a congregation that had *Ruakh*. They set forth as a community into the unknown, pushed through the pains of birth, bringing forth congregational life.

The band Chicago sings, "Does anyone really know what time it is?" If we truly ask ourselves this question, we put ourselves smack in the middle of our wake-up call. As individuals and community, it is up to us to read the writing on the wall, or more accurately, the hour hands on the clock. It is up to us to serve the future while honoring the past, and this necessitates moving forward in our journey to reclaim a living and vibrant Judaism that speaks to who we are today, this hour, this minute. Nothing is static; everything is changing. The only wrong response is no response.

The word *Torah* is derived from the Hebrew word *lirot*, which means "to shoot." It was an archer's term implying direction, and ultimately that's what Torah is meant to be, the direction in which we move within our lives. And halacha, though often translated as "Jewish law," literally means "the path." Torah is the direction, and halacha, the ins and outs of Jewish living, is the path on which we walk. Judaism was never meant to be static. By definition it is liberating, calling us to journey, setting us in a direction. Of course, there are parameters in place to keep us collectively on the path, but the boundaries are far more expansive than usually presented, and the choices are far more abundant than we ever imagined. These choices are here to be made and celebrated. Our synagogues, as living and breathing holders of sacred space, must allow for and applaud these various expressions and embrace a spectrum of possibilities. When we fail to do so, we constrict the lives of the congregants and the path of inspiration. With no choice, there can be no *Ruakh*. With no breath, there is only death.

Ellen's Story: On Being Seen and Having Choice

Though I was born a Jew, I'd have to say at this point in life, I am a Jew by choice. If people had told me a few years back that I would be attending Shabbat services on a weekly basis, I would never have believed them. After all, my childhood experiences in temple were uninspiring, my questioning and seeking were not encouraged, and the distance between me as a congregant and my rabbi felt as big as the Red Sea—but this time, there was no parting of the water, no place to meet in the middle. My decision not to go to temple was a choice in itself, as I chose to walk away.

Ten years ago, as my daughter was preparing for her Bat Mitzvah, I felt the constriction of the temple walls. While I continued to bring my children to the shul, wanting them to have their own experience as opposed to imposing mine, when entering temple I held my breath, as if I were literally holding in my *Ruakh*. And though I was used to sacrificing choice when it came to my spiritual needs within my synagogue, I wasn't going to hold my tongue when it came to advocating for my daughter. She alerted me to something that was bothering her in the service in which she would participate as she became a Bat Mitzvah.

"Mom, when I read the prayer that mentions the patriarchs, I want to mention the matriarchs, too," she told me. Allie pointed to the prayer book, showing me what she meant. Her request didn't surprise me. When she was in fifth grade, she began spelling *woman* as *womyn*. From that moment onward I had a budding feminist at my side. So her request in reading the matriarchs made sense in terms of both who she was and who she was becoming. I told her I would speak to our rabbi, since I was meeting with him that week.

I explained the situation to him, expecting that what, to my mind, was a simple request from a girl navigating her way toward a meaningful Bat Mitzvah would be both welcomed and celebrated. Instead, it felt like the many times I shared my thoughts and my spirit with the rabbis of my youth and was not seen for who I was. Now my daughter was not being seen for who she was. Yet again, we were left with no choice.

He told me he couldn't honor this request because the prayer book being used mentions only the patriarchs and it's too confusing for the congregation to make changes. I could feel the anger boiling inside me, the old wounds of being dismissed in the temple of my youth reopening. I remember following my breath then, trying to connect with the peace I was experiencing while practicing my meditation. So I stood there breathing, and he stood there breathing, but it felt like the oxygen was being sucked out of the room.

Allie read beautifully during her Bat Mitzvah, but she was unable to proclaim out loud her connection with the women who came before her. With a focus on the one-size model, our rabbi was unable to really see my daughter and, in doing so, missed an opportunity to partner with her and facilitate her movement toward self-expression and the celebration of her spirit.

And so, three years later, when it was time for our son Matt's Bar Mitzvah, I, too, learned that changes have to be made to reflect a dynamic and changing family. That was when we decided to have a creative Bar Mitzvah under the guidance of Rabbi Alan Ullman, the nonpulpit rabbi with whom we had been studying for years. We journeyed together with *Ruakh*, but it was outside the synagogue, for we had failed to find it within those walls where we lacked choice in our journeys.

Coffee and Choice: A Sign of the Times

There was a time when people were happy with a cup of mediocre, weak, black coffee. Maybe some would jazz it up with milk or others would get a little wild and throw in some sugar. Today, hardly anyone drinks plain, black coffee. Even if the coffee is black, it's hardly simple. Do you like beans grown in Africa or those harvested in South America? Do you like it bold or medium or mild? Or perhaps you no longer even drink coffee, as you're now addicted to espresso or cappuccino or lattes—lattes with milk, lattes with soy milk, lattes that are skinny or dry or no foam or extra hot or sweetened—and the list of sweeteners is a book unto itself.

The point is clear: we live in a world of choice. Our society celebrates choice, expects choice, and demands choice. The bottom line is that if Judaism and our Jewish institutions, particularly our synagogues, are going to thrive, we are going to have to start honoring choice and offering choices. And it's not just most shuls' coffee that is lacking a variety of flavors, richness, and boldness. Just as there's one type of coffee, usually really bad coffee being served at the *Oneg Shabbat*, there's also only one type of prayer experience, and it's usually about as enticing as that watery, weak, flavorless coffee of years ago. What synagogues need today are real choices. We need choices for Jews to express themselves and their individual needs within community and choices that can wake up the soul, regardless of being caffeinated or decaf!

One of the first things I'm asked as a rabbi is, "What type of rabbi are you?" And, I feel duty-bound to challenge their question.

"A good one, I hope," is often my reply.

"No, no, I mean, what kind of rabbi are you?" they'll say again, wondering if I'm really a rabbi at all.

"Oh," comes my rejoinder. "A Jewish rabbi," I'll respond, knowing full well this might do them in, and on it goes.

Of course I know what they are asking. They want a label. They want a neat, tidy package to place on their understanding of my Judaism—their understanding of me. In this world, we are hung up on labels, and Judaism is no exception. Labels, labels, labels.

"Reform Judaism says ..."

"Conservative Judaism stands for ..."

"Orthodox Judaism declares ..."

Reconstructionist Jews do this, Renewal Jews do that. There are Humanistic Jews, JuBus, HinJus, Agnostic Jews, Atheist Jews, fifty-one flavors of ultra-Orthodoxy, and the list goes on. In the end, I have no problem sharing that I am a Conservative rabbi, proud of much of what Conservative Judaism has to offer. My Jewish journey began with inspirational Conservative rabbis like Daniel Gordis and Bradley Shavit Artson during my time in rabbinical school. My admiration for the movement continues when I hear about the *Ruakh* emanating from our Schechter Day Schools and Camp Ramahs. However, for me, it often feels as if this label tells only part of the story. There have been so many influences on me from many other movements, like my mentor and teacher Rabbi Mordecai Finley, a Reform ordained rabbi and spiritual leader of Congregation Ohr HaTorah, in Los Angeles, where I served as a rabbinical intern for over five years. The earliest inspirations on my Jewish journey were Orthodox teachers such as Rabbi Michael Rosen (of blessed memory), founder of Yakar in Jersualem, and Rabbi Daniel Landes, head of the Pardes Institute in Jerusalem. So, instead of limiting my label to one definition, I feel compelled to answer the question "What type of rabbi are you?" by echoing Dr. Alan Morinis once again: I am an Under-constructionist Jew.

"What type of synagogue is this?" is another question I'll get. I tell them it is a Jewish one, a dynamic one, a work in progress, running the gamut of possibilities and expressions, experiences and choice. It's usually not a response they are expecting. They want a clear-cut answer. They want to know what movement we belong to as they try to figure out how to glorify or demonize exactly what we do. This, however, is not a movement issue. Frankly, most, if not all, the movements equally fail to recognize this truth about choice. Sure, a Reform temple may have chosen a very different path from an Orthodox shul. However, by and large, within those walls there is still far too little choice.

People are hungry for choice in this day and age. Jews demand it in the marketplace, in their grocery stores, their cafés, and bookstores. And though they aren't necessarily demanding it from their synagogues because they hardly think of it as an option in this particular venue, when they are offered choices they will respond. At CSH, for instance, over the past seven years of our existence, hundreds of new individuals and families have joined. They haven't joined because of the label or our Conservative affiliation. In fact, like Ellen, sometimes they have joined in spite of it. What modern Jews are looking for is not a brand name, but a brand-new experience anchored in something ancient, rooted, and inspired. Whatever the movement, a synagogue in the twenty-first century needs to span the spectrum of choices. Choice isn't always about being contemporary and new. It's about allowing options within boundaries that point toward the Jewish spirit and guide its practitioners down a Jewish path. People want to be seen for their unique journeys and want to experience pieces of that journey within a Jewish context and their spiritual home. Congregation Shirat Hayam is a community that celebrates their paths and knows we are richer for having them in our midst. "What kind of synagogue is CSH?" they ask. A synagogue that is, in the deepest sense, "pro-choice."

The Synaplex Revolution

Growing up in Omaha, Nebraska, I used to love going to the cinema. At my favorite theater, like most theaters of that era, there was only one movie showing at a time. It worked way back when. I was happy to sit in front of the large screen and watch whatever was playing. Having few choices was indicative of the times. After all, what did the movie theaters have to compete with then? Network television? Big deal. There was no cable. There were three channels to choose from, and it was a big event when a fourth one was added to the roster, though not nearly as monumental as the invention of the remote control.

Then along came cable television and everything changed. Music channels. Movie channels. Multiple channels. No more national anthem followed by that off-the-air signal playing late into the night. No more having to watch something you had no interest in simply because you had no choice. The revolution of cable TV was a reflection of the larger revolution that was under way: the revolution of personal choice.

We wanted and demanded choice. The businesses and industries that responded to our needs for choice ultimately survived. My beloved theater didn't make the leap. They held fast to the belief that "one size could fit all." They staked their claim on the belief that people would still come out of loyalty, out of a desire for that grand viewing experience. And they, like almost every other business that did not adapt to a highly individualized, personalized, and nuanced marketplace, disappeared.

The venue where movies are shown in many theaters under one roof—not just one—is called a cineplex. What is unique is not the *cine* of cinema, but the *plex*, which drove the real revolution. "Plex" added to the end of a word transforms the subject into a space with multiple locations, divisions, or options. It's not coincidental that the first-known use of this term came in the mid-1980s, a time of shifting from little choice to an expectation of many choices. During this same period, shopping malls began to feature food courts, workout gyms became fitness centers, grocery stores became supermarkets, and of course, Starbucks and coffee-how-you-like-it burst onto the scene. You take your pick of industries and this was a time of expansion and choice. People now demanded options to suit their personal preferences. One size never really fit all, but now we not only knew it, we engaged it. We had the ability to watch, wear, and eat whatever we wanted, wherever we wanted, and whenever we wanted it.

Although Jewish communities and synagogues need to be distinguished from merely being a business or part of the larger marketplace, it's time to start rethinking them as part of a choice-driven society. If we don't, we'll continue down the path where we are headed, the path of that one-size-fits-all bankrupt movie theater.

Synaplex is the honest and necessary outcome of a consumer culture, one defined by choice. Instead of *cine*, it is *syna*, as in *synagogue*. The *plex*, however, remains the same. A Synaplex, a name created and trademarked by an organization called Synaplex Transformation and Renewal (STAR), is a synagogue offering a multiplex of programmatic options. Particularly, though not necessarily exclusively, this takes place on Shabbat. It is a one-stop shop of Jewish offerings that speaks to this era's expectations, if not demands, that one size doesn't fit all.

And though some might reel at this notion of offering multiple pathways within our synagogues, claiming that multiple venues of self-expression are new age, it's as old as Jewish tradition and Torah itself. This is why, according to the Midrash, when God speaks to Moses, God says, "I am the God of Abraham, the God of Isaac, the God of Jacob ..." It says *God of* separately each time. It could have, after all, been said more succinctly. Why wasn't it? Because the Rabbis teach us that Abraham's experience of God was different from Isaac's, whose was different from Jacob's.

God is dynamic, and each human being is unique. No two human beings have the same fingerprints. No two people have the same DNA. So it would make sense that no two seekers of the Divine would express themselves, their desires, their *Ruakh* in the same way as anyone else.

Later at Sinai, when God spoke to Moses, the Midrash teaches us that God spoke to all the Israelites and to everyone who was present, everyone who was not present, those born and those yet to be born. God spoke to each fetus in the womb who stood at the base of that mountain. God spoke to them on their terms—every man, woman, child, embryo, and future soul who would one day come into this world. They were spoken to and connected with as individuals, brought into covenant on their individual terms. Yes, it was and continues to be a community, but a community of individuals with different voices and different choices.[1]

God spoke *panim el panim*, literally, "faces to faces." There is no singular word for *face* in Hebrew. No one, least of all God, has "one face." The face itself has over seventy muscles. Contracted one way, we have one type of expression. Contorted another way, we have an entirely different look. The permutations create a huge spectrum of possibility. The manifestations of God are infinite, and so are the ways each one of us expresses ourselves to the Divine. Therefore, the desire to speak to God on our terms, with the expectation that we will be heard, seen, and felt by the Source, is an authentic urge rooted in Jewish tradition. It is understandable that people are seeking a spiritual home within their synagogues and Jewish communities that not only recognizes this desire, but celebrates it as well. This is essential if we are to reclaim *Ruakh* at the center of our spiritual homes.

Of course, Synaplex would have been utterly foreign to our forebears, but that is the point. God speaks to us where we are, in ways we know, through means to which we can relate. "What is Your name?" Moses demands to know of God, to which God finally responds, "*Ehyeh asher Ehyeh*—I will be what I will be" (Exodus 3:13–14). It's not that God will be different; God is unchanging. Rather, we change and our needs change. It's as if God is saying, "I don't want a label; I can't be quantified or tied down to space and time." Our Jewish communities and synagogues need to reflect this aspect of God: *I will be what I will be,* the God of the eternal but the God of change as well. Synaplex is not a new age, commercialized Judaism. Rather, Synaplex is ancient and rooted in tradition.

Additive Change: Offering More, Not Less

Once when a great rebbe died his son assumed the mantle of leadership. However, much to the chagrin of the rebbe's disciples, the son altered many of the time-honored practices of his father. Some of the older followers approached him to complain, challenging him as to how he could make such changes.

"What do you mean?" asked the new master. "I am, in fact, doing exactly as my father did!" Seeing the looks of consternation on the disciples' faces, he went on.

"When my father became master, he changed many of his father's practices. Thus I am doing exactly as my father did."[2]

Change happens. Jews, and Jewish institutions in particular, tend not to admit this, but it is true nonetheless. *Chadesh yamenu k'kedem,* we read as we place the Torah scrolls back into the ark, "Return us to the days of old" (Lamentations 5:21). However, the days of old weren't all that they were cracked up to be. And even if they were, they are behind us. The future is before us, and if the Jewish enterprise is going to move into that future, we'd better stop waxing nostalgic about the past and make some changes in the way we do things today.

"Rabbi," a cantor colleague said to me, with a warning tone in his voice the day I arrived at my first congregation, "whatever you do here; don't make changes. But if you have to make changes, don't make them too often or too quickly." He also warned me, after hearing me sing, "Leave the singing up to the cantor, please," just to give you a sense of where he was coming from. And he was not alone in either of his sentiments. He spoke for many of my colleagues and many of my congregants as well.

The problem, however, is that most of the Jews weren't in the pews. Perhaps he spoke for the few who were in attendance, but as the saying goes, if you do what you've always done, you'll get what you've always gotten. Or, in the words of Albert Einstein, "Insanity is doing the same thing over and over again and expecting different results." So we'd better take a different road and make some changes. Of course, those who show up every week are fine with the status quo, but all those people who have left the synagogue aren't coming back unless we make changes—and lots of them—fast!

We also read, with Torah scrolls in hand, "Not upon angels do we rely, nor upon miracles do we depend." Yet too many of our Jewish institutions sit around seemingly waiting for the miracle that Jews will somehow change their minds and flock to our synagogues once again. So we change little and hope a lot, and we're left with empty seats as we wait in vain, hoping and praying for miracles that will never occur.

So I was done sitting around and waiting for miracles. I decided it was time to make a change, and that's what I did. And it was a disaster. Although it might be nice to get it right the first time without making any mistakes, in life this rarely happens. It certainly wasn't the way I learned how to create and sustain a well-functioning Synaplex. Although CSH currently runs a successful, weekly, Shabbat morning Synaplex, it only came about as a result of my previous, failed attempts in my former shul.

While trying to implement the Synaplex in my previous position, the biggest mistake I made was violating the fundamental notion of Synaplex—that of choice. Originally, I attempted to bring a whole host of different offerings to the synagogue all at once, into the same venue, to the same constituency, rotating the offerings week by week. One Shabbat was traditional davening. Another Shabbat was camp-style singing. Another time it was a meditative service. And once and only once, I had the "regulars," the over-seventy crowd dressed in suits and dresses, doing very, very mild yoga poses. But while the yoga was mild, their reaction to the change was far from it, to say the least, and to repeat that offering would have been insanity, to be sure. Needless to say, it bombed. Each and every time there were people who loved the newly minted offering, but most did not. And though the spirit was there, its expression was misguided and ultimately failed.

Still, even if my efforts were misdirected, that didn't make that old, crotchety cantor right. He was wrong, too. The problem wasn't change. I reject the popular sentiment that synagogues and Jewish communities will refuse to embrace change. Rather, they tend to reject a certain type of change, a change that takes away something near and dear to their hearts. Too much change wasn't the problem; rather, it was the method used to implement that change that failed.

Since then I have learned my lesson and have instituted what I call *additive change*. Unless one is talking about a very small congregation with a very narrow set of interests and expectations, additive change is the way to go. What is additive change? It's just what it sounds like—change what is being offered at synagogue by adding to offerings, rather than subtracting, substituting, or creating a situation where people still have no options, no choice.

At CSH, instead of taking away what was already being offered—namely, the traditional minyan—we added multiple offerings simultaneously in adjacent settings. There is still traditional davening, but now there are also alternative services. The regulars still have their beloved, unchanged service, while others, including but not limited to the unengaged, unaffiliated, alternative types, have choices of their own. There is, of course, still the Torah service, but simultaneously there is a Torah study, too. Yoga, family options, children's options—they are all implemented simultaneously, and instead of removing someone's slice of the pie, we have simply begun offering more slices and more pies in our Shabbat buffet. Rather than resenting the new additions, congregants express frustration that they can't do it all, and that is a glorious problem to face.

So often my colleagues will share with me in bewilderment how amazing it is that we can pull this off week in and week out. At their shul they will offer a Synaplex once a month or every other week. Maybe they'll offer an option here or an alternative offering there. But in many ways, the Synaplex is all or nothing. The truth is that without the certainty and regularity of a weekly Synaplex, without the energy and critical mass of many simultaneous offerings, we could never make this work. Ironically, a little change would be harder than a lot of change. Additive change that comes too slowly, too incrementally, or in ways that are simply not all that substantial may be harder for a congregation to embrace. However, when blitzed with tremendous, staggering, awe-inspiring amounts of change, there can be an energy, a synergy, and an experience of possibility that is ignited, creating a community and a culture of change that builds on itself. With that said, just as the Creator worked for six days with a seventh day of rest, so, too, CSH, our professional and lay leadership, and even our congregants need to take a break. Although our Synaplex runs every week, we do take a hiatus in the midst of summer, though still offering a handful of choices. Come late August, we are refreshed, reenergized, and back in full swing.

Living Shuls, Dying Shuls

Living shuls are constantly changing;
Dying shuls don't have to.

Living shuls have lots of noisy kids;
Dying shuls don't.

Living shuls' expenses always exceed their income;
Dying shuls take in more money than they can spend.

Living shuls focus on people—keeping them growing;
Dying shuls focus on the building—on keeping it neat and clean and quiet.

Living shuls dream great dreams;
Dying shuls rehearse nightmares.

Living shuls don't have "can't" in their vocabulary;
Dying shuls have nothing but.

—ANONYMOUS

If synagogues fail to allow for change and choice, the spirit of those within their walls becomes constricted and the congregation is left gasping for air. There is an old Zen story about a student who complained to the Master that paying attention to the breath in meditation was boring, and certainly there must be a better and more interesting way to reach enlightenment. The Zen Master didn't say a word, but proceeded to submerge the student's head under water and held him there while the student struggled. When the Master let the gasping student up for air, he asked him if he found breathing boring or interesting while he was under water. The student got the point and the breath became a great teacher for him.

The truth is, you're either breathing or you're dying. Our breath flows in and out like the waves of the ocean, like the rustle of the breeze. When we pronounce God's name, *YHWH*, the sound that comes out is the breath. And, as Jews, the central place where we gather our collective breath is within our synagogue, a living and breathing synagogue that mirrors the inhalation and exhalation of our collective being.

To choose life means to stop and be present to the moment, to enter the world of discernment, where ongoing choices are made in the service of moving forward. This is what our patriarchs and matriarchs did; this is the model that they set. Now it is our turn to stop and pay attention to the call, to say *hineni* individually and set forth on our individual journey, and to say *hinenu* collectively and travel the path in community. The truth is, for the past generation, many of us have been suffocating. Like that Zen student, gasping for air, what will revive us is *Ruakh*. Although there are some synagogues breathing life into the Jewish community, there are still so many others that have failed to heed the call for change, and congregants have responded by silently walking away. Like Abraham and Moses, we can be the ones to hear the call, to step up and move forward, even with our hesitations. Like that Zen student, like Abraham and Moses, the question for us is this: Are we ready to hear that call, to take that breath and *lech lecha*, go forth and choose life, so that we and our children may live?

Part II
From the Known to the Unknown

And the Divine called to Abram: Journey forth, *from the known* [from your land, from your birthplace, from your father's house] *to the unknown* [the land that I will show you]. And I will make you into a great nation, and I will bless you, and I will increase your name, and you shall be a blessing.

—GENESIS 12:1–2

4

The "When" of *Ruakh*
Erotic Shabbat

Rabbi B's Intoxicated Shabbat

Although I had gone through the motions of Shabbat growing up, the experience was what many people have come to call "pediatric Judaism." I'll never forget my first real adult encounter with Judaism, quite literally rated "R," which I discovered was worlds apart. I was in my mid-twenties, and I'd just moved to Israel and signed up to begin a wonderful program called *Livnot U'lehibanot*, based out of the mystical mountain city of Tzfat. Although it was a program geared for young, secular Jews, nonetheless, there was still an expectation that we would minimally observe Shabbat.

I wasn't interested, to say the least. The working and hiking aspects of the program were why I was there, or so I believed. The thought of going to a shul at age twenty-five, when my parents weren't even there to witness it and earn me some mitzvah points, was more than I could bear. I wasn't interested in arcane rituals, pietistic prayer, boring sermons, and a wasted Friday night. I was heading out on the town to celebrate Shabbat with a drink. The bars, beer, fun—that was my idea of a good time. That was my idea of Shabbat and that's what I set out to find.

However, living in the Old City of Tzfat, the home of not only Jewish mysticism but *Kabbalat Shabbat*, it wasn't so easy to find anything open on Friday night, let alone a place to go have a drink. Still, I somehow managed to find the only bar around. It was me and a handful of other Shabbat protesters, made up of a bunch of European wayfarers and a couple of Arab Christians, none of whom spoke English. A few Goldstar beers later and I had had enough of my depressing Shabbat night out on the town. That boring old shul where everyone else had headed wasn't sounding so bad after all. I caved and ventured over there, prepared to have a bad time.

As I was walking the streets making my way, I was delighted by the sounds of what I thought must be a party. I could only imagine that it was coming from someone's home—maybe they had a keg, certainly they had a DJ, as they were singing so loudly. Imagine my surprise when I found that, indeed, there was a party. However, it wasn't coming from someone's home; it was emanating from the shul.

It was loud, really loud. It was lively, incredibly lively. And it was a party, a blowout party the likes of which I had never seen or imagined taking place in a synagogue of any sort. This, however, was an Orthodox synagogue, and I was completely and utterly blown away. Although there was no DJ playing or guitars jamming, nonetheless a serious party was taking place. It went on like this deep into the night. They kept pouring me shots of Slivovitz, and the party continued on to someone's home as we raised our glasses high, toasting *l'chayim*, singing, dancing, and celebrating well into the dawn.

It was then that I realized my assumptions and ideas about Judaism might have been skewed, partially formed, or in many ways just plain wrong. From that night on, I understood the difference between Friday night and Erev Shabbat. Friday night at a bar could bring fun, but Erev Shabbat would bring joy.

I had no regrets about my Friday night excursions. They were good times. However, at best they were only ever fun. My Shabbat encounters were not merely fun; they were joyous. Fun is fleeting. Fun is finicky. Fun is hit or miss, hard to have, and even harder to re-create. Joy, on the other hand, is simple, it's sustainable, and it runs deeper than tapping out a keg. Shabbat joy, or *oneg Shabbat*, is most of all an experience of being part of something much larger than yourself. That Shabbat I was intoxicated, not with the Slivovitz but with *Ruakh*—*Ruakh* that woke me up, sparked a flame, and sent me down a different path. As we read in Psalms, *"Ivdu et HaShem b'simchah*—Serve God in joy" (100:2). That is what I did that Erev Shabbat and almost every Shabbat since.

Rushing through Our Lives

The truth of the matter is we need not observe Shabbat, or even wait until Friday night, to begin to tap into *Ruakh Shabbat*. *Ruakh* is the spirit of the Divine within us, around us, always available, always accessible, any time and anywhere. That is in theory. Life, on the other hand, is not lived in theory; life is real. And in real time even though *Ruakh* is present, too often we are not. We may be there in body, but our spirit is often somewhere else.

And who can blame us? We are so incredibly busy. We are bombarded with duties, responsibilities, expectations, and obligations, all coming at us from every which way in this modern, technological, frenzied age. We are distracted in ways our parents could never have imagined. We are rushing around generating a whole lot of wind, but not always a whole lot of *Ruakh*. We are, in the words of Dr. Wayne Dyer, human doings when, in fact, we were created to be human beings. To be human means to stop rushing, to stop doing, and to start being present in the moment. For when we miss moment after moment, we end up missing our lives.

This point is brought home by a great Hasidic teacher, Rebbe Nachman of Breslov:

> Looking out of the window on a weekday morning, Reb Nachman noticed his disciple, Chaim, rushing along the street. Reb Nachman opened the door and invited Chaim to come inside. Chaim entered the house and the Rebbe said to him, "Chaim, have you seen the sky this morning?"
>
> "No, Rebbe," answered Chaim.

"Have you seen the street this morning?"

"Yes, Rebbe," he answered.

"Tell me, please, Chaim, what did you see in the street?"

"I saw people, carts, and merchandise. I saw merchants and peasants all coming and going, selling and buying."

"Chaim," said Rebbe Nachman, "in fifty years, in one hundred years, on that very street there will be a market. Other vehicles will then bring merchants and merchandise to the street. But I won't be there and neither will you. So I ask you, Chaim, what's the good of rushing if you don't even have time to look at the sky?"[1]

Although we know the lesson of this story, knowing it and living it are entirely different things. After all, we know what's good for us, more often than not, in almost every area of life. That, however, doesn't mean we do what is good for us. We know we don't need that extra helping of mashed potatoes when we're already full, but we have it anyway. We know we need to quit smoking, get out of that relationship, go back to school, turn off the TV and read a book. It's hard to change, even if we know what to do.

In regard to our busy lives, we know we are pushing too hard. We know we can't keep giving our lifeblood to our job and also expect our home life to flourish. We know we can't continue to leave our relationships unattended and expect to feel passion within them. We know we are missing the point when we choose to lie on the couch and watch a ball game when our child is begging us to get up off that couch and toss a ball around. And we also know that we can't keep up this frenetic pace—no human being can—not for long and certainly not forever. We know that we are burning up and burning out, and we know that if we don't stop soon, our engine will explode or eventually we will crash.

We know and yet we go and go and go. It's not enough to know. Knowing won't keep us from becoming slaves; it certainly didn't prove enough for the Israelites back in Egypt. The Israelites probably knew that Egypt was a bad place to be a Jew. They probably knew that their civil liberties were dissipating, their plight worsening. They never intended to bow down to Pharaoh, or later to idols in the desert. However, slowly, over time, knowing what they knew, they lost their way nonetheless. You can only ignore "the call" for so long before eventually it slips away, too.

> Moses spoke to the people of Israel; but they listened not to Moses because of their *kotzer Ruakh* [cut-off spirit] and because of the *avodah kashah* [backbreaking work].
> —Exodus 6:9

The only thing that seemed to wake these people up from their stupor were God's signs from above, like frogs hitting them on the head. Do you know how to boil a frog? You don't throw it into a pot of scalding water. It will react, it will fight you, it will find a way to jump out or die trying. Rather, you put that frog in room-temperature water. You make it feel "comfortable." You lull it into a stupor. And you slowly turn up the heat. The frog won't know what happened. Even if it knows, it won't seem to care. It will sit there for you, boiling in its own juices for you, willingly giving up its freedom for you.

The Israelites were not enslaved in a moment. Rather, their enslavement came slowly, over time. Pharaoh stripped them of their identity through *avodah kashah*—backbreaking work. Their bodies were kept busy so they wouldn't have the energy to think or the time to feel much of anything at all.

According to the mystics, this work led to their *kotzer Ruakh*, literally their "shortness of breath." The harder they worked, the less they could breathe. Over time, their breath not only dissipated but their *Ruakh*, their spirit, also became *kotzer*, cut off, too. Soon they were like that listless frog, sitting there, unmotivated, uninspired, unable to even dream of freedom, let alone to act on it and jump out of the pot—jump to freedom.

The true definition of slavery is not incarceration behind metal bars. Great men and women throughout history who have been imprisoned—people like Nelson Mandela, Natan Sharansky, and Viktor Frankl—may have been imprisoned, but each one was always free. How? In the words of Frankl:

> Everything can be taken from a man but one thing: the last of
> the human freedoms—to choose one's attitude in any given set
> of circumstances, to choose one's own way.[2]

Buddhist nuns incarcerated for their cries to free Tibet, civil rights
activists in the 1960s who were imprisoned for standing up for equal
rights, and great men and women like them have always understood that true freedom comes not from the outside but from within.
Mitzrayim, Egypt, is not merely a geographical place. Rather, it is a narrow, constricted inner reality. When we can no longer hope, no longer
dream, no longer feel, we may not have shackles on our feet but we
have shackles around our spirit.

Over and over again, the text says that the Israelites "could not
hear." They couldn't hear because ultimately they could not feel. Their
breath was shallow, their spirit was cut off, they lost their call and they
lost their way. Ultimately their passion for life waned, and eventually
there came a day when they could no longer even imagine what it
would mean to be free. They lived lives of quiet desperation with the
greatest curse of all: they were indifferent; they were apathetic. Or, in
the words of Elie Wiesel:

> Indifference to me is the epitome of evil.
> The opposite of love is not hate, it's indifference.
> The opposite of art is not ugliness, it's indifference.
> The opposite of faith is not heresy, it's indifference.
> And the opposite of life is not death, it's indifference.
> Because of indifference, one dies before one actually dies.[3]

Erotic Shabbat

Before that wildly exciting but foreign experience of Shabbat, I, along
with so many other Jews I know, claimed we were indifferent: indifferent to Shabbat, indifferent to Judaism, and indifferent to all things
Jewish. Turns out, I was wrong.

I remember asking a Kabbalist whom I had met in Tzfat how a
synagogue could have celebrated Shabbat with drinking, dancing, and

so much joy? Wasn't Shabbat supposed to be solemn? Wasn't Shabbat supposed to be subdued? Wasn't Shabbat supposed to be about respectful, quiet rest?

And his answer was illuminating, life changing, and it motivated me to engage my Judaism a whole lot more. He answered, "Shabbat is not about rest. Shabbat is not about prayer. Shabbat is not about Torah study. Shabbat may include all those things, but the Kabbalists understood Shabbat to be about sex!"

And this changed everything. My indifference was no more.

What we were never taught in Hebrew school was that Moses was not the real reason behind the Israelite uprising, the journey of the Exodus, or the purpose of having a seder thousands of years later. And what you are about to hear probably won't be talked about around your *zayde*'s seder table, though some *bubbes* might welcome this as a change of pace. According to the Midrash, it wasn't Moses who inspired the Israelites to cast off the shackles that bound them as slaves. Rather, it was the radical women of the time who led the way. They didn't do it by battling Pharaoh directly. They did it by battling the apathy that had quashed the spirit of their men. They started a rebellion by igniting their husbands' desire, and that desire began with sex.

The Radical Women of the Exodus

Rabbi Avira expounded: As the reward for the righteous women who lived in that generation were the Israelites delivered from Egypt.[4]

Who were these righteous women of the Exodus? They were the midwives who stood up against Pharaoh and his evil decree to kill the first-born Hebrews. They were the powerful women who worked behind the scenes to keep Moses alive—his sister, Miriam; Yoheved, his birth mother; and Batya, the woman who raised him in Pharaoh's palace. In the words of Avivah Zornberg: This is a conspiracy of three women, who return the baby to the mother's breast, its natural place.[5] These women were courageous, visionary, and bold. It was a conspiracy beginning with the two midwives, continuing on through these three matriarchs, and carried further by women of that time.

According to the Midrash, what the rest of the Israelite women did was outrageous, given their circumstances. Whereas the men were beaten down and resigned to being slaves, the women fought back through a spiritual revolution of their own. When these women weren't engaged in backbreaking work, they were using what little energy they had left to busily scheme and carry out the biggest prison break in history. Although they left the logistics of getting out of town up to Moses and the men, nonetheless, they were behind the scenes, pulling the strings and setting the stage for that escape.

What did they do? What was the battle they waged? How did they ultimately win the war against Pharaoh? It was simple. They took their husbands out on a date.

These women would save up scraps of food all week long. They would make themselves up for their husbands. And they would each take turns creating diversions for one another, sneaking over to the men's barracks, finding their husband, and stealing away down to the river to make their own little midday Shabbat break.

At that river they weren't davening the afternoon prayers. They weren't studying Torah or talking about the "do's and don'ts" of halachic observance or debating why we can or cannot rip toilet paper on Shabbat. All they had was one another and one ritual object in hand. It wasn't a siddur, a Torah scroll, or a *Kiddush* cup. Rather, they sanctified their Shabbat through one single, solitary handheld mirror. And what did they do with this ritual object, this mirror? They played sex games, of course. Those mirrors were used during foreplay before they engaged in the mitzvah of making love.

> And when they had eaten and drunk, the women would take the mirrors and look into them with their husbands, and she would say, "I am more comely than you," and he would say, "I am more comely than you." And as a result, they would accustom themselves to desire, and they were fruitful and

multiplied, and God took note of them immediately.... In the merit of those mirrors which they showed their husbands to accustom them to desire, from the midst of the harsh labor, they raised up all the hosts, as it is said, "All the hosts of God went out of the land of Egypt" [Exodus 12:41] and it is said, "God brought the children of Israel out of the land of Egypt in their hosts" [Exodus 12:51].[6]

How did this mark the beginning of the Exodus? you might ask. Is this really just about sex? you are wondering. Of course not. After all, sex, in and of itself, is not holy. Animals have sex. Sex can be used and abused in a myriad of ways. Sex is simply sex. This, however, is not about sex. Rather, this is about the erotic, about eros, about the Divine.

It's unfortunate that in our culture we have relegated the magnificent concept of eros to pornography and "gentlemen's clubs." It is more than sex, even more than making love. What these women did was awaken the sleeping giants lying dormant within these slaves. They "drew forth" that which was covered over, hidden deep within. This wasn't about sex, this was about desire, imagination, and the power of freedom that lies at the core of every human being. For the first time in a long time, instead of feeling like animals, like slaves, they were made to feel like men again. More than the sex, the playfulness, the ecstasy, and the eroticism, the joy and the love given to them by their beloved wives opened up something deep within them. In that moment they remembered who they were, remembered what they were. They were a tribe of men and women who faced life's struggles, adversity, and darkness and never gave up, never gave in, never abandoned their journey. As God said to Jacob in his transformation into Yisrael, "for you have wrestled with God and with the man and you have prevailed" (Genesis 32:29). This was their legacy. This is what it means to be *B'nai Yisrael*, the children of Israel.

Although Moses came along earlier, crying out for them to follow him to the Promised Land, it wasn't until they were truly ignited by the radical women of the Exodus that the journey could begin. It was only then that Moses could live out the meaning of his name, "to draw forth." And it was only then that the Israelites could live out the true meaning of their name, *Yisrael*. They were no longer indifferent. They were no longer asleep. Finally they had awakened to *Ruakh*.

Eros and Igniting the Soul

Too often halacha, in general, and Shabbat observance, in particular, are stifling rather than liberating, quashing our ability to feel. But a *Ruakh*-filled Judaism and Shabbat experience can and must be freeing. This is why the Jewish mystics created *Kabbalat Shabbat*. *Kabbalat Shabbat*—the prayers we read to begin this sacred day of spirit—don't begin with a bunch of do's and don'ts. It's not about the rules, but about feeling, about the erotic, about eros.

Song of Songs, after all, is what is traditionally chanted to begin this erotic day. And make no mistake about it, Song of Songs is ancient erotica, which is why it was banned in certain periods, within certain groups. In pre–Hugh Hefner days, young boys were known to find their way into their father's study and sneak a peek at the words of the "lewd" language of King Solomon's description of Israel making love to the Bride.

It was not coincidental that this book was called the "Holy of Holies" by Rabbi Akiva. He understood what the creators of *Kabbalat Shabbat* understood. At the end of the week, after our *avodah kashah*, our backbreaking work, what we need are not rules and regulations to stifle our spirit. Rather, we need to have our minds unfettered, our feelings unchained, and our spirits unleashed. A little ancient erotica is how it was sparked.

However, when we recite *Kabbalat Shabbat*, the night is still young, there is much more that will help us find our way. On Shabbat we don't talk about God in the masculine as *Avinu Malkeinu*—our Father, our King. On the contrary, on Friday night God is the feminine, the Queen, the Shabbat Bride. We don't "daven" *Kabbalat Shabbat*, trying to gain the attention of the Judge on High. Rather, we chant love poems like *Yedid Nefesh*, "My Soul Mate," or *L'cha Dodi*, "My Lover," trying to awaken the Bride above and within. And it is not coincidental that the popularized notion of the "double mitzvah," which usually needs no explanation, is perhaps one of the most important aspects of Shabbat. Indeed, it is a mitzvah, a divine imperative, to have sex with your partner at the right time, in the right place, for the right reasons. But it is a "double mitzvah" to have sex with your partner on Shabbat.

Shabbat is not about sex; Shabbat is about eros. Eros is not a physical act, but a spiritual act. Eros is about feeling, about passion, about desire. Desire is what was awakened within those Israelites and set them on the path toward freedom. Desire, imagination, and inspiration are what we crave. We want to breathe again. We want to feel again. We want to be inspired again. We want to dream and to live out those dreams. When we rekindle our desire, it ignites our imagination and we are on our way from *Mitzrayim* to *Yisrael*, from suffocation to breath, from slavery to redemption. We are on our way to the Promised Land.

Later on, after the Israelites had arrived in the Land of Israel, God commanded them to use those mirrors once again. God instructed Moses to take every mirror to be melted down and incorporated into the *Beit Mikdash*, specifically to be transformed into the bronze mirror before the Holy of Holies. Why? Because the mirror was the last place the *Kohen Gadol*, the High Priest, would look prior to standing before God and pleading the case of the people on Yom Kippur to be given another year of life, of spirit, of *Ruakh*.

What God wanted from the High Priest, what God wanted from the Israelites, what God wants from you and me, from our Jewish communities and synagogues, is to reclaim the secret of those mirrors—the secret our spirit and the spirit our community is crying out for. Shabbat is our weekly invitation. Freedom awaits.

Rabbi B's Story: Mirrors—In-To-Me-See

Too often religion, halacha, Shabbat, and synagogue observance are, in the stinging words of Karl Marx, "an opiate for the masses." Those of us in the twenty-first century don't need ancient, archaic, backwards religions to live a meaningful life. We're free. We're successful. We don't need a crutch like Shabbat or synagogues, or so the reasoning goes.

Let me tell you about a recent experience I had of being "free." It was a Friday afternoon and, as usual, I was rushing around to get all my necessary preparations done for Shabbat. First there was the bank. I needed to deposit money and so, to save time, I hit the ATM. I waited in a line with other people, not making eye contact, not exchanging meaningless pleasantries, not saying a word. I had to drop off dry cleaning, but to avoid the line I simply dumped the laundry bag through the slot in the wall. There was the "self-serve" automated gas pump, and groceries to be purchased through the do-it-yourself, automated line. In the course of an hour or two I made multiple stops, passed by dozens of people, and I don't think I spoke to a single one. I was busy. I was independent. I was free. But if this was independence, if this was freedom, then why did I feel like such a lonely, calloused, isolated automaton and slave?

One of my favorite movies is *Avatar*. Though there are many significant moments in the film, none are more insightful than the way they acknowledge one another. Instead of saying hello or goodbye, the *Navi*, or blue aliens say, "I see you." More than the words, they stop, they look, and most of all they truly see. This is similar to the greeting in Southeast Asia, where palms are placed together as if in prayer, eye contact is made, and the word *namaste* is offered. Translated, it means "the Divine in me sees and honors the Divine in you."

Isn't this the point—to see one another? Isn't this why we are here? Isn't this what is supposed to happen in our daily lives, the monumental encounters we have with our family, friends, and neighbors or even the seemingly trivial encounters at the bank, the gas station, or the grocery store? Isn't this what Adam was stifled by in the Garden, feelings of *l'vado*, loneliness, and his need to overcome them? Isn't this what all human beings seek in their lives, this desire to be seen, to be understood, to be known? Or in the words of Wayne Dyer, *intimacy* is really *in-to-me-see*. Our duty, the task at hand, is to see and to be seen. However, the hustle and bustle of our busy lives hardly leaves room for intimacy, hardly makes it possible to see or be seen.

The next day, after the automated, frenzied grind, was Shabbat. As I was walking to services, I was about one hundred yards behind a couple also walking to synagogue. This couple went to a different shul. I didn't know them, but I'd seen them before. She looked to be about

107 and she was clearly the younger of the two. They walked so slowly they must have set out on Thursday. While I was in hurry, walking fast, and would make the journey in a matter of minutes, they were en route to be touching down around *Havdalah*. They walked slowly. They walked lovingly. They walked hand in hand.

So often in our mad, rushing, youth-obsessed society, we look on an old couple like this with pity; they are at the end of their lives, they move through the world so slowly, feebly, dependent on one another. But as I walked passed them, I felt a sense of admiration, even jealousy. They had so much peace, so much patience, so much intimacy. I was even a little embarrassed, as if I were a voyeur of sorts, barging in on a private, erotic moment, even though they were only holding hands.

At shul, amid the energy of the Synaplex, as hundreds of people are going this way and that, there is something different about the vibe than the outside chaotic world. This is "holy chaos" where the hustle and bustle is infused with a sense of community, even intimacy. Sometimes these encounters come through the formal offerings, but often they occur when people are walking and talking or sitting and schmoozing. The community that is being built and the relationships that are being fostered are in many ways a referendum on the unholy chaos of our frenetic, modern lives. What I see happening at CSH is that this is more than a return to the synagogue and a reclaiming of Shabbat observance. It is a radical revolution of spirit, calling out for God, for *Ruakh*, for intimacy. Shabbat is a collective mirror allowing for reflection, allowing us to see and be seen.

The famous Israeli poet Ahad Ha'am is quoted as saying, "More than Jews have kept Shabbat, Shabbat has kept the Jews." There is a rhythm to Shabbat that is like nothing else. There is a power in orienting individuals, a synagogue, and a community to this holy day. We can transform modern Judaism by reclaiming this ancient gift. We can reclaim our power and freedom once again when we respond to the invitation of a *Ruakh*-filled Shabbat.

5

The "What" of *Ruakh*
The Synaplex Experience

What Happens in Our Holy Home

Shabbat Synaplex Schedule:

> *Boker Tov* Breakfast beginning at 8:30 a.m.
> 8:30 a.m. Early Mystic Meditation Minyan
> 8:45 a.m. The Renewal Minyan (chanting, drumming, and dance)
>> Blessings from the Heart—*Birchot HaShachar*
>> Songs of the Soul—*Pesukei D'Zimrah*
>> Morning Prayers—*Shacharit*
> 9:00 a.m. Traditional Davening in the sanctuary with Cantor E.
> 10:00 a.m. Traditional Torah Service and *Musaf*
> 10:00 a.m. Alternative Offerings:
>> The Yoga Minyan
>> Nosh and *Drash* (Torah study) with guest rabbis and scholars
> *B'yachad*—For Everyone:
> 11:15 a.m. Healing *Chavurah*
> 11:30 a.m. Torah Reflections: The Rabbi's Message
> 11:45 a.m. *Ruakh* Rally
> 12:00 p.m. Shabbat Café Lunch for all!

What Makes Up Our Spiritual Homes

If synagogues are going to thrive, they are going to have to return to the past and reclaim the nuance of our once dynamic tradition, becoming spiritual "homes" for our present and future. Jewish spiritual homes, after all, were never called *synagogues*. This word isn't organic to Hebrew; it's Greek. It is not our own word, nor has it grown into a concept that ultimately reflects our goals.

A "synagogue" has come to represent an organization or an institution. Although this is partially what our spiritual homes need to be, we don't want this to be our primary experience. The Yiddish term *shul* hearkens back to an era gone by, to the shtetl with little gathering places to pray and literally to learn. A shul is simple and in some ways captures the simplicity and informality of what a sacred communal Jewish home could and should be. However, it is only part of the whole. Shuls tend to be missing much of the institutional, organizational know-how and sustaining power that is necessary in a complicated and competitive world. Finally, there is *temple*, the word du jour and the most popular of all the terms. Frankly *temple* is anathema, quite literally, to what the vast majority of Jews today are seeking. *Temple*, after all, implies a focus on the place and space and hearkens back to the formal rites and rituals performed by the High Priest, not to mention the blood and guts of a sacrificed animal.

The traditional and authentic name for our Jewish homes was just that, a home. The Temple was called the *Beit Mikdash*, the Holy Home. This is why the Rabbis termed each of our respective individual homes as a *mikdash me'at*, a little *Beit Mikdash*. Homes are central to our lives. Our home is where we spend most of our time, form our deepest relationships, our identity, and where the *Ruakh* most fully comes into our lives.

If *Ruakh* is to return to Judaism, it will only do so once we start thinking of our temples, our synagogues, and our shuls in terms other than as institutions, organizations, or buildings. Rather, spirit will animate our religion once again when we reclaim the language of the home speaking to the comfort, nurturing, nuance, and intimacy of that sacred space.

A *beit mikdash* is ultimately made up of three distinct experiences, three activities that take place in our spiritual homes:

- *Beit tefilah*—house of prayer
- *Beit midrash*—house of study
- And, above all, *beit knesset*—a house of gathering

Beit Tefilah: A Home of Prayer

First and foremost, our Jewish spiritual homes must reclaim prayer at their core. Traditional Jewish prayer in Hebrew is called *tefilah*. To engage in *tefilah* is a move inward, taking stock of who we are, what we feel, how we think, and what we believe. It is an opportunity for what our mystics call *cheshbon nefesh*, or soul searching. And it is a process not only of self-evaluation but of self-replenishment, filling ourself up with faith, imagination, and *Ruakh*.

For many Jews, traditional notions of davening still accomplish this end. A Synaplex should continue to offer traditional pathways of *tefilah*. Regardless of our personal wants and needs, there is something profound and powerful about participating in or witnessing a *beit tefilah*, where the formal structures of the Jewish prayer service are the focus. Traditional *tefilah* is an important offering in a Synaplex. Perhaps it is even the "main" offering in a space with multiple venues. However, it should not be the only offering. For some, experiencing *Ruakh* may come through traditional prayer; for others it might come through seemingly nontraditional expressions.

Silence: Early Mystic Meditation Minyan

We learn in the Mishnah that before the actual morning prayers would convene, the *Hasidim rishonim*, the early mystics, would sit for an hour to prepare to pray. And how would they prepare? They would recite *Pesukei D'Zimrah*, Psalms of David—psalms from their soul. In all probability they would simply sit quietly, finding God on their terms and in their own way.

One of Abraham's defining moments was not up on Mount Moriah amid the Binding of Isaac. Nor was it only *Lech lecha*, when he set out on his big adventure. Perhaps the moment of greatest clarity for Abraham came when he was merely sitting at the entrance of his tent:

> Now the Lord appeared to him [Abraham] in the plains of Mamre as he was sitting at the entrance of the tent during the heat of the day.
>
> —GENESIS 18:1

And what was he doing sitting there? Nothing, absolutely nothing—which is exactly the point. *Shabbat* literally means "to sit." Shabbat is about sitting and being, sitting and not doing. There is a beautiful Zen poem that reads, "Sitting quietly, doing nothing. Spring comes, and the grass grows by itself." Or, in the words of the Jewish Buddhist author Sylvia Boorstein, "Don't just do something; sit there." Synaplex provides the space for the peace and quiet so many of us crave. We need places and spaces in the holy chaos of the day for quiet communal contemplation. Meditation is offered as a way to touch that *Ruakh* within, filling us up with the breath of life. At CSH, we offer the space for meditation early Shabbat morning. Other synagogues, like Beth Elohim in Wellesley, Massachusetts, offer a weekly evening group that gathers to meditate and pray in silence, recognizing the fact that, throughout time, Jews have made silent meditation an important piece of their spiritual lives. Other synagogues are following suit, so much so that there are now organizations devoted to Jewish meditation, such as Nishmat Hayyim: Jewish Meditative Collaborative of New England and The Institute for Jewish Spirituality, teaching our Jewish leaders the art of Jewish meditation. This ancient mystical path is spreading its roots and continuing to blossom.

> A great and strong wind cracked the mountain and shattered boulders, but God was not in the wind. And after the wind there was an earthquake, but God was not in the earthquake. And after the earthquake a fire, but God was not in the fire. And after the fire, a still small voice.
>
> —1 KINGS 19:11–12

Traditional davening has its time and place. It just can't be the only method and manner of talking to God, and clearly there is great Jewish precedent to make this claim. Sometimes God is in the noise, but sometimes, as with Elijah, God is in the silence. The Ba'al Shem Tov, who spent much time in meditation and quiet reflection, explained, "Through silence, one can meditate upon the greatness of God and bind oneself to God more completely than through speech."[1] Prayer is an expression of longing and yearning of the soul, and sometimes our souls need to feel the rhythms expressed in the sounds of our formal, traditional services. Other times, however, or for other types of spiritual seekers, those prayers need to be experienced in the fullness of silence.

Artur Schnabel, a great Austrian pianist, was once asked by an ardent admirer, "How do you handle the notes as well as you do?" The artist answered, "The notes I handle no better than many pianists, but the pauses between the notes—ah! That is where the art resides." At the beginning of our Renewal Minyan, there is time and space for quiet meditation and contemplation, for experiencing the pauses between the notes. As in the days of the early mystics, there is an opportunity to prepare oneself to fully enter into prayer by stopping and paying attention to the present moment and finding that quiet, still center.

Voice: The Renewal Minyan

After our early morning meditation, we move into the alternative *tefilah* offerings. This particular community is not interested in going wide across the pages of the siddur, from *aleph* to *tav* of the *Shacharit* (morning) service. Rather, they want to go deeper, to rise higher. They are less interested in *keva*, structure, and more concerned with *kavannah*, intention. That spirit comes through primal, repetitive Hebrew chants. Instead of reciting the entirety of Psalm 150, we'll chant the last verse repeatedly. Instead of saying all of the *Birchot HaShachar* in Hebrew and not understanding it, we'll chant in "Heblish," half Hebrew, half English, tapping into the ancient Hebraic blessing formula with words resonating within our soul, while filling in the end with words in English that resonate within our mind. Sometimes we'll share alternative readings or poems from other traditions that help us reflect on the week's parashah. Other times we'll return to the silence or sounds of the breath, which, according to Kabbalah, are the sounds composing the name of *Adonai*.

Please rise, please sit means nothing in this venue and is only applicable to a rising of spirit or a sitting in stillness of the mind and the soul. It matters not in here what we do or say; rather, it matters what we feel. And hundreds have returned through this experience. Young and old, traditional and alternative, Jews, semi-Jews, and non-Jews come together in the Renewal Minyan, all sharing and enriching the Synaplex experience.

Music: The Pews Are Alive

One of the harsh blows to hit an inspired Jewish experience has been the loss of music, particularly musical instruments in our services. And when it is present, too often the cantor sings and the congregants listen. The choir performs while the "spectators" passively observe. Services have become a show rather than a participatory experience.

However, a phenomenal shift in modern *tefilah* within all movements in Judaism has taken place since the later part of the twentieth century. This was the era in which we saw the emergence of the late, great Debbie Friedman, with her easily accessible, camp-style tunes that inspired a new generation of Jews and transformed worship in so many of our synagogue services. This was also the era that began the Carlebach revolution. Rabbi Shlomo Carlebach came along in the late twentieth century at a time when Jews were awakening to their need for a personal experience of God and reminded us that God doesn't just want our words, God wants the heart. Carlebach-style davening doesn't require a beautiful voice—Reb Shlomo certainly didn't have one—but a beautiful soul. Reb Shlomo's daughter, Neshama Carlebach, continues to inspire us, and we sing the chants composed by Shefa Gold and the modern Jewish pop and liturgical music of Craig Taubman, Rick Recht, and so many other voices of a new generation. We all have a soul that is waiting for the opportunity for full expression once we can peel away the worries, doubts, and fears. We simply need to be given opportunities to express ourselves in our *beit tefilah*, our holy home of prayer—a place where we can open up and sing. In the words of Rabbi Aaron of Karlin, "Jews expresses their faith most fully and most joyfully when they sing out unreservedly."[2] Song, for some, is the pathway back. Joyous song is perhaps one of the greatest forms of prayer. If we are going to touch upon *Ruakh* in our *tefilot*, in our prayer offerings, we're going to have to learn to sing out unreservedly and offer opportunities and venues to open our mouths and our hearts. A synagogue, however, does not need to incorporate musical instrumentation into its services to reclaim *Ruakh*. In Orthodox synagogues, it is forbidden to use instruments on Shabbat. However, there are many Orthodox minyanim (services) where *Ruakh* is alive and well through singing, clapping, and dancing. In New York City, for example, the spirited services led by Eli Kranzler or those at Congregation Kehilath Jacob—The Carlebach Shul welcome hundreds into their *Ruakh*-filled prayer.

In the Conservative movement, although many synagogues use instrumentation on Shabbat, others still continue to debate the acceptability of doing so. At Ikar, although they refrain from using string instruments, they allow for drumming and have created a *Ruakh*-filled experience drumming their way to the Divine. Across the country, synagogues are redefining Shabbat *tefilah* through an explosion of song and sound. There are the trailblazing Rabbis Marshall Meyers (of blessed memory), Rolando Matalon, Ari Priven, and Marcelo Bronstein at Manhattan's B'nai Jeshurun and their *Kabbalat Shabbat* extravaganza. In Los Angeles, under the inspirational leadership of Rabbi David Wolpe and Craig Taubman, there is Temple Sinai, where thousands gather for Friday Night Live. Down the street from them you can find Rabbi Naomi Levy of Nashuva leading monthly Friday night services with the Nashuva Band, which is a partnership between Nashuva and the Westwood Hills Congregational Church. Playing music from across the globe, this celebration of sound and spirit welcomes both community and Shabbat. Out in Chicago, you can find Rabbi Lizzi Heydeman hosting Music Jam, and at CSH we have one simple policy, BYOB—bring your own bongos, and get ready to rock and roll.

Ellen's Story: Rocking, Wild, Baptist-Style

I have been attending the Renewal Minyan each Shabbat, and every Saturday morning my heart soars in the ecstasy that defines the energy of this space. The chants take on a life of their own, while the voice sings and the body responds. Rabbi B plays his African drum to the rhythm of the song, and others bring in their own instruments. There is a young boy who comes each week with his own drum. Sitting beside his father, tallit draped around his shoulders and yarmulke on his head, he plays his drum in sync with the rabbi, and I find myself mesmerized by his drumming. When I look at him, I see the future. As a beautiful aside, this boy is from an interfaith marriage, is African-American, and has been given a choice as to what religion he wants to express. He is expressing it joyfully every single week as a Jew.

There's a gentleman who brings his flute and women who come with tambourines and add beautiful sounds and vibrations to the songs that are so alive. Some chants become so lively that every foot in the room is tapping, hands are clapping, and bodies are swaying. These are people of all ages, and who knows what the virtual Renewal Minyan participants are doing in the comfort of their own homes. Some in the room stand up and dance, some shake maracas, some just do their own thing. Others sit as if in meditation, the chants and vibrations transporting them to a place of deep experience. Over time, I've learned how certain people typically express themselves, and I find myself counting on their expressions as part of the gestalt of the experience. It is synergy: each one of them—whether up dancing and twirling in rhythm, or sitting in chairs or cushions clapping their hands, or standing and swaying—brings forth a force that is beyond the individual. It is a communal expression of connection to each other and to something beyond.

I have always loved the wild Baptist style of worship, so foreign to any of my shul experiences. I love the idea of people calling out "Amen" and "Hallelujah," in rapture with the experience of connecting to something beyond place and time. Toward the end of the Renewal Minyan, when we are singing "Amen" and "Hallelujah," I understand that this wild dance of song isn't just for other religions to experience.

These are Hebrew words, part and parcel of our Jewish tradition. When I sing them out wildly, audaciously, and unreservedly with a growing community, I know that a revolution of Jewish spirit has been ignited, illuminating sanctuaries that have long sat in the dark.

The Yoga Minyan: Finding the OM in *ShalOM*

We dealt much in soulfulness; we forgot the holiness of the body. We neglected physical health and strength; we forgot that we have holy flesh, no less than holy spirit ... our *teshuvah* [return] will succeed only if it will be, with all its splendid spirituality, also a physical return, which produces healthy blood, healthy flesh, might, solid bodies, a fiery spirit radiating over powerful muscles. With the strength of the holy flesh, the weakened soul will shine, reminiscent of the physical resurrection.[3]

An authentic Synaplex experience must offer a plethora of opportunities for a myriad of different types of people, personalities, and seekers looking to experience *Ruakh*. *Ruakh* is dynamic; therefore, our attempts to connect with God must be equally dynamic. Some connect through the mind, others through the heart, and still others through body movement. If we are truly going to open up our synagogues as a home of prayer, then we are going to have to offer rooms within our home for people to move their bodies as well their hearts and spirits. Experiencing *Ruakh* through the body is not new. Dianne Bloomfield, author of the book, *Torah Yoga,* and Rabbis Sheila Peltz Weinberg and Myriam Klotz, at the Institute for Jewish Spirituality, have been incorporating yoga into *tefilah* for years. In other communities, such as Anshei Emet in Chicago, Jewish yoga is taking root and flourishing. And at Temple Micah in Washington, D.C., Rabbi Daniel Zemel has partnered with congregant and choreographer Liz Lerman to introduce body movement into prayer. But the truth is that moving one's body as a form of prayer goes all the way back to the Bible and the book of Job. When Job said, "through my flesh I see God" (19:26), he was not simply speaking in metaphor. Human beings have been using their bodies in spiritual worship for thousands of years. Dance has always been integral to tribal prayer. In Hinduism, the mystics developed the body movement of yoga as a way to engage not just the spirit through soul but the spirit through flesh as well. And when most of us think of our return to *Eretz Yisrael*, we picture Jews celebrating by dancing the hora as an expression of joy.

At CSH, one of the major breakthroughs and game changers has been what we call the "Yoga Minyan." Although yoga is not organically Jewish, ancient religious groups have always been borrowing, co-opting, or adapting other religious traditions, rituals, and practices and making them their own. Unlike Hinduism, Judaism never developed a spiritual body practice. Some might argue that the fact that we don't have such a practice is proof that it isn't Jewish or that we weren't meant to express ourselves in this way to God. However, our tradition and texts have much to offer in formulating body prayer experiences in this day and age. Great Jewish thinkers like Maimonides, the Ba'al Shem Tov, and Rebbe Nachman have all addressed these issues. For example, the Rambam (Maimonides) cared not just that the food being eaten was kosher but that it was also healthful both in amount and quality of what was being ingested. For him, kashrut was about well-being. And the Ba'al Shem Tov was highly focused on the body. He discouraged fasting and self-affliction, and he prayed with shouting, dancing, and singing. For him, prayer involved not only the mind but the body as well. In the words of the Psalmist "All my bones shall cry out: Lord, who is like unto You?" (Psalm 35:10). We need to pray with our mouths, but we need to pray with our bodies, too. We need to expand our thinking and have the courage to make room for movement in our synagogues.

In addition, what makes the Yoga Minyan Jewish is that each week it is oriented around the themes of the parashah. Poses, and the intention underlying them, are in harmony with the instructor's prompts about the spiritual teachings of the text, tradition, and *tefilah*.

Instead of background music in chants of Sanskrit, peaceful and meditative Hebrew songs spill softy into the room. The Yoga Minyan ends with the singing of *Oseh Shalom*, and the Jewish yogis are able to truly feel the universal *Om* but on their terms, in their hOMe, the OM in *ShalOM*.

Rabbi B's Story: Mourning through Movement

When my father died, what I remember struggling with most, after the initial shock and the first few waves of emotion, was the fact that I couldn't cry. Although as a rabbi I know there's no right or wrong way to respond to the death of a loved one, I still wanted, needed, to cry.

Nonetheless, I couldn't. I thought it was because I was angry at my father. I thought maybe it was because it was a suicide and that just left me in a confused emotional state. Whatever the reason, I couldn't cry. Even after the funeral I was unable to shed a single tear.

I would go to the synagogue to say *Kaddish* for him, but my eyes remained dry. I would write about him every day during the weeks that followed his death and, still, no tears. Then one day while I was jogging, the floodgates opened and the tears started flowing. When I jogged, I would cry. When I stopped jogging, the crying stopped. I couldn't cry while davening. I couldn't cry while writing. I couldn't cry while talking about him. I could only cry while I was out on the running trail, while my body was moving and my endorphins were pumping. In time, the tears stopped, but only after the grief was released. And the grief was released, in no small measure thanks to the gift of movement. It wasn't through moving my mouth, pen, or even my mind. Rather, moving my body ultimately moved my heart.

I cannot tell you how many people have approached me after I've told this story to concur and share experiences of their own. They tend to relate God encounters they have had while dancing or biking or walking along the beach. Often they'll share teary-eyed relief that they are not the only one who has felt little in traditional Jewish prayer services. They carry with them guilt, resentment, and feelings of failure or inauthenticity at not having connected to traditional modes of *tefilah* or having been made to feel that their body prayer practice was "not Jewish." Regardless of whether the Synaplex offers yoga or Israeli dance or tai chi, what matters most is that for those who want to move their bodies in service of the Divine, there is a venue and an opportunity to do so.

Dressing *Ruakh* Up and Down: Fig Leaves and Fashion

Creating a community and culture that not only offers alternative pathways but welcomes those who walk them is an essential part of the Synaplex. It requires courage and open-mindedness to begin offering such options. One of the first hurdles we ran into at CSH with the introduction of the Yoga Minyan was the dress code.

Like most temples, the two from which we merged were far more formal and thrived in an era where that was the norm. This formality was evident in many ways, including dress. However, if you invite people to partake in a Synaplex Yoga Minyan, you can't expect them to show up in skirts and suits. To move the body obviously necessitates a different style of clothing, so one of the first things we did, and had to do repeatedly through writing and through speaking from the bimah, is remind everyone that Gucci, Armani, and Dior were not Jews. Levi Strauss, however, *was*, and his jeans are kosher in our home.

There is no holiness in formal clothing. There is no holiness in clothing at all. It is as meaningful as the meaning we give it. Although CSH isn't entirely clothing-optional, once you have your fig leaf, you are good to go. Beyond that, there is no dress code other than you arrive and leave dressed!

Formal attire, street clothes, workout apparel, football or soccer uniforms, too—no one is turned away because of what he's wearing. Though it took time to transform the culture, eventually it became a moot point. Today no one cares what anyone else is wearing. There are options not just in how to pray but in what kind of clothes you choose to wear while praying, or not praying, as the case may be. We have learned to let go of judgments and superficial standards of acceptability. We are now unconcerned with what is being worn. Rather, we are more concerned with people's spark and our wish to have them share that gift freely in our—and now their—home. That gift can be shared in a suit as easily as in yoga pants. Our goal is to create an atmosphere of self-expression and acceptance in style of prayer and style of dress, too.

Beit Midrash: A Home of Study

The majority of American Jewish men and women are college-educated. Judaism has always placed a high value on education. "An ignorant Jew cannot be a pious Jew," says our Talmud.[4] To be fully engaged in Judaism, you must be literate. And literacy in Judaism isn't just about reading and writing, as we make our way to the upper echelons in secular academia. Rather, it means being literate in regard to Judaism and the continued pursuit of Jewish education. The pioneering work of Experiment in Congregation Education (ECE) is one such example of how educational initiatives continue to transform synagogue life. There's the innovative work of Rabbis Irving "Yitz" Greenberg and Irwin Kula at CLAL and Rabbi David Hartman at the Hartman Institute in Jerusalem, all doing tremendous work of building bridges within the Jewish community and beyond through Jewish text study, cutting-edge programing, and promoting Jewish education as a cornerstone of Jewish community and Jewish living.

Jews have always viewed the pursuit of *Talmud-Torah*—the study of holy Jewish texts—not only as an intellectual exercise but as a sacred rite and expression of prayer. As Rabbi Louis Finkelstein, a twentieth-century Jewish scholar explained, when we daven we speak to God; when we study [Torah] God speaks to us. From a Jewish perspective, the Divine communicates to us in a myriad of ways, not the least of which is through the medium of our holy texts.

For too long, Judaism has been outsourced to the rabbis. Undoubtedly, what synagogues need today are charismatic, motivational rabbis who can inspire their congregations to new modes of thinking and higher ways of living. However, unlike other religious traditions, Judaism is not a religion with a middleman. Moses may have functioned as an intermediary at times, but ultimately he was just a man schlepping along through his life with his own imperfections and challenges, his own path to walk, his own work to be done.

There's nothing wrong with Jews looking forward to their rabbi's Shabbat sermons or orienting the day around a rousing talk. However, "the Jews in the pews" must be invited to reengage in a living Torah. This isn't to suggest that sitting down at night, alone, and reading through the Five Books of Moses is the answer. It's nice, but it's not the defining change. Rather, part of our Synaplex offerings have to be pathways in for those looking for Torah to come alive in their lives while they expand their minds.

While the traditional service continues in the main sanctuary and the Yoga Minyan is under way in the *tefilah*-studio, every week we offer the option of Nosh and *Drash* (Torah study) with guest rabbis and scholars. Instead of listening to a teaching and sitting quietly, this is a lively exchange of thoughts, questions, insights, debates, and holy arguing. After all, Jewish study is not about a single voice, but many voices. Every page of our Talmud has layers of conversations being spoken not only across the page but across generations. Jews study Torah, look at commentary, and most of all jump right in, adding their unique, distinctive voices to it. The destination in Torah study is truly the journey itself. Exploring the ancient texts and making them come alive and speak to us today is exhilarating. Offering this forum to join with others is another way people come together to celebrate both Shabbat and each other. For so many seekers, indeed, it is the pathway home.

Ellen's Story: Noshing and *Drashing* Just Like at Home

Nosh and *Drash* reflects the diverse group of people that CSH attracts. When studying a text with a guest rabbi or scholar, the discussion has the potential to unfold in a variety of ways. Recently we were studying *Vayigash*, the story of Joseph revealing himself to his brothers. You could feel the energy in the room expand, and so did the tension. People had strong and opposing ideas of the meaning in the text. In some ways, it reminded me of the Thanksgiving dinners of my youth. With close to thirty people at the table, I can remember the political debates that were served up each year along with the turkey and mashed potatoes. There was the one relative who was going to side every time with the most liberal position, and there was the other relative who would invariably side with the most conservative. Then there were all the others who fell somewhere along that continuum. As a young child, I didn't follow much of what they were arguing about and debating, but as I grew older, I was able to participate and share my views. These were almost like sporting events in my house, and sometimes I think one relative, in particular, liked to throw punches just to get a rise out of the dinner crowd.

That spirit of engagement is what defined this recent Torah study. There were strong opinions on both sides, with people arguing with some, while agreeing with and supporting others. My interpretation fell in line with a more Kabbalistic understanding of the portion, and there soon developed a faction that supported this insight. Others explored it in a different way, but it was clear that there was intense focus and investment in the process itself. "*Eilu v'eilu divrei Elohim chayim*—Both these and those are the words of the living God."[5] We can interpret sacred texts in ways that speak to us and we can engage in debate not to prove that one side is right or wrong, but to grow deeper in our spiritual quest for meaning.

The conversation and discussion followed us from the room in which we were studying out into the hall, where many of us had a little nosh. This conversation was integrated into the rabbi's sermon, and as he spoke, hands popped up as students from the Nosh and *Drash* wanted to continue the conversation. And the rabbi not only invited them into his sermon, but seemed to shape his talk by the Torah exploration that was being created together as we all merged our minds, our hearts, and our *Ruakh*. That, too, was like the Thanksgiving dinners of my youth. Yes, we could argue and debate, but we were united not only in the food of our meal but by the spiritual sustenance of our tradition, which nourished our bodies, our minds, and our spirits, too.

Beit Knesset: A Home of Gathering

Last but not least, we end as we began. When all is said and done, Judaism is a people and a community. Our synagogues need to be reclaimed not as communal institutions but as communal homes. We need spaces and places for us to meet, to gather, to congregate. Our holy home needs to be a *beit tefilah*, a house of prayer; a *beit midrash*, a house of study; and a *beit knesset*, a house where we simply gather as well.

I cannot tell you how many times I have heard people say that they wanted to come to the synagogue, but they weren't sure if they'd be welcomed. They aren't members, so they didn't think it would be okay. Or they don't want to come for the entire day, so it would be more respectful, more acceptable, if they didn't come at all. Above all else, if they come but they don't enter the sanctuary, don't engage in traditional davening or the Torah service, it will have been an incomplete Shabbat experience and they will feel judged.

The Mercaz: The Central Meeting Place

Judaism never conceived of a clear divide between people congregating and people worshipping. In many ways they are one and the same. Congregating can mean coming together to speak words of the siddur in unison. Congregating can equally mean coming together and speaking our own words, not just to *HaShem* but to one another as well.

"And I shall be sanctified in the midst of the children of Israel," God says to Moses and the Israelites (Leviticus 22:32).

Where is God found, according to the Torah? God is found in the midst of God's children—in our relationships and within our community. Wherever we gather, there is God. Whenever we come together, that's where *Ruakh* is found and felt. For this reason a Synaplex must offer spaces and opportunities for informal gathering—to sit, to schmooze, to talk, and of course, to eat. This isn't a marketing tool. This isn't a consolation offering. This is and needs to be presented as a legitimate, authentic pathway into the *beit mikdash*, into our spiritual home, into the Shabbat experience, and into the Divine.

At CSH we have reclaimed the Atrium—a place once used only as a thoroughfare to shuttle people to the sanctuary as quickly as possible—into a destination unto itself. We have changed its name to reflect this shift. No longer is it merely a lobby. Rather, now it is the Mercaz—the Center—the center of our building, the center of our *tefilot*, *Talmud-Torah*, and our relationships. Although no formal offerings take place in this space, it is at the center of our Synaplex experience nonetheless.

In the Mercaz people can sit on sofas, sip coffee, or have a nosh, as we offer a full coffee bar and breakfast table at our Boker Tov Café. They can talk; read Israeli newspapers, local journals, and Jewish community bulletins that are out on the table; or just play with their babies or toddlers on the carpet. Although all our offerings are kid-friendly, since we have a "no shush policy," still, this is the place to let loose, to crawl, coo, and cry.

Along with multiple plasma TVs broadcasting the various services from around the building, there is a constant stream of people going from one venue to the next, flowing in and out of one another's conversations. But for dozens of people who may not have found their way to a Torah or *tefilah* offering, they have found their way home nonetheless, not merely to and through those conversations in the Mercaz but through connecting with others smack-dab in the middle of the synagogue and in the center of their hearts and lives.

Healing *Chavurah*

A new addition to our Synaplex is a perfect example of the blend of tradition and additive change. Like many synagogues, we used to offer the *Mi Shebeyrakh*, healing prayers, quickly and without much fanfare, amid our Torah service. Although we expanded this a bit, it was still almost an afterthought, certainly not a service unto itself. But then one day a congregant lovingly chastised me. "Rabbi," she said, as only a ninety-year-old *bubbe* knows how to do. "You tell us to pray for them, to visit them, to cook them chicken soup. However, you read the names so fast I don't even know whom I'm cooking for or where to deliver the prayers or the soup! Any chance you could slow down your recitation of the names of the sick so that maybe I could actually understand whose name it is you're saying?"

And she was right. I was telling people to believe in the prayers. To listen to the words. To feel the experience without truly providing a context for the content to be fully received. As Rabbi Larry Hoffman stresses in his book, *Rethinking Synagogues*, for synagogues to flourish today they must reclaim being a center of healing. "Permission is given to heal, says the Talmud, but Nachmanides ups the ante when he says, 'This permission to heal is really a *mitzvah*.' The Tosafot explain, 'Where humans cause damage, humans should repair what they caused. But for illness that comes from heaven [that is, as if from God], cure is like opening up a divine decree that has been hidden away."[6]

So the *Ruakh* Rally band got together and designed a *Mi Shebeyrakh* experience. There is mood-appropriate music, the reading of healing poems, and the experiencing of meditations and visualizations in what we now call the "Healing *Chavurah*." It is a stand-alone offering where people can drop in or tune in online just for this worthy and inspirational experience, an experience so deeply and desperately needed. "Thank you so much," one cyber-Jew wrote in. "I have been battling cancer alone. I have no synagogue near me where I live, no faith community I feel like I'm part of. But then I tuned in, and now I have come to depend upon this weekly experience. It has truly changed my impression of Judaism and experience with my disease."

That is additive change. Nothing was lost. No one had to sacrifice her experience. Instead, something was created, something magical that has provided a pathway in for souls who might have otherwise been left out of our home. An ancient prayer was simply expanded and reimagined into an experience that goes beyond rote recitation. This is an example of reclaiming an authentic prayer experience, one that came about because we were willing to admit our mistakes—okay, my mistakes—adjust our focus, and experiment with new directions.

The Miniplex: Changing Directions for Our Children

Of all the issues plaguing modern Judaism, perhaps none is starker than the state of our Hebrew school system. When I poll a room full of Jewish adults who have attended Hebrew school and ask them, "Who loved Hebrew school?" at most one hand shoots up—there's always one in every crowd. When I ask them who even "liked" the experience, still only one more person will raise his hand. Then, when I ask who hated Hebrew school, not disliked but actually hated it, practically every hand shoots up in the air. It's nearly unanimous. Generations of Hebrew school students have matriculated through a fundamentally flawed, if not outright broken system.

The crazy thing is, so many of those who hated their Hebrew school experience send their children to that very same type of Hebrew school. It begs the question why. Why, knowing full well that their children are as miserable in Hebrew school as they were, do they continue to enroll their children? Why wouldn't they get involved with it and change it or demand change? Typically their response is either, "I suffered through it and so they can suffer through it, too," or they just look at me as if they've never thought about it or can't imagine another way. But for modern American Jewish parents who are choice-oriented, proactive, and visionary in other aspects of their lives to respond with such resignation, pessimism, and lackluster vision is disconcerting, to say the least. They know Hebrew school is broken. They know that it is counterproductive and probably causing an increasing number of young Jews to walk away from their Judaism. Still, they keep on sending their children there without making any demands for change. If Judaism is going to thrive, if we are going to breathe *Ruakh* back into our collective and individual Jewish lives, it is going to have to include a transformation of Hebrew school. *Ruakh* must be front and center not only in our lives, but in the lives of our children.

While Hebrew school has failed, other Jewish youth efforts have succeeded. Trips to Israel for our older kids have made, and continue to make, incredibly positive contributions to Jewish identity. Youth groups are wonderful experiences as well. Except for Jewish day school, which is a different genre altogether, perhaps nothing has proved itself as successful or invaluable in fostering the identity of our Jewish youth as summer camp. Jewish summer camp is one of the single most influential determinants of whether or not Jewish kids will remain Jews and continue identifying and connecting with the Jewish community.

In those camps they experience Judaism in action and in community. Whether in arts and crafts, sports, or the subtle aspects of their camp life, Judaism infuses their days. Time is lived according to Jewish rhythms, with Friday evening welcoming Shabbat and with *Havdalah* transitioning the campers back into their activity-filled week. Campers take an active role in creating a vibrant, Jewish experience, filled with songs, prayers, and fun throughout the day.

Jewish summer camps have done a tremendous job of conveying *Ruakh* to countless young Jews. Sadly, however, when so many of these energized kids return from camp wanting to carry that *Ruakh* into their shul, they hit a closed door. They go to their synagogue expecting to feel what they felt at camp, hoping to continue celebrating their Judaism as they had all summer, experiencing the music, dance, and prayer. But Hebrew schools are the opposite of their camp experiences—joyless instead of joyful, and confining rather than liberating. At Hebrew school, they are told to get out their *machberet* (notebook), memorize prayers, recite haftarah trope. They are told to sit down, sit still, and "*Sheket b'vakasha*," shut up and listen. It's time to admit that while Hebrew school served its purpose for a particular time and in a particular era, that time and era has come and gone. Jews have always abandoned practices that were no longer appropriate, applicable, or served us. We stopped offering animal sacrifices centuries ago, yet we continue to offer our children as sacrificial lambs on the desks of those Hebrew school classrooms week in and week out. It's time to say good-bye to Hebrew school before our young Jews say good-bye to Judaism.

Different Era, Different Needs

Our Hebrew schools have failed because the premise on which they were built is no more. It is like the old story about the woman who always prepares a brisket by first cutting off both ends. When one of her children asks her why she does so, she is puzzled; she's never thought it through. She simply learned to do this from her mother, and her mother learned it from her mother. When she asks her *bubbe* why the family does this, what she believes to be a Jewish mystical practice, *Bubbe* sets the record straight. She explains that back in the

Old Country they were poor and didn't have a pot big enough for the roast so they had to cut off the ends. So here was this modern, affluent, American Jew continuing to cut off the ends of the roast, thinking she was perpetuating something meaningful when, in fact, she was foolishly wasting her resources and a perfectly good brisket.

Like that woman, we continue to perpetuate a Hebrew school structure whose time has passed. There is no doubt that Hebrew school served a purpose in a different era, for a different generation of Jews. It grew out of a time when Jews were clearly identifiable as Jews, more or less observing Judaism, Jewish holy days, and Shabbat. Early to mid- twentieth-century Judaism was deeply ingrained with Jewish observance, culture, ethnicity, and living. Even secular Jews were only secular in religiosity, not in cultural terms. Their world and worldview was Jewish through and through. So it made sense that they needed *supplemental* Jewish education to supplement what they were seeing in their homes or what was being practiced all around them within their Jewish community.

It was also a time when there were very few demands made on the lives of Americans—families or youth. Work defined adult life, while school defined the lives of youth, with a handful of other diversions in between. There weren't the after-school programs and activities that overschedule American children in this generation. Today, I literally have to sit with sixth graders BlackBerry calendars in hand—theirs not mine—trying to find time in their overly programmed schedule and lives to work the old rabbi in for a Bar Mitzvah appointment or two. While they are busy to the hilt, their parents are run ragged providing shuttle services from activity to activity, not to mention taking out second mortgages to pay for it all. Times have changed, and our youth, for better or, probably, for worse, lead very busy lives.

Even more problematic is that within these busy lives the weekend is the time of the week that is the most programmed of all. Saturday or Sunday—the Jewish Sabbath or the Christian Sabbath, take your pick—is often busier than the days of the workweek. The weekend is not a weekend at all; their week does not end. If they do come to the synagogue on the weekend, they will not come both on Sunday for Sunday school and Saturday for Shabbat services. So they come only once, if they come at all. They come on the day we have insisted on, on Sunday, the Christian Sabbath, leaving behind the Jewish Sabbath for another time.

And what do they do on Sunday in Sunday school? They study about Shabbat, of course. They study about the day they are missing, the day they are expected to celebrate in shul but hardly ever do. Does this make sense to you? Supplemental education is based on the fundamental idea that there is something that the education is supplementing. But the vast majority of these children are not living in families where they are receiving an education by experiencing Jewish prayer and observance in the home. So, in essence, supplemental Jewish education needs to be renamed as primary Jewish education, reflecting that this is the central place for them to learn and experience their Jewish selves and lives. And if that is the case, Jewish education cannot continue to be simply *learning* about Jewish things but not having the opportunity to *engage* in Jewish things. In Hebrew schools today, kids are reading about Judaism, perhaps talking about Judaism, but they're not *practicing* Judaism. They're not experiencing Judaism. Is it any wonder these children become uninspired?

If Jews won't or can't come to the synagogue both days of the weekend, then doesn't it make sense for us to bring them on Saturday, on Shabbat? No amount of talk about Shabbat, no amount of discussion about prayer, no amount of understanding about Judaism can, will, or should substitute for the real deal. It's what Jewish campers have been demonstrating all along: living, breathing, and celebrating their Judaism through action and interaction provides a *Ruakh*-filled experience that is truly without measure.

The Shabbat Learning Experience

For this reason, at CSH we no longer offer Sunday school. Like Adat Shalom in Bethesda, Maryland, or Ohr HaTorah in Los Angeles, we did away with that old model in exchange for what we call Limud Shabbat, which literally translates as "Learning Shabbat," but which we often refer to as the "Shabbat Experience." The move was more than a shift from our Sunday program to the same old, same old simply on a different day of the week. Rather, it was a shift from practice to play. Limud Shabbat is the day when our kids, like our adults, suit up, sometimes literally, as they come in their soccer or football uniforms and get in the Jewish game.

We still have a weekday supplemental program that functions much like the programs with which we are all familiar, though certainly with some monumental changes in philosophy, feel, and vibe. Now, however, we are supplementing the Shabbat experience on Tuesday but experiencing Shabbat on Shabbat.

On Shabbat, instead of writing out the rules of Hebrew grammar, we are speaking Hebrew, leaving writing and frontal classroom instruction for the week. For too long Jews have learned to memorize Hebrew without understanding what they are saying. Instead of studying about prayer, our youth are praying. They are engaged in the words not merely in their heads but within their hearts. And their engagement, though primarily focused around tradition and traditional modes of davening, is not without elements of what their parents are experiencing down the hall in the Synaplex.

What we want is for these kids to be moved, as they are at camp, by *Ruakh*, so we have a mini-Synaplex (or Miniplex) of offerings and experiences for our kids as well. Beyond the traditional davening, we have them rotating through a family service, the traditional sanctuary service, the Renewal Minyan, and body movement expressions of prayer like the Yoga Minyan and tai chi, too. Kids are no different than adults in this regard. They, too, live in a world defined by choice and self-expression. As we read in Proverbs, "*Chanoch lana'ar al pi darko*—Educate a child according to their own unique path" (22:6). Some of these kids like the traditional, but others march to the beat of the bongos.

Most important, beyond the skills and fluency that we are committed to providing and these kids are demonstrating as never before, they are learning to love Judaism. They are not fighting with their parents about coming to Limud Shabbat. They are not rushing out the door when it is over. On the contrary, the climax of the Synaplex, the *Ruakh* Rally, is an explosion of *Ruakh* that spreads across the generations.

Pain in the But, But, But:
Why We Can't Do This in My Shul

"But Rabbi, it won't work at my synagogue," a visiting Hebrew school director will say to me, something I have heard time and again. "Parents will never go for it," they say, defeated before they even begin.

"But Rabbi, we [a Conservative shul] can't write on Shabbat."

"But Rabbi, we can't afford to offer twice as many classes."

"But Rabbi, we can't afford this kind of programming, period."

The list of *buts* I get is endless. At these times, I am reminded of the axiom stated in the book *Spiritual Strategies*, where the authors point out that no matter how unlikely, if something exists, it must indeed be possible. Each issue is often substantial and real, *but* let me assure you of this: to keep on keeping on with Sunday school is a guaranteed failure. There are no *ifs*, *ands*, or *buts* about it. Yes, there are challenges to deal with. We have dealt with them. "Necessity is the mother of invention," said Plato. We have necessity. We have invented an inspired Hebrew school experience. So can you.

Is it challenging for us to pull it off without writing on Shabbat? Of course, but it's not impossible. Is it difficult, pedagogically, for teachers to engage in only experiential learning for three hours on Saturday morning? Certainly, but they have risen to the challenge. What is the biggest challenge? You can probably guess. It's not halachic or pedagogic; it's the holy of holies—Saturday sports and activities. Soccer in the spring, football in the fall, ballet performances and piano recitals, you name it—if our kids practice it, you can be certain that in our world it will be played on Shabbat. And so we send off our Jewish children to play in all these other arenas, knowing full well that they'll most likely never grow up to become professional athletes or ballerinas or concert pianists. Okay, maybe your kid will, but the rest of ours won't. What they have a chance of being when they grow up, however, is Jewish, but only if we provide the opportunities for them to be inspired on our playing field.

At CSH, Saturday sports have not trumped the Shabbat school experience. Of course, at first parents were up in arms at the thought of our proposed shift. The same arguments came up for us as they have for others, and will for any synagogue that makes this move. They aren't, however, deal breakers and in the end aren't that difficult to overcome. From the outset we made a principled decision not to fight. Our members are our customers, and the customer is always right.

"You can't do this," they said. "You can't make us come on Saturday."

"Okay," we responded. "We won't make you."

"We go skiing in the winter and can't make it back for Shabbat during that time of year."

"Fine," was our response. "Come when you are in town or tune in online."

"We have games in fall and can't come until winter."

"Not a problem," was our reply. "You can make it up by coming more in the spring."

Some of our faculty were clearly doubtful and concerned about our attitude and policy. "But no one will come," or "They won't come often enough," or "They won't come consistently," we were warned repeatedly. But this is not what happened. In fact, the opposite proved to be true.

When we offered Sunday school, between all the vacations and Jewish holidays, we were in session roughly twenty Sundays a year. Shabbat, however, happens every week, and we run Limud Shabbat, or a downsized version, throughout the school year. We've doubled the offerings, and many families send their children or, better yet, join them, week in and week out. Many, however, come half the time but still come more than they did when we had the Sunday model. Most come somewhere in between. It is not an all-or-nothing proposition. We encourage kids, just like their parents, to come early, to come late, to come when they can. And when they choose to go to their ball game, on numerous occasions many kids come off the playing field asking their parents, "Can we go now? If we leave early, we can still catch the *Ruakh* Rally and lunch." But the bottom line is that now it's worth coming because it's joyous, it's the place to be, and it's about celebrating Shabbat.

The *Ruakh* Rally

This brings us to the apex of the day and one of the two key ingredients that makes the Synaplex work. As the "plex" offerings begin to wind down, with people making their way into the main sanctuary for the rabbi's talk or discussion, CSH erupts into an explosion of spirit. Hundreds of souls join together in what we call the *Ruakh* Rally.

You can repeatedly tell your children or grandchildren that they should be Jewish, love Judaism, and perpetuate this ancient, holy, and inspirational religion. However, like anything else in life, our children will do as we do, not as we say. If we drop them off at the shul to practice Judaism for us or the family as we head off to the golf course or the mall, they will see through the ruse. They will play along with the game only as long as they have to, and then they won't. They'll be out of there quicker than you can say "sacrificial Shabbat lamb," which is exactly what they are and why they'll resent Judaism and their Jewish identity.

At CSH, our *Ruakh* Rally is an inspirational opportunity for all. Hundreds of kids come marching in to join with parents, grandparents, and the rest of the congregation. Instead of being told to feel inspired, they experience that inspiration firsthand. They experience their parents and grandparents not merely telling them to feel pride, but modeling that pride. Singing out at the top of their lungs, with fists pumping and feet stomping, *Am Yisrael Chai*—the Jewish people are alive and thriving. These kids see it for themselves.

At the *Ruakh* Rally children are not told to sit down, face forward, and be quiet. Rather, they can stand or sit, mingle up on the bimah, or dance the hora around the *amud* (lectern). Some grab drums and others are handed a microphone. Some sit and observe, but most stand and sing. We have consciously chosen to end our day's experience with Israeli rock songs about peace, Zionist hymns about Jewish survival and joy, and proudly chant in unison *HaTikvah*, understanding that what was once our hope is now our reality—hope etched on their impressionable minds, psyches, and spirits. These kids will grow up being part of a living, growing, vibrant Judaism.

These moments of joining together in spirit are crucial to making the day work. Synaplex has many moving parts, and what keeps us together, what binds the respective day's offerings into a coherent whole, is this grand finale. We may not look the same, dress the same, have the same inclinations, or choose the same pathways to walk in our life. However, standing together arm in arm, adults and children, individuals and families, young and old singing together, we are indeed *am echad, lev echad*—one people with one heart, and that is experienced at the *Ruakh* Rally.

One People, One Lunch

As a rabbi I spend much of my week inviting unengaged members, unaffiliated Jews, and members of our community—Jews, semi-Jews, and non-Jews—to come join us on Shabbat. I tell them you don't need to be a member, you don't need to be Jewish, and you don't need to come to our services—just join us for lunch! Needless to say, it is shocking to most people that they'd be welcomed in our *bayit*, our home, with no expectations that they become members, that they adopt a certain set of beliefs, or that they pray before they can eat. Pay to pray and pray to eat in our holy home is not only foreign to CSH; it's simply not Jewish.

What is Jewish is joining together in community for the *Kiddush* lunch or, as we call it, the "Shabbat Café." The Shabbat Café has become the "challah and butter" of CSH and the Synaplex experience, without which Synaplex would not and could not work. It happens every week, 12:00 noon on the dot.

It is a full, sit-down lunch. It is costly but can be adjusted for expense. Regardless of the money involved, it is worth its weight in gold. It is the unifying force of the day. It is the one time during the week when multiple generations sit around a table together. It is a time when young families sit together, talk together, and none of them is looking at a watch. An hour or two into it and people are still schmoozing the day away. Sometimes we tack on programs during this time slot: Shabbat Sports for Kids, *Shulchan Ivrit* (Hebrew conversation), Israeli Dance, or speakers of all sorts. But the most important aspect of Shabbat Café is that there is ultimately nothing to do, nowhere to go, and everyone is invited, period. You can come for the day. You can come just for the Shabbat Café. But if you come at all, you are encouraged to stick around, to join us, and, of course, to eat.

A monumental and crucial shift is that Shabbat is never canceled. Fifty-two weeks a year, regardless of secular holidays, regardless of B'nai Mitzvah, there is always one full lunch. No matter how many hundreds of people we are talking about, B'nai Mitzvah families are required to minimally sponsor our lunch even if they don't stay, opting instead to take their lunch outside of CSH. While this happened quite often in the early years, it is now seldom that a Bar or Bat Mitzvah family and guests will choose to have lunch elsewhere.

Did this involve a contentious change in policy? At first it was incredibly difficult, to say the least. There was, and is, in most synagogues today, a sense of entitlement and elitism that B'nai Mitzvah families unfortunately exude. They traditionally made up the vast majority of those in attendance. They most certainly staked out the day as theirs, on their terms, and though the rest of the congregation was tolerated, they were hardly welcomed and certainly not getting their hands on that Bar Mitzvah boy's hard-earned lox.

At CSH, however, the tides have turned. Now there is clearly a culture that the Synaplex belongs to no one but to everyone. The Bar or Bat Mitzvah family and guests are invited to join in not as the center of attention, but rather as part of a whole. And though they don't always love the thought of having to provide food for the congregation, it can be made affordable and it can be made relatively intimate as well. But, most of all, what they have come to find is that it is ecstatic, it is *freilach* (joyous), it is more enjoyable than anything else they could imagine. China and silverware, high-end caterers, or Bat Mitzvah themes are no longer necessary and hardly missed, as the *Ruakh* of the day returns to center stage.

Three Pillars of the *Beit Mikdash*

Every Shabbat, friends and family of the B'nai Mitzvah, members of Ritual Committees checking us out, and visiting guests to CSH respond in a similar fashion. They make a beeline for me, sometimes literally grabbing me by the collar, saying, "I have never seen anything like this!"

This response is not only priceless, it always instills in me so much hope. Jews are hungry—and for more than just bagels—and people are seeking what Judaism has to offer. Synagogues are poised to redefine themselves, reinvigorate their congregants, and reimagine Judaism and Jewish community in the twenty-first century. But this can and will happen if, and only if, we reclaim the *beit mikdash* not at the center of Jerusalem but at the center of our communities and our lives.

An authentic *beit mikdash* rests on the traditional three-legged stool on which Jews have always leaned: a house of prayer, study, and community. This is what has made and sustained this religion for thousands of years. This is what an inspirational Judaism and Jewish community must offer. The central organizing principle of our philosophy at CSH is a *Ruakh*-filled vision and the building of personal relationships. Experiencing Shabbat through our Synaplex format enables people to enter the blessing of both Shabbat and community. If we can rethink our communities in general and our synagogues in particular as being a home with many rooms, many doors, and many openings to the sacred, we will know *Ruakh* and move from merely surviving to truly thriving. Jews will find their way through one of the open doors; they will find their way home.

6

The "Who" of *Ruakh*
Re-Membering the Tribe

Rabbi B's Story: Radical Animosity

Congregation Shirat Hayam is only a few years old. It is a merged congregation of two formerly Conservative synagogues that, strangely enough, were across the street from each other. You'd think that a merger of two shuls a few hundred feet apart would have been seamless enough, but if you thought that, you would have been wrong. These communities, as I was about to find out, were miles apart in terms of spirit.

When I first arrived at CSH, the merger brought them under one roof, but that was about the only thing that united them. Although they hid their congregational warts during the interview process, by my first Shabbat as their rabbi they were letting it all hang out, warts and all.

The former members of one of the temples would sit on one side of the pews. The former members of the "other" temple would sit on the opposite side. They would hardly talk to one another, still referring to their respective beloved temples in the present tense. They vowed they would never embrace this new congregation with the strange name, nor would they embrace this new rabbi, also with a strange name. The place was polarized and unwelcoming, to say the least.

It was so bad that after one of those initial Shabbat services, an irate congregant came up to me after the Torah service. "Rabbi, how dare you give out four *aliyot* to members of Temple Israel when you only gave out three to members of Temple Beth El? We knew you liked them better. That's why 'our people' didn't want to hire you in the first place!"

I just smiled, despite how I felt on the inside, and reassured him and the others it would all work out. The problem was I wasn't exactly sure how to make that happen. In that moment I felt like Moses, who had pleaded with God not to give him the job, not to make him lead these people, to find someone else, anyone else, just not him. Or in Moses's words:

> I am not able to carry all these people alone, because it is too heavy for me. And if you deal thus with me, *hargeni nah*—kill me now....
>
> —Numbers 11:14–15

Kill me now, God, kill me now, because it was about to get a whole lot worse.

Over the next few months I repeatedly heard the language of "us versus them," not only in terms of the two warring factions under our roof but toward the world at large. There were the "Jews down the street"; Chabad was at one end and a Reform temple and Conservative synagogue at the other. Chabad was trying to "steal" our members, though at that point they didn't have to steal them—I was ready to give them away. The Reform Jews were "not Jewish enough," and the Conservative shul was supposedly "the most unwelcoming bunch in town."

The "them," however, wasn't just limited to Jews. I heard the nastiest things about interfaith families in the community and the handful of them, God knows why, who actually belonged to our shul. Although our synagogue policies stated that interfaith families were welcome in theory, they were hardly welcomed in practice and certainly not with open arms.

"The neighbors" were all "goyim," I was told in no uncertain terms. They wouldn't let us into their beach clubs or country clubs, though that was thirty years ago, and that's why we weren't going to give them the time of day, not that they were actually asking for it.

I heard derogatory names for every group under the sun. *Schvartzes, schiktzas, shegitzes, goyisha kopfs, feigeles,* you name it and I heard it said within the walls of this "holy" place. It was like being rabbi to the Jewish version of Archie Bunker, and all I could think of were Moses's words: kill me now, God; kill me now.

But God didn't kill Moses. He wasn't getting off that easily and, I guess, neither was I. I decided that if there weren't going to be any divine lightning bolts in my immediate future I was going to have to turn the Un-Love Boat around. So I set a new course for a new adventure, proclaiming it from the bimah, in personal interactions, and in writing every chance I got. The days of Radical Animosity were over. This ship was setting sail toward the Promised Land, the land of warmth and kindness, the land of open minds, open hearts, and open arms. This congregation was heading toward our new home; the voyage toward Radical Hospitality was about to begin. We would either arrive or die trying. And, truth be told, at the time I thought I would certainly have to go down with the ship, or more likely be thrown over the side of the boat.

Members of the Tribe

We have been called "*Am Yisrael*—the people of Israel," reaching back to our origins not on the high seas, but in the desert. Along the way this people diversified, began to speak different languages, expressed themselves through different cultures, even became different races. We are as nuanced as the colors of the rainbow or the shades reflected by a setting sun over the land of Canaan. At least in theory.

Unfortunately, today most American Jewish communities are hardly diverse. We are primarily of Ashkenazic descent. We are white, relatively affluent, college-educated Democrats who like fifty-one versions of smoked fish. We tend not to believe in God or translate our beliefs into Jewish practice. We are highly successful and increasingly assimilated into the mainstream culture. Yet, no matter how far we travel from our tribe, the tribe still exists. We still find ourselves on the lookout, scanning the movie credits for the Jewish names or noticing the mezuzah on the doorposts of the houses we jog past, feeling this identification with a fellow MOT (member of the tribe). We are highly successful, motivated, and, frankly, a highly insular group, to say the least. Though today this might be slowly changing, this is descriptive of the Jewish communities in which most of us grew up.

Our modern, American, suburban Jewish tribes must be re-created, reconstituted, or re-"membered" once again. Let us start by rethinking about who is actually a Jew. When we define who's a Jew, many denominations turn to the halachic definition of being born to a Jewish mother. But this definition is hardly sufficient any longer in defining who is in and who is out. It certainly does not speak to who will be an inspired Jew or an active participant in the tribe. And, as we have clearly seen, it is not enough to predict who will remain a Jew.

The truth of the matter is that a great number of those who were born Jewish will walk away from Judaism. They are "choice-less Jews." Yes, they were born into the tribe, but in an age where everything is a choice, inaction itself is also a choice. Many Jews simply choose not to choose, making the passive choice to drift away, to assimilate, to leave Judaism and the tribe.

Ellen's Story: Choosing to Come Out

Over time, I avoided going to temple as much as possible, even skipping the High Holy Days. At some point, it just seemed silly to put myself, as an adult who could make her own choice, in a space that felt both stifling and aggravating. I can recall the sermons on Rosh Hashanah where rabbis bemoaned the fact that people don't come to shul enough or contribute financially enough and told us everything we were doing wrong. I remember thinking to myself, "Well, we're here now, so maybe you can stop berating?" I didn't have the power to change the service, but I had the power to decide not to take part. I also found the way in which Jewish organizations solicited contributions so offensive that I eventually told them to put me on a "Do Not Call" list. I had, in a sense, become an anti-Jewish Jew.

My connection with my Jewish heritage was rekindled as I studied Torah as a spiritual path, with both Jews and non-Jews. All of this, however, had been outside of any synagogue, because I was unable to find this openness, acceptance, and deep spiritual reflection within a shul. Whether by chance, by karma, or *beshert*, I discovered CSH. And what happened? I had to start lying. My family knew my Buddhist heart still chilled at the idea of stepping foot into a temple. My kids were now in college, and while they didn't bat an eye whenever I left for a few weeks to trek in the Himalayas or go on a silent meditation retreat, the idea of their mother now joining a shul and becoming an active member would be, I imagined, too alarming.

After all, despite belonging to a temple when they were growing up, they learned to look over at me to gauge my reaction to a sermon, got used to me complaining about the insular Jewish community, the "us versus them" themes that I couldn't stand. They were used to me reading Buddhist quotes to them each morning at breakfast but had never seen me light the candles on Friday night.

Now I was celebrating Shabbat nearly every Saturday and I felt as if I had to go undercover. I imagined they would react to this news as if I were possessed by some strange and inexplicable alien creature who had brainwashed me. I would say to my husband, "If the kids call, don't tell them I'm at shul; tell them I went to the health club or the grocery store." Steve would meet me later in the morning for the Healing *Chavurah*, the rabbi's sermon, the *Ruakh* Rally, and lunch. As soon as I saw him, I'd ask, "Did the kids call? Where did you tell them I was?"

As the weeks went by, I came clean. I told my kids what I'd been doing. "It's so different from the temples we've known," I'd explain. After their initial surprise, we talked about why CSH has become so important in my life. I told them how I don't have to cut off parts of myself; my spiritual leanings can be expressed fully in this community. I see others, and I feel seen. I laugh when I think about the irony of feeling that coming out with my kids about Judaism was like telling them I've converted. We're Jewish. But for so long, I felt like the "other" in my own tribe. Coming clean, coming out, and coming home never felt so good.

Jews by Choice

Judaism is not an ethnicity, culture, or race. Judaism is a religion, and a religion is about God, about faith, about choice. You can be born Jewish, and you can choose to become Jewish, too. Judaism, after all, was founded by converts in Abraham and Sarah. Judaism has always wanted and welcomed converts, even if Jews have not always been so welcoming. Non-Jews do not need to convert to Judaism to be a good person, to be deemed worthy of God's love, or to be "saved" and ensured a place in the world to come. However, an authentic Jewish tribe has always been accepting of non-Jews who choose to become Jewish or, as we call them in this day and age, Jews by choice.

To become a Jew may be rigorous by the standards of some movements or rabbis. But that doesn't make it authentically Jewish. Some Jewish schools of thought throughout history have made it quite easy to convert and enter the tribe:

> When a person comes to be converted, one receives him with an open hand so as to bring him under the wings of the Divine Presence.[1]

Other traditional voices and thinkers have not only made it acceptable to receive converts, they have made it an imperative:

> Every Jew should endeavor to actively bring non-Jews under the wing of God's presence, just as Abraham did.[2]

Actively bring non-Jews to Judaism? Tell that to the writers of *Sex in the City*, where Charlotte, a non-Jew, attempts to convert but is turned away by the unwelcoming rabbi. Tell that to too many choice-less Jews who are threatened by Jews by choice. After all, if these people choose to be Jewish, embrace Judaism, and engage it passionately, which they tend to do, what does that say about the choice-less Jews stuck in their dreaded pews? Ironically, it is often those among the more religiously liberal and secular segments of our tribe who tend to be the least welcoming of converts.

If Jewish communities are to prevail, we are going to have to radically rethink our approach to non-Jews seeking to convert. Of course, they do not need to convert to Judaism to be part of our communities. However, they also need to be told and, more importantly, shown that they are wanted and they are welcome within our tribe. Our tribal tent flaps were thrown open by Abraham and Sarah thousands of years ago, and it is our duty to follow their example by expanding our notion of the "tribe" and welcoming fellow seekers into our midst.

The Limitations of Language

Let me tell you a story about Dana. In a congregation of a few thousand souls, Dana's is one that burns brighter than most. She is a passionate student of Torah. She is deeply committed to growing in both Jewish knowledge and practice. She takes her life seriously and sees it through a filter of *Yiddishkeit* like few other Jews I have met. Dana is not a born Jew. Dana is a Jew by choice.

The truth of the matter is that Dana is hardly alone. Quite often, the most sincere, passionate, and committed Jews in synagogues and Jewish communities are Jews by choice. They tend to exhibit the best of what Judaism has to offer and examples of what Jews could and should be. That is why we not only need new attitudes but new language, too.

"Rabbi, I don't mind if you call me a 'convert' or a 'Jew by choice,'" Dana said to me before her conversion. "Neither are offensive and I understand the need for labels. However, knowing how you talk about authenticity, I was wondering if there is a better term for describing myself as a Jew." Dana got me thinking. She's right. We need new names, better names, for the journey she and others like her have taken. To *convert* means to become something else, something other than what you were. Dana and others like her have hardly converted. Dana was not leaving something else. Rather, she was becoming a Jew, what she felt she always was. And *Jew by choice* is not only clumsy, it also isn't true. As Dana and so many others share with me, "What choice did I have?" Dana didn't become a Jew to marry a Jew. Dana was choosing to become Jewish because that was where her heart and soul were leading her. Growing up, it was a menorah she longed for, rather than a Christmas tree. She wanted to go to Passover seders and attend the shul for the High Holy Days. "I was born with a Jewish *neshama*," she said. "I was simply born into the life of a gentile. Now I have found my way home."

Her Jewish journey was finally completed. Maybe that makes her a "completed Jew," but that sounds too messianic. Dana experienced herself as a Jew and now she simply revealed it to the rest of the world. Maybe that makes her a "revealed Jew," but that's too suspicious sounding. Dana was on a journey to become a Jew; maybe that makes her a "becoming Jew," but that's a bit too attractive sounding. Her pathway into Judaism was truly inspired, so maybe we should call her an "inspirational Jew," but that brings images of Tony Robbins to mind. And though Dana had returned home, I think calling her a "home Jew" somehow misses the point and makes me want to break out into a rap song and dance. So, until we come up with a better label, for now we'll simply call Dana a Jew—a member of the tribe who found her way home.

Semi-Jews: Not Jewish But Not Not Jewish

This brings us to the problem of language and labels in our modern Jewish tribes. Most of our labels are outdated and no longer make sense. For instance, the term *non-Jew* in an interfaith marriage is inaccurate. *Non* means "not," "nothing," or "opposite." Is a woman who is not Jewish but married to a Jewish man a "non-Jew"? Is a Christian-born father who is paying for his Jewish child's Bar Mitzvah, making sure his son is dutifully entered into the Jewish covenant, a "non-Jew"? Are parents who are not Jewish, with no faith tradition of their own, but married to a Jew and raising their children as Jews, really "non-Jews"? And even the term *interfaith* needs to be rethought. The vast majority of Jews I know who marry outside the religion are not marrying devout Christians, Catholics, or Muslims. If they are, then *interfaith* is an accurate description. Interfaith, after all, implies two faiths, whereas, at best, most of these marriages only contain one and oftentimes none. Or in the words of Rabbi Harold Schulweis, one of the pioneers of outreach to the interfaith community, these unions are often more aptly "inter-faithless" marriages, as neither partner brings a faith to the marriage. We need new language in describing these marriages, and we need new language in describing partners in marriage who support, sustain, and contribute to our tribe. At CSH we often refer to such members as "semi-Jews" to show our appreciation for them, though, admittedly, the label is far from perfect. Clearly, we need better labels. But more important, we need new attitudes in the way we approach holy souls who call our synagogues their home. To be more accurate, we need old language, old labels, and old approaches. We need to return to the Torah so we can move ahead with authenticity once again.

In biblical times, the tribe of the Israelites was far less rigid and far more porous than it is today. For instance, there were always what the Torah calls "*ger'ei toshav*—resident aliens." These were "semi-Jews" who lived within the Jewish tribe. They weren't "Jewish" per se, but they weren't "non-Jews," either. Rather, they had particular responsibilities and privileges within the Jewish tribe, and the Jewish tribe had certain affinities and obligations toward them in return. They may not have technically been *mishpacha*, family, but they were allies and friends and therefore spiritual brothers and sisters.

Since the time of the Torah and onwards, there have always been "*ger'ei tzedek*—righteous gentiles" in our midst. These were men and women of other religious traditions, beliefs, and practices who lived side by side with Jews. For instance, Moses's father-in-law, Yitro (Jethro), was such a man. Yitro was a Midianite priest and yet he was also Moses's mentor and advisor. Think of the many gentiles during the Holocaust who risked their lives and the lives of their families to hide

Jews, save Jews, and keep Jews safe. Think of all the mentors, teachers, and great figures in your life who guided you along your path. To describe such "righteous gentiles" as merely "non-Jews" is simply inaccurate. They may not share our religious beliefs or heritage, but we share a common set of values that mandates mutual care and concern for one another, as we are all children of the One.

Rabbi B's Story: Second-Class Citizens

Having just graduated from rabbinical school, I, along with almost every newbie in almost any field, thought I knew it all. My talmudic exams were still fresh in my mind, and halacha was still my primary modus operandi. I felt ready to take on my shul and transform it into the halachic centerpiece it was meant to be. I was rigid in my intention to reclaim Torah for my congregants out in the cornfields of Iowa, so off I went. But there was that old saying again, "Man plans and God laughs."

One of the first encounters I had at that shul was with a "non-Jewish" mother of two girls, both of whom had converted to Judaism. She and her Jewish husband were members of our synagogue, and the girls both attended Hebrew school. Her name was Margaret, and in a couple weeks' time, her youngest daughter was going to become a Bat Mitzvah. The mother was incredibly kind and respectful, and she was also very, very worried. She was so worried, in fact, that she summoned what must have been a tremendous amount of courage to make an appointment with me, the rabbi, a title she revered in ways I had only ever witnessed in either religious Orthodox communities or at rabbinical school, where we were intoxicated by the sound of that title next to our names.

Margaret sat with me and broke down in tears. "Rabbi, I'm so grateful that you would see me, 'a gentile.' And Rabbi, please don't misunderstand what I'm about to say as anything other than gratitude to you and the Jewish people. I'm grateful that you have allowed me and my husband to raise our girls as Jews in this synagogue. But Rabbi, I don't know if I can attend my daughter's Bat Mitzvah if what happened the last time happens again. As proud as I was in that moment, it pained my heart and my family's heart that I couldn't come up, not to the Torah, not to the bimah, not even to the front of the room to make a short speech for my little girl."

The policy at that point was just that: non-Jews could in no way, shape, or form take part in any of the rituals or even non-rituals within the synagogue and particularly not on Shabbat during *tefilah*. While I knew this to be a traditional, "halachic" dictate, though as I've come to discover it is hardly grounded in Torah, it broke my heart. But not as much as what she shared with me after that.

"Rabbi, I'm not sure if you are aware of this, but we don't live in this community. We live fifty miles outside of the city in a little farm town. This is the closest synagogue. We drive in twice a week and have done so every week for the last seven years. Rabbi, I'm honored to do it. I'm even happy to do it and I'll keep on doing it no matter what you decide. I just don't think I can sit through my younger daughter's Bat Mitzvah and feel like a second-class citizen again."

In that moment I didn't hear God laughing. Instead, I felt God crying, through Margaret's tears.

"Margaret," I said, "not only will you give your daughter a Bat Mitzvah blessing, not only will you do it from the bimah, but you will do it at the Torah. Although you won't be reading from the Torah or saying the blessings recited by the one receiving an *aliyah*, which your husband can do, you will stand up finally as a member of this shul. On behalf of this synagogue, I am so sorry for your pain. On behalf of the Jewish people, I want to thank you for giving your daughters to us and providing for their Jewish education as you have done so graciously. And on behalf of myself, I want to thank you for waking me up, setting me straight, and teaching me Torah. Margaret, *todah*, thank you from the bottom of my heart."

Margaret was the first "non-Jew" in the history of that hundred-year-old congregation to set foot on the bimah during a Bat Mitzvah, to be called up with her husband as he had an *aliyah*, and to formally kvell over her children.

I can assure you that convincing the Ritual Committee of my decision was not an easy process, but it was the right thing to do. I can also assure you that once the change was made, it was as if the congregation took a collective breath. The committee members, even those who were adamantly opposed at first, eventually came around. Margaret was a turning point not only for me but for that congregation as well. In that moment we all felt the *Ruakh* return.

The Dreaded "P" Word

Growing up in Nebraska gave me a unique view into the life of Evangelical Christianity. It was there I was given a firsthand glimpse into the world of the dreaded "p word": *proselytization*. When I was growing up, my school friends, almost exclusively Evangelical Christians, often brought up my Judaism, questioned my disregard for Jesus, or outright asked me to convert. Periodically we'd get that "knock on the door," from an Evangelical cold caller or from our neighbor, a born-again Christian, who loved us so much she couldn't bear the thought of us burning in hell.

Understandably, this word—more accurately, this idea—strikes fear in the hearts of most Jews. We have been hounded over this issue. We have been treated as second-class citizens over this issue. We have been persecuted, tortured, and murdered over the ugly "p word." No wonder we shy away from it when it comes to reaching out to those in our midst who aren't Jewish.

But maybe as Jews it's time to rethink our aversion to reaching out to the non-Jewish world. If Judaism is going to survive, we are going to have start doing serious, aggressive outreach, not only to the choice-less Jews, but also to the many could be, would be, and frankly should be potential Jews by choice.

Before you hyperventilate, take a deep breath. This does not mean we should become Evangelical Jews. From a Jewish theological perspective, non-Jews need not be Jewish to be saved. Jews should not canvass the neighborhood sniffing out Sunday ham suppers, nor should they stake out the local church on Christmas Eve, inviting the congregants out for a movie and Chinese. That said, Judaism is a good, holy, beautiful, and meaningful way of life. Judaism is compatible with your average secular American's life and lifestyle. And Jewish values and spirituality are deeply and desperately needed in the lives of so many, particularly those who are without a formal path, which is the vast majority of the people we know. If someone is unchurched, if someone is looking for a worthy, meaningful, compatible way of life with their secular American values, walking a Jewish path may be that needed step. We should be inviting and welcoming them into Judaism.

This is not new age; outreach has been around since the beginning of the tribe. It is said that Abraham and Sarah were not only converts, but that they spent their time along their journey "making Jews," inviting others into their tent and onto their newfound Jewish path. In the Talmud, Rabbi Elazar goes so far as to say, "The reason for the destruction of the Second Temple and ensuing exile was for one reason alone—to acquire more Jews."[3] If indeed that was the case, then clearly we have failed. Almost every religion is outpacing us in the convert department—Baha'i, Sikhism, even the Zoroastrians are doing a better job at outreach. Judaism has hardly ever been a viable option for most "non-Jews." We've hardly reached out to the non-Jewish world and invited them into our spiritual homes. This partially comes down to a problem of inspiration. We tribal members need to be part of a Judaism that inspires us so profoundly that we wouldn't want to keep it to ourselves and couldn't if we tried. This is the real reason why most Jews don't reach out to other Jews, semi-Jews, or non-Jews. The real reason for our collective reticence is that we are uninspired, and our spiritual homes and Jewish congregations are devoid of *Ruakh*. Of course, it's hard to ask people to join such a tribe. Once the tribe is infused with *Ruakh*, don't worry—your job is taken care of; the *Ruakh* will speak for itself and you can't help but reach out. In this modern, open, and ecumenical era in which we find ourselves, it is not only time to open the flaps of our tent, it is time to reach out and formally invite others in.

"Spiritual Friends" Membership

Still, no one need be Jewish to join us, and at CSH anyone can join our tribe. Let me tell you about my good friend Jay. Jay knows Hebrew. Jay davens with fervent conviction from the siddur. Jay drums with me, side by side, in the Renewal Minyan. Jay plays in our *Ruakh* Rally Band. Jay is at CSH every single Shabbat. Jay is one of the best Jews I have ever met, except he is an Evangelical Christian. He is not a Jew. He is not a "non-Jew." He lives in two worlds and this is one of his two spiritual homes. On Shabbat he is with us. On the Christian Sabbath, he is at his church. In his church he is a member. At CSH he is what we call a "spiritual friend."

So what is Jay doing at CSH? What are other "non-Jews" not married to a Jew doing at a shul? Jay, and many others, have found their way to us because of the *Ruakh*. They come for the davening. They come for the *chevra* (fellowship). They want to patronize us, support us, and help spread our *Ruakh* into the world.

It is simply inconceivable to most choice-less Jews that these "non-Jews" would care so much about Judaism. It is baffling to members of other synagogues who can't get their own people to attend services that these "non-Jews" would show up and participate every single week in ours. And it is offensive to too many rabbis that a Conservative synagogue would have a seat at the table for anyone other than a Jew. But we do have a seat for our growing cadre of "spiritual friends" at our table.

This is why CSH offers an affiliation category called "Spiritual Friends of CSH." This is for "righteous gentiles," for anyone who is not Jewish, for our spiritual brothers and sisters who want to join us, sustain us, and give to us as we have given to them. They aren't technically members, complete with voting rights, nor do they want to be. They are supporters, sustainers, and friends of CSH. Once you open up the floodgates of *Ruakh*, you simply have no idea how it flows or where it will go. You must be prepared to steer into uncharted territory with all those new, excited, and engaged souls who join you along the way.

Re-Member the Tribe

In the end, the Jewish tribe can thrive once again if and only if we open it up and loosen our grip on rigid definitions, borders, and boundaries of who's a Jew. The modern obsession with "who's in and who's out" is stifling our spirit. The Jewish tribe is a sacred community made up of souls housed in containers coming in all shapes and sizes, from all backgrounds and ethnicities, races, and beliefs. We don't have a membership problem, we don't have an assimilation problem, we don't have an interfaith problem, we don't have a continuity problem; rather, we have a *Ruakh* problem. Reclaiming *Ruakh* in our synagogues, Jewish institutions, and Jewish communities will begin when we remember that we are a tribe and when we evolve our understanding and language for being a part of the tribe. Above all else, what is needed today is acceptance, open minds, open hearts, and open arms. Today what is needed is radical hospitality.

Radical hospitality is not merely tolerance for interfaith families. Radical hospitality is not merely acceptance of "converts" or Jews on the fringe. Radical hospitality is not a mere "nod" to the righteous gentiles among us. Rather, radical hospitality is just that—radical, energetic, intense, active, and directed hospitality. It is about standing up and greeting others. It is about running to meet them where they are, on their terms, without judgment, without qualification, without an agenda. Radical hospitality is what Abraham and Sarah demonstrated to the "strangers" in their midst only later to find out these were no strangers at all. Indeed, these were not even people; they were *melakhim*, angels and emissaries of God.

Rabbi B's Story: Radical Hospitality

It is possible to turn this ship around, and that is exactly what has happened at CSH. We put our capital campaign and building plans on hold. Instead, we focused on becoming a congregation, merging our spirits into one people, and opening our hearts to our fellow Jews and "non-Jews" in our midst and down the block. We bombarded our congregants with a vision of where we were headed. We stated the message clearly and succinctly. Radical hospitality was our clarion call and we said it time and again. We asked anyone who wasn't onboard with our direction to leave the boat. Radical hospitality was the direction we were sailing, and radical animosity was thrown over the side.

Fast-forward a couple years later and imagine the day. Now, instead of a handful of grumbling seniors, we have a room full of people of all ages, all demographics, all colors, all sexual orientations, with many religions represented, and we've even picked up a Republican or two along the way.

There we were on a lovely Shabbat morning as I was standing there with a few hundred of my newfound closest friends. Hardly any of those early kvetchers on the Un-Love Boat were kvetching at this point on the trip. Still, as I was standing there that day, preparing to officiate at a double baby-naming ceremony, I had my doubts. The shattering of the repressive interfaith policies was one thing. The fact that black Jews, Latino Jews, and a whole host of converts had come onboard over the past few years was yet another. The creation of a membership category for non-Jewish supporters was a stretch for many. The formation of a joint Jewish Evangelical rock band, or an Interspiritual Council putting on Sufi dances, or demonstrations by psychic mediums was something else indeed. But all these offerings were always off to the side, elective opportunities that people could opt into or opt out of. This was front and center. This was in their face.

This was no typical baby naming, though the idea of "typical" at CSH was clearly a thing of the past. This particular baby naming was truly unique. It was for a lesbian, interfaith couple raising African-Latino American children. This one was going to set us back for sure. Some of the family members thought it would be best to do this on a weekday, behind closed doors in the rabbi's study. They wanted it to take place on Shabbat in front of their friends and community, within the vibrancy of our Synaplex, but feared drawing attention to themselves and didn't want to cause friction. Although I assured them they were mistaken, that this would hardly rock the boat, I had my doubts.

And so we called up both moms and the children to the bimah. The Jewish mother recited the *brachot*. The semi-Jewish mother recited poems about mothering, nurturing, and love. We named the children right there at the Torah as they hugged, kissed, and cried. We threw candy. We sang, danced, and literally embraced this couple and these children as part of our congregational family, indistinguishable from anyone else. There wasn't a holler. There wasn't a resignation. There wasn't an angry letter to the president. There wasn't a hitch or a hiccup.

There was nothing other than clapping, cheers, and sounds of celebration. And those were among the sweetest sounds I have ever heard.

No one batted an eye that day because our vision of community and tribe had been transformed. It was then that I realized I could take off my life preserver because this captain wasn't going down with the ship, nor were they going to throw me overboard, which was touch and go there for a while. We had embraced not only this particular family, but a new way of thinking, a new way of behaving, and a new way of being Jewish. It was no longer about "us versus them." It was no longer about the "other." It was no longer about clear categories, clean divisions with some on the inside but most on the outside. Most of all, CSH was no longer a place of radical animosity. Instead, we had truly become a place of radical hospitality, and it has been that way, growing stronger, ever since. Authentic Jewish community has been reclaimed as we have re-membered our tribe.

Part III

And You Shall Be a Blessing

And the Divine called to Abram: Journey forth, from the known [from your land, from your birthplace, from your father's house] to the unknown [the land that I will show you]. And I will make you into a great nation, and I will bless you, and I will increase your name, *and you shall be a blessing.*

—GENESIS 12:1–2

7

Vision and Visionaries

Roots of Leadership

Remember that little blue *tzedakah* box that sat on your family's shelf when you were a kid? You know the one. The box that we grew up placing our spare change into and sent off to the Jewish National Fund to plant trees. From the get-go, Jews were taught the importance of planting trees in Israel. It's our duty, our mission. It makes a really nice Bar Mitzvah gift, or so I was told by my mother after she saw the disappointed look on my face after having received thirty-three of them as gifts. Have you ever wondered why? Why are Jews so obsessed with planting trees?

While there are many reasons, a primary one is brought home to us by a story in the Talmud:

> Once Honi Ha'magel was walking on the road and saw a man planting a carob tree. Honi said, "You know a carob tree takes seventy years to bear fruit; are you so sure that you will live seventy years so as to eat from it?"
>
> "I found this world provided with carob trees," the man replied, "and as my forebears planted them for me, so will I plant for my offspring."

115

Honi then sat down to eat and was overcome with sleep. As he slept, a small cave formed around him, so that he was hidden. And thus he slept for seventy years.

When he awoke, he saw a man gathering carobs from that same tree and eating them. "Do you know who planted this carob tree?" Honi asked.

"My grandfather," the man replied.

"I must have been like a dreamer for seventy years!" Honi exclaimed.[1]

L'dor vador, we say in our prayers, "from generation to generation," is our mantra. We plant not only for ourselves but for our future. Moreover, the act of planting is literally *tikkun olam*, repairing the world. It is so important that Rabbi Yochanan ben Zakkai, a rabbinical scholar in the first century taught: "If you are holding a sapling in hand and someone tells you, 'Come quickly, the messiah has come,' first finish planting the tree and then go to greet the messiah."[2]

Those little blue *tzedakah* boxes responsible for planting trees aided our Israeli brothers and sisters across the ocean. This was a visionary response by a generation of leaders to deal with the challenges at hand. Upon returning to our homeland, Israel needed trees to reclaim the barren landscape. We raised money for trees, we planted trees, and Israel bloomed. But trees and what they represent are just one example of why Israel flourishes. Perhaps an even better example is Israel's fish industry—fish raised, of all places, in the desert.

Fish in the Desert

Israel is hardly a lush oasis, laden with natural resources. In the words of Golda Meir, "Let me tell you the one thing I have against Moses. He took us forty years into the desert in order to bring us to the one place in the Middle East that has no oil!" There's no oil and there isn't enough water. Yet Israel is transforming its landscape through cutting-edge technology, excelling in green tech, clean tech, and agricultural technology and innovation. One of many examples of this is detailed in the must-read book, *Start-Up Nation: The Story of Israel's Economic Miracle*, by Dan Senor and Saul Singer. Senor and Singer report that Israel is turning back the desert through, of all things, desert fish farming.

Deep beneath the Negev they have discovered water, albeit hot, unpotable salt water. Instead of writing off that water, the desert kibbutzniks found a use for it. They pumped it up, filled ponds, and began raising fish. If that weren't enough, they figured out that the waste in the water made excellent fertilizer, pumped it out, and began watering olive and date trees, bringing forth fruits and vegetables. In other nations, deserts are considered wasteland. In Israel, however, there is no such thing as wasteland, no such thing as impossible.

Was it even deemed possible at first? Hardly. "It was not simple to convince people that growing fish in the desert makes sense," said Professor Samuel Appelbaum, an Israeli fish biologist. "But it's important to debunk the idea that arid land is infertile, useless land."[3]

While fighting multiple wars, amid unprecedented immigration absorption, while facing global economic downturn, and in spite of increasing world anti-Zionism and external threats, Israel not only survives, *Am Yisrael Chai*, Israel is thriving! With vision and a pioneering spirit, Israelis and Jews created forests in a barren land and a fishing industry in the desert. That is what we do. That is who we are. As Jews, whether living within Israel or in the Diaspora, we need to reclaim the *chalutzim*—the pioneering spirit.

Chalutzim: The Pioneering Israeli Spirit

The *chalutzim* were the survivors of the Holocaust, stripped of so much, yet carrying within them this fighting spirit. Escaping the horrors of Auschwitz, they made their way to Eretz Yisrael, picked up a rifle, and battled for independence and freedom. Then the *chalutzim* put down that rifle, trading it for a shovel and turning swamps into an economically thriving country, where of all things, fish are harvested in the desert. And the *chalutzim* were the Jewish immigrants of this country, not speaking English or knowing a soul and with only a pocketful of change, who came here to make a better life. They came and peddled from carts, working all day, every day to provide opportunities for their children and grandchildren.

These Jewish pioneers worked not merely for themselves, but for their children, family, and community. Like the man planting the tree taught Honi H'magel, the *chalutzim* work *l'dor vador*, for future generations of Jews.

Every era had pioneers, leaders who carried us forward. Where do we look for that vision today? Who are our pioneers, visionaries, and leaders? "From where will my help come?" we read in the Psalms (121:1–2). Although it answers, "My help comes from God," our tradition is not one where we merely sit around and wait for God's intervention. God meets us halfway. God expects us to do our share of the work. God has implanted within us the pioneering spirit. Our help comes from such men and women, patriarchs and matriarchs, leaders and visionaries in every generation. Who will lead us toward that vision, back to our spirit, to a path of *Ruakh*?

Café Confessional

I'm a rabbi in a relatively small town where it's nearly impossible for me to disappear or blend in, especially with a *kippah* (yarmulke) perched on top of my head. Even if people don't know me personally, it's not hard to tell who I am or what I do. On any given day I'm likely to be found in one of the local cafés writing or meeting with someone. On a regular basis, members of my congregation will approach me to confess, "Rabbi, I keep meaning to come to shul, I really do. I will try to come this Shabbat." Feeling like the priest holding confessional, I'll respond, "Say seven *Shema*s, two *Oseh Shalom*s, and show up this Shabbat. I'll save you a seat."

They feel guilty. They want to get that guilt off their chest. I remind them that it's okay. It's still their synagogue; they are welcome and need not feel like they are on the outside. However, what strikes me during my Starbucks confessional hours are not the congregants who confess as much as the non-congregants who have the need to purge as well. Oftentimes the un-synagogued, disenfranchised, seemingly alienated Jews will stop me and say something like, "Excuse me Rabbi. I just want to share with you that I haven't been to a synagogue in twenty years." Then they share with me their thoughts:

I hated my Hebrew school experience.

I find services boring and uninspired.

Why do bad things happen to good people?

How could God allow for the Holocaust?

The bad news is they ask while I'm trying to pour some sugar into my cappuccino as I'm late for an appointment and trying to rush out the door. The good news is they aren't really looking for an answer. Rather, they are frustrated with their religion. They are looking to vent. And so they find someone they consider to be one of God's spokesmen on earth. That's why they stop me. That's the reason they unload.

Although I'm flip with the congregant who feels a little guilty and somehow thinks that confessing to me will let her off the hook, with these frustrated and disenfranchised Jews, I just listen. They are sincere and I am sincere. They aren't sharing with me their frustrations or even anger toward Judaism or God because they don't care. They wouldn't be wasting their time with me if that were the case. Instead, something deep within them, in spite of their *Ruakh*-less Jewish and Jewish communal experiences, is calling out to them, and now they are calling out to me. What I have discovered is that these "outsiders" in their own religion are tired of being on the outside. They want to be heard, to be seen, and though they may not be conscious of it, they long to be on the inside, to reconnect, and to find their way home.

The Spiritual Outsiders

The truth of the matter is that these outsiders, and others like them today and throughout history, are crucial to sustaining Jewish community and leading us into the future. They are also the most beloved in the eyes of God.

In the place where the returnee to Judaism stands, even the completely righteous are not able to stand.[4]

Judaism has always made room for such people, those who have walked away from Judaism or outright rebelled against it, because when they return they have something significant to offer. "Jewish outsiders" who become "insiders" have always brought with them fresh perspectives and insights that have shaped, reformed, and transformed Judaism and the nature of Jewish community.

As we've already seen, Judaism was founded by outsiders in Abraham and Sarah. Their grandson Jacob had to leave home, essentially leave the Jewish community he was a part of, before returning and fully taking the reins of leadership. Joseph disappeared into Egypt, rose to second in command under Pharaoh, and in the end his vision saved the Israelites and saved the day. And Moses was literally an outsider to Judaism. Raised by Pharaoh's daughter in Pharaoh's palace, Moses didn't even know he was Jewish. It wasn't until he was older that he woke up to his Jewish identity and began his return. Because he was an outsider, with an outsider's eye, he was able to see the plight of the Israelites and see the pathway to their freedom. It had to be an outsider that led these people down the path of the Exodus—from slavery to freedom. In the words of Albert Einstein, "Problems cannot be solved by the level of awareness that created them." Like Moses, outsiders throughout Jewish history have often served as the solution to the problems the Jews were facing, whether they realized they were facing such problems or not. Oftentimes it is the outsider who is best able to point out our shortcomings and flaws and is best suited to lead us home.

One of the most famous "returnee" stories in Jewish history was that of the great Rabbi Akiva of the second century. Rabbi Akiva was perhaps the least likely candidate to become a rabbi. He was an unlearned Jew who didn't even know the Hebrew alphabet, and by the standard of the times, he was an old man who thought it was too late to follow his dreams.

However, behind every good man there is usually a good woman who raises him up and sets him onto his path toward greatness. This is exactly what Rabbi Akiva's wife did. She encouraged him to follow his dreams and go to school. Back then, there was no online distance learning or commuting back and forth during the week. She sent him off for over a decade so he could pursue his calling. The man humbled himself as he started from scratch, started in Jewish preschool if you will, simply learning the *aleph-bet*. Not only did he become one of the finest talmudic minds in Jewish history, he redefined the way Jews learned. Whereas the insiders seemed to be fine with the status quo, Rabbi Akiva asked outsider questions: Why are we not more methodical, our texts better organized? Why is it so difficult for outsiders to make their way inside?

Because of these questions, we now have the Mishnah, a logical, ordered compendium of Jewish law. Rabbi Akiva not only became a rabbi, but because he was an outsider with fresh eyes and an unassuming heart, he transformed Judaism for the better. Rabbi Akiva was not, and is not, alone. Many rabbis and Jewish leaders, such as Theodor Herzl, have been a force for change in Judaism or Zionism. But it isn't just individual outsiders who have transformed the Jewish enterprise. Russian and Ethiopian Jews are transforming Judaism, Jewish culture, and Jewish practice as they continue to return to Israel. Fresh eyes, new perspectives, and a spiritual hunger continue to reignite both Jews and Judaism itself in rich and dynamic ways.

That is why today, when you look around at some of the greatest leaders in Judaism—professional or lay—they are often the once unaffiliated, disenfranchised, or Jews by choice. They might have once been far removed from Judaism or Jewish community, but today they are central to an inspired Judaism. Their *Ruakh* is transforming Judaism and Jewish community, leading us forward, like Abraham and Sarah, into the great unknown.

It was striking to me that in rabbinical school some of the most interesting, engaging, and insightful teachers I had were *ba'alei teshuvah*, returnees to Judaism or converts who not only chose to become Jewish but eventually chose to teach it, lead it, and ultimately transform it. So many of my fellow students and now rabbinic and cantorial colleagues were once outsiders. It often seems that there is a direct correlation between how far they traveled from Judaism and how great their impact has become upon it when they return. They see Judaism more clearly. They challenge the status quo, casting aside assumptions that others, who don't have a wider perspective, simply cannot do. They ask a different set of questions and consequently get a better set of answers.

It is humbling, awesome, and inspiring to be in the midst of true *ba'alei teshuvah*, people who have chosen to return and to fix what they find broken, to rise up in their lives and claim their spiritual heritage with *Ruakh* and joy.

While there are great leaders that have come from within the Jewish world, some of our greatest Jewish leaders are from the periphery. Whether we are talking about lay or professional leaders, we need to create an atmosphere of openness and respect for new people, those too often considered "outsiders," because quite possibly the next Abraham or Sarah is on the outside just waiting to come into the tent.

Ellen's Story: From the Inside Out and the Outside In

Years ago, I was sitting with a rabbi and told him that I didn't feel as if I could connect on a spiritual level to the services of his congregation. I offered some ideas and suggestions about what I thought was missing and what I could envision. He kindly explained to me that this synagogue was not focused on spirituality. Rather, this was a place where Jews connected on a cultural and social level, engaging in *tikkun olam* as a community, but that if I was looking for spirituality, I needed to find that elsewhere. He suggested perhaps a walk in nature. I argued that while I could connect with the Sacred in various ways, I felt the services offered in synagogue should provide the space for that connection as well. He explained to me that the great percentage of his congregants weren't looking for that kind of experience and that things would stay as they were.

It didn't matter that I had been a member of this synagogue for many years; I felt like an outsider. While the door of our synagogue was open, there seemed to be one way to walk through it; eventually, I simply walked out. It was clear to me that I was on the periphery of this particular Jewish community and it was time for me to find the center, my center, somewhere else.

Now, years later, many of my friends who had told me in the past that I wasn't "really Jewish" because I was frustrated with synagogue life and kept on searching are now turning to me and saying that they are craving something more. They are frustrated by the lack of spiritual connection they have in their temples and the lack of congregant participation. They are in a different part of their life cycle now, empty-nesters whose kids are no longer in Hebrew school or in youth group. Now, they're focusing on who they are, as individuals and in community, and what this new stage means for them. Despite feeling that once they were on the inside, now they are living more on the outside, on the periphery. They are asking if they can join me at CSH. Some are interested in the drumming and chanting and meditation, others want to explore Jewish yoga, still others crave Torah study or the *Ruakh* Rally, or want to feel part of a spirited community.

Like me, many members of CSH have explored other paths and have returned, deepened by their experience. The modes of expressions are endless, with each of them offering their talents and gifts to the community. There is Jessica, a Jew by choice, who has stepped in as leader of the Renewal Minyan when the rabbi is away. With her deep connection to Jewish wisdom and her gentle, encouraging voice, she guides others in experiencing the *shalom* of the Sabbath morning. Jonathan, another Jew by choice, excels in business and has offered his keen insight and intellect into leading CSH in the development of a groundbreaking business plan to revolutionize the synagogue's financial platform. There is the woman who has studied shamanism and has tapped into her artistic gifts. She now paints beautiful Hebrew letters and leads workshops on the art of transformation. There is the man who, along with his Judaism, practices Buddhism and offers up his leadership to guide meditations on loving-kindness. We are people who were once on the outside and who have returned. We have been both welcomed back and valued for where our paths have taken us and the richness we offer the community.

One of the greatest aspects I see in this process is that you can't tell who has been at the synagogue for years and who is newly arrived. There is such a sharing of experiences, an openness to explore, and a willingness to take the reins of leadership—leadership not only doled out to the who's who of a temple board but to the once-outsiders as well. This honoring of people is from the inside out and the outside in. It's about not only opening the space for people to offer their inner spirit and gifts, but also opening up the board and committees for people who've been waiting to be heard and to lead.

People are leaving synagogue life for a reason, and it is imperative that we ask those who have left and are returning to share what they have discovered. Fresh ideas, perspectives, and energy—this is the way that *Ruakh* can infuse Judaism once again. It is this type of culture that moves Jews and Jewish institutions forward. It is this organic process that moves us from being enslaved in the past to finding freedom in our future.

Leaders and the Ship

There are a myriad of ways we turn away the outsider, whether we realize it or not. Take the position of executive director, for instance. Having recently gone through an executive director search, I heard the outsider bias loud and clear. The committee's default position was to hire an executive director from another synagogue. After all, these candidates would know the ins and outs of the business and would hit the ground running. As insiders, they would be best suited for the job.

However, as Albert Einstein warned, when you are part of the problem, you can't see the solution. Our synagogues, Jewish institutions, and Jewish communities need fresh faces, minds, and ways of looking at the world. Of course, there are wonderful executive directors, but the culture in which they work often carries institutional complexities and dysfunction that inhibit moving forward. The motto is to hurry up and change things as long as you don't change anything. Other times, executive directors may be so marinated in the culture that they are unable to find new ways of dealing with old problems. Take the financial problems most synagogues face. How many synagogues, if they weren't synagogues, would still be open for business if judged purely on their financials? Most would not. Many of these institutions have at their helm an executive director who perpetuates the financial challenges as they continue to sail forward into the dangerous waters of perennial synagogue deficits.

Thanks to a fresh new group of "outsiders" now in lay leadership positions at CSH, we set forth in new directions. Instead of simply limiting ourselves to executive directors from other synagogues, one of our new, young leaders insisted that we head out into the business world. Thanks to him and the support of this new crop of visionaries, we not only hired the right person from the business world, but we recrafted the position entirely, much more in line with a CEO, to take us forward onto paths unimagined, paths that will transform our destiny.

We need to hire more business-minded leaders. Our top priority in appointing leadership positions should be not merely familiarity with Judaism but also business acumen. While we shouldn't turn our Jewish institutions into secular corporations, there's nothing Jewish about running our institutions into the ground or having to survive on charity alone. If we don't start reenvisioning ourselves along these lines, we won't last long. To get there we'll need new faces and new leaders, including CEOs, marketing and PR professionals, IT specialists, and people for other positions we expect to find in the business world. Instead of promoting exclusively from within, we need to attract from without, from the outside. We need to invite outsiders in if we are to thrive in a *Ruakh*-filled community.

All Aboard in the Boardroom

This holds true for our lay leadership as well. One of the biggest challenges facing synagogues and Jewish institutions is that the lay leaders who are often involved aren't necessarily the best qualified to lead the organization, while those who are best suited to lead the organization are often uninvolved. Unless we deal with this dilemma, our synagogues will ultimately fall by the wayside. Let me tell you a story about Sam and Ron.

Right out of rabbinical school, I knew nothing about the business of synagogues and had no clue what I was stepping into regarding synagogue politics. I had never served on a board in any capacity. At my first board meeting, however, I quickly learned that I was the only outsider in the boardroom of the dying shul for which I was now the rabbi. Each of them was a native to the community, had grown up in that congregation, and had been selected to be on the board primarily, if not exclusively, because they were insiders. Nobody was more of an insider than Sam.

Sam didn't know the first thing about the business world. He was an academic with a large family inheritance, a deadly combination in any volunteer setting. In addition, he knew a fair amount about halacha, was a minyan regular, and was the rebbe when it came to anything and everything that related to the synagogue. Here's an example of his power. He was the only one who knew how to operate the thermostat in the ancient sanctuary, and when he was mad we would all *shvitz*! Although he wasn't president during this term, he had been before and would be again. I think he even wrote the bylaws, and the shul was over one hundred years old. President or not, he ruled that synagogue with an airtight mind and an ironclad fist. It was his way or the highway, and nothing mattered other than that good old mantra: We've always done it this way—always have and always will. This attitude is the kiss of death in any organization, and it certainly was proving true in ours. Because of it, and largely because of him, there were never any new faces around that table, no new ideas entertained, and no new directions charted. Sam was simply steering that ship in one direction; it was going south, and I don't mean Miami Beach.

Then there was Ron. Ron was an entrepreneur, an incredibly successful business mind, and an outsider through and through. He was a transplant to the community. He was raised in a secular Jewish home with hardly any knowledge about Judaism. The main reason he was at that synagogue was because he was married to a longtime member. Ron was considered a genius by his peers in the business world and considered an idiot by Sam and that board when it came to the synagogue. Ron knew how they felt and approached me to see how he could break in.

While he may not have known much about Judaism, he had a spark when it came to Judaism, Jews, Jewish community, and Israel. Ron wanted to get involved, connect, and offer his expertise and business acumen. He approached me to see what I thought. Having endured perhaps half a dozen visionless, closed-minded, *Ruakh*-less bored/board meetings, my first thought was to get him "on board." The synagogue was running a serious deficit and deeply needed what Ron had to offer. I thought it would be a slam dunk. I was wrong. This is how too many synagogues and Jewish institutions are run: the Rons are kept off the court while the Sams insist on playing every quarter without any time-outs.

So Sam and his cronies benched Ron's participation even before it had begun.

"He doesn't keep kosher," one person said.

"He doesn't keep Shabbos," another chimed in.

"He doesn't come to the daily minyan or Shabbat services," and on and on it went.

They were a kosher board, except for the pepperoni pizza that they would eat at restaurants; they observed Shabbat, except when the local football team had a home game on Saturday; and they attended the daily minyan, except when they didn't show. They were insiders and were not going to allow some "outsider" to infiltrate their midst. Perhaps this may have been a necessary standard for a different era or a very narrow type of community or congregation. But in this day and age and in this community it was not only misguided but detrimental to the synagogue's well-being. I could understand how this might be pertinent if Ron were asking to sit on the Ritual Committee, but all I heard around the board during those miserable meetings were primarily kvetches over financial matters. The shul was failing financially and in no small measure due to Sam's poor leadership and the board's business folly. The synagogue's finances were being handled by "insiders" who were, ironically, well outside their area of expertise.

The synagogue board struggled with more than just finance problems. They were lacking creativity, technological know-how, marketing savvy, artistic expression, a sense of customer service, and human resource sensitivities, to name just a few shortcomings. It may have been the twenty-first century, but they might as well have been back in the shtetl. They lobbied. They argued. They rallied against Ron and other would-be leaders. Like a longtime dictator refusing to step down, Sam ruled until his death, when his old worldviews and the old board loyalists finally came to an end.

Eventually, Ron not only came onto the board but became president. With Ron's leadership came fresh perspective, business know-how, and a whole cadre of other "outsiders" wanting to be on the inside and get involved. For the first time, people in interfaith relationships were allowed on the board, representing a growing constituency and lending their voices. People with tech skills, artistic direction, marketing minds—you name it—were asked to join and got involved. Did they keep kosher, observe Shabbat, or refrain from *shatnetz* (wearing a combination of cotton and wool)? Who knows? Who cares? This wasn't rabbinical school, the yeshiva, or the shtetl. This was a synagogue board in the business of running a business, and that's what Ron and his modern, energetic, creative team of "outsiders" set out to do.

Without the Rons in our community, we will default to the Sams, to the same old tired, closed, and *Ruakh*-less ways. We will continue to push away the outsiders as the insiders crowd together, making room for no one else. We will continue to have board members who will consistently steer our ship down a boring, uninspiring, and ultimately devastating course. The outsiders wanting to come into our midst will only wait so long. Eventually, they'll go elsewhere and get involved with other efforts, other boards, where they will lend their talents, their know-how, their expertise, and their *Ruakh*.

The days of deciding who is invited into the position of president, executive committee member, or board member based on financial contribution, religious observance, or institutional involvement as the sole determinants of invitation need to come to an end. When we stop incestuously doling out leadership positions to the inner circles and invite the outsiders in, who knows? Maybe we'll find our Rabbi Akiva, our Theodor Herzl, or our Ron and witness a new visionary with new ideas, enthusiasm, inspiration, and *Ruakh* to help us steer our ship back toward the horizon.

Not for Prophets

Six years of rabbinical school. Thousands upon thousands of dollars in tuition and costs. Hours upon hours spent poring over ancient texts in the library and receiving instruction in the classroom from learned professors. Still, this is not where I learned the key ingredient to successful leadership as a rabbi. It wasn't until a few years later when I was having my own leadership crisis that a friend pulled me aside. This friend, a highly successful author, speaker, and leader within his industry told me, "Leaders lead. What you have to do may not be easy, it may not be popular, but you know what you have to do.... Be a leader. Leaders lead."

It is obvious and yet it was the first time that I heard it put in such stark terms. In rabbinical school there are courses on practical rabbinics. However, there weren't enough classes on practical, effective, or inspirational leadership. Though rabbis are charged with the mission of heading off into the trenches of Judaism and leading the troops, without this charge most are doomed to get caught in the ant mill.

What is the ant mill? An ant mill is a phenomenon where a group of army ants separated from the main foraging party lose the pheremone track and begin to follow one another, forming a continuously rotating circle. The ants will eventually die of exhaustion.[5]

Too many of our not-for-profits are really not-for-prophets. That is, they discourage prophetic, forward-thinking, visionary leaders. Instead, they opt for leaders who are willing to step into the ant mill. We have created a system designed to fend off change, to get group buy-in, to seemingly vet each and every decision before it is presented to an institution or congregation. "Change things, Rabbi, but just make sure you keep it all the same" is too often the synagogue tagline across the country. Green light. Red light. That's what most of our rabbis and leaders are told implicitly, if not explicitly. Although we have already mentioned a handful of shining examples of courageous, visionary rabbis and Jewish leaders, too many others take their place in the circle and follow the person in front of them as they march around, and around, and around.

Though there are many reasons for this, a major problem is that we continue to operate in fear. Take the story of the spies in the book of Numbers. The Israelites are panicked at what they believe awaits them in the land of Canaan. They vote to send twelve spies to scout out the land. The fearful majority return, saying the Israelites must not enter. They declare, "The land we explored devours those living in it. All the people we saw there are of great size.... We seemed like grasshoppers in our own eyes, and we looked the same to them" (Numbers 13:32–33). Only two spies, Caleb and Joshua, urge the people not to be afraid. But like visionaries in a synagogue, they come up against a people who let their fears of change and moving forward run amok. There's arguing, panic, and revolt—and, in the end, death. Whether it's the Israelites saying they never should have left Egypt, or the temple board holding steadfast to their own narrow vision, in the end what's left is a whole lot of kvetching and inaction. Failing to listen to those who would lead them out of the desert, they wander another forty years to reach the Promised Land, which was always right there in front of them. How long will synagogues circle around their own promised land, while their flock either dies off or turns away?

Foggy Leadership

Why are so many Jewish institutions floundering and far too many synagogues failing? It isn't due to demographic challenges or economic downturn or merely the fact of congregants' resistance to change. Although these concerns figure into our complex challenges, frankly, these issues are nothing new. The primary reason we are failing comes from the top down. Leadership that fails to inspire and breathe life into our ranks is still too prevalent in many of our institutions. Until our leaders imbibe vision, spirit, breath, and Ruakh, as a community we will lack these attributes as well. Our rabbis need to be our teachers and preachers inspiring the flock. Without such guidance, Jews, Judaism, and Jewish institutions will be like wandering sheep, desperately searching for a shepherd to lead them home.

In his book, Heaven, Randy Alcorn tells the story of a woman named Florence Chadwick. The year was 1952 and she was about to attempt to swim the channel from Catalina Island to the California coast. She was an accomplished, long-distance swimmer and had already swum the English Channel in both directions. She entered the chilly waters in a fog so thick she could barely see the boats that were accompanying her. She swam for hours upon hours through the cold, deep fog and by the sharks that were kept at bay through rifle fire. And then, when she could endure no more, she asked to be taken out of the water.

Her trainer begged her to keep going, knowing she was close to the coast but not knowing exactly how much farther there was to go, since no one could see through the dense fog. But she couldn't do it, and finally, before her goal was reached, Florence gave up less than a mile from realizing her dream.

Later she said, "I'm not excusing myself, but if I could have seen the land I might have made it." It wasn't the cold or fear or exhaustion that caused Florence Chadwick to fail. It was the fog.[6]

But the truth of the matter is that it wasn't even the fog that kept Florence from succeeding. Rather, it was her trainer's lack of vision through the fog and his failure to inspire her in the face of the unknown that kept her from her realizing her dream. So many of our institutions are operating in fog. They don't know where they are going and don't know how much farther they must travel to achieve success. Without visionaries, they are giving up on moving forward, content to sit in the fog, floating in their little raft, stranded in blindness and fear.

What we need are captains of the ship, men and women able to see through the fog and paint a picture for their followers to envision, as all visionaries since Abraham and Sarah have been able to do. Then they must have the courage to share that vision. That is their job. When they fail to stand up, step out, and offer the gift of that vision, we congregants and would-be followers secretly, or not so secretly, resent them because deep down, we know we are adrift in uncomfortable, if not dangerous waters.

"Leaders lead," my mentor said, and he was right. At some point along the journey of my formal Jewish studies, I should have been taught this. My rabbinical school was a wonderful place and light-years beyond many other alternative venues for study. However, in this area my teachers failed to instill in me the leadership skills I would need to transform a synagogue and inspire a Jewish community. An exit Talmud exam should not have been the only test I was given to prove my worthiness and readiness to be a leader of the Jewish people. What this generation of Jewish leaders needs is to return to the Torah as a leadership manual. We should be dropping off our would-be Jewish leaders in the Sinai Desert to prepare them for the task of facing desert crises and learning how to lead their complaining, scared, but yearning and hopeful flock into the Promised Land.

Common Struggles Jewish Leaders Face

A rabbi knows that she needs to eliminate the *Musaf* service, knows that for her congregation it is hindering rather than helping to create an inspired service, but knows that her Ritual Committee will never sign off.

A cantor is tired of the formality of the High Holy Days, wants to make it more informal, more modern, more relevant, but knows that he'll get push-back from many longtime congregants.

An executive director is clear that the dues and ticket system is turning people away and has imagined a better alternative, but is too afraid to speak up and face his board.

A Hebrew school principal is well aware that the Sunday school model is failing and knows that a Shabbat school alternative would revitalize the program. But she also knows that parents won't receive this well, might even rebel, as it could infringe on their children's sports activities.

"Rabbi," I've heard my colleagues visiting my synagogue or consulting me about ritual changes, musical additions, or Shabbat school transformations begin, "this is great—necessary even—but in my shul it would never fly!"

"Why?" I ask, knowing full well what they are about to tell me, as I've heard it fifty times before.

"Because my Ritual Committee [or my *ba'alei batim* (bigwigs) or my students' parents] won't entertain the conversation, won't pass it through, won't let me make the change."

And herein lies the crux of the problem. This is not a Ritual Committee problem but a leadership problem, not a board approval problem but a leadership problem, not a parental problem but a leadership problem. Followers follow and leaders lead. If a rabbi, cantor, executive director, principal, or lay leader is afraid to make change in these crucial areas, it will take its toll on her ability to make changes elsewhere, too. Far too many of my colleagues would do well to heed the words of the great Rabbi Yisrael Salanter, who said, "A rabbi whose community does not disagree with him isn't really a rabbi; but a rabbi who fears his community is not really a man."

The Israeli Defense Forces (IDF) exemplify such leadership. "The famous cry of the officer is 'Acharai,' after me. The fact that senior officers take front-line combat positions means Israel suffers, proportionately, the highest officer-to-soldier casualty rate in the world. However, the IDF believes that leading by example increases respect for the officer corps and instills greater motivation among soldiers."[7]

Though Jewish leaders in our nonprofits might technically be considered noncombatants, make no mistake about it: they are soldiers who must be ready to do battle. Not only must we be willing to send our troops into battle, but we must be willing ourselves to go to the front lines for our cause. Although no rabbi or cantor has yet lost his or her life going head to head with a congregant, Ritual Committee, or even an entrenched president, nonetheless there are still casualties in the war of words, the wounds to spirits, and the fractured relationships that can ensue, not to mention the question of a renewed contract. If we are afraid of this, afraid of taking a stand or unwilling to charge ahead, crying out, "Acharai—after me," then we are not truly suited for a position of leadership. There are many examples of bold rabbis and cantors who continue to break new ground. We need trailblazers. We need leaders to lead.

Turning the Impossible into the Possible

We read in the Talmud a discussion of what it takes to be a true leader of the Jewish people, in this case to have a seat on the Sanhedrin, the Jewish supreme court. "Rabbi Yohanan said: None are to be appointed members of the Sanhedrin [high court], but men of stature, wisdom, good appearance, mature age.... Rabbi Yehuda said in Rav's name: None is to be given a seat on the Sanhedrin unless he is able to prove the cleanliness of a reptile from biblical texts."[8]

What's strange, indeed shocking, is this last line. How can you prove the cleanliness, the spiritual cleanliness, of a reptile? You can't. It's not possible; that is the point. What Rav is demanding is that our leaders take on the impossible with the commitment to and expectancy of transforming it into the possible. As Eleanor Roosevelt said, "You must do the thing you think you cannot do."

Abraham and Sarah reassess their direction and lead into the unknown; Moses faces his fears and fixes the problems he walked away from; Joshua and Caleb break from the ant mill and are up for the challenge that lies ahead. Each one of them cries out to their followers, "*Acharai*—after me." If you can't do the thing you fear, if you won't take a step back now and again and reassess your vision, and most of all, if you don't see this as part and parcel of your primary mission as a Jewish leader—lay or professional—then regardless of your strengths, you will not be a great leader. Leaders lead into the unknown, into new directions, and into the world of making the impossible possible. To enter the land of milk and honey, be it in the Holy Land or in the center of our own synagogue, we need our leadership to paint a picture of our destination, even in the midst of darkness and fog, especially in the darkness of fog. We need our leaders to set forth into the unknown. We need our leaders to illuminate the darkness. We need leaders to lead.

8

Future
Shul

Make for Me a *Mikdash* and I will dwell within them.

—Exodus 25:8

Don't Judge a Book by Its Cover

Don't judge a book by its cover. How many times have we heard this? It's a cliché that we have been telling ourselves for most of our lives. But when it comes to our shuls, JCCs, and Jewish institutions, we should judge the book by its cover, so judge away. The physical structures, the "book cover," does indeed reflect the enclosed pages, what is happening or not happening within those walls and that organization, providing a pretty accurate read about what is being offered. In criminology, "broken windows theory" refers to the effects of urban disorder and vandalism on additional crime in those neighborhoods. There seems to be a correlation between how bad the place looks and how badly some of the citizens act. Clean up the crime by cleaning up the neighborhood and fixing those broken windows, or so the theory goes. Whether or not this is true in regard to neighborhood crime, it is certainly true in regard to our neighborhood synagogues.

Broken windows may not be commonplace but broken doors, broken chairs, broken signs, and especially broken down, dirty, or just plain dilapidated bathrooms can tell you the state of a shul or Jewish institution. The physical spaces of far too many of our Jewish institutions are old, run-down, and uninspiring. Yet Jews in America are disproportionately educated, successful, and wealthy. We expect a very high standard and quality in almost every aspect of our lives, except when it comes to our Jewish institutions, particularly our synagogues. "That smell is nostalgic," we tell ourselves, it reminds us of growing up in that synagogue, the same one we tried to escape from during our Hebrew school days and beyond. "Those 1960s couches in the lobby are quaint," we've convinced ourselves, a bit of the retro look right here in our modern, sophisticated lives. Somehow we have come to believe that there must be something from the Torah itself that requires us to have a *beit mikdash* that looks this way, feels this way, and, yes, smells this way, too.

Our synagogues need to be transformed not just programmatically but architecturally as well. It may be acceptable to have a space that looks, feels, and smells uninspiring if we don't intend to use it more than three times a year. However, if our synagogues and Jewish institutions are going to be central to our lives, they are going to need to be rethought, transformed, and absolutely aired out.

Rabbi B's Story: The Whiff, Your Nose Knows

When I was interviewing for my current position I had multiple stops along the interview path. One of those places was a synagogue that felt far more promising on paper, in theory, and even during the initial phone interviews than it did during my actual visit. I knew this the moment I was standing in front of the synagogue doors.

Prior to swinging those doors open, which was no easy feat, I was hopeful that this was the place for me. But those doors only said one thing to me, or any would-be visitor or outsider: go away. They were heavy, imposing, and in many ways impenetrable. Still, I wrote it off with the rationale that they were only doors. A building is just a building, I had told myself, and I was hopeful that they were not reflective of the people or experience on the inside. So I persevered. I made my way into the building, and any remaining hope I had was erased in a single whiff of stale, stagnant air. What that whiff smelled like is hard to explain. However, in the words of a U.S. Supreme Court justice commenting on pornography, "It may be hard to define, but you know it when you see it." That smell told me that the interview was over even before it had formally begun.

As a teacher of mine, Dr. Ron Wolfson, has said, you can tell a lot by how a congregation smells. And he was right. In a matter of moments I had summed up exactly what their challenges were, how the interview would proceed, and why this would never turn into a *shiddach* (a match), at least not for me. For the next twenty-four hours, the tension that my new ideas, vision, and even presence created within those walls was palpable. There were those who knew the synagogue "smelled" and wanted change. However, too many, and frankly the loudest opponents, echoed Sam and his mantra, claiming nothing was wrong. They weren't looking for change and certainly didn't want a change agent. Needless to say, I didn't get the job. The reason given to me, off the record, was that they felt my ideas were too big for such a little place, which happened to be a congregation of five hundred families, which in its heyday was one thousand families. I shared with them a saying from American writer and humorist Peter Finley Dunne, putting my occupation into his quote, which sums up a rabbi's mission: A rabbi's job is to comfort the afflicted and to afflict the comfortable.

Suffice it to say, that particular synagogue may not have had to endure my afflictions, but they nonetheless had afflictions of their own. They've since gone through multiple rabbis, and last I heard, they were considering the ultimate affliction, closing up shop. In the end it was not only the stale air, but the stale approach that led to their demise. What they needed was a whiff of *Ruakh* and a fresh new vision.

Signs That Say Go Away

When I arrived at CSH, it wasn't only the smell that we had to navigate through, but quite literally we needed directions, period. This is a problem many synagogues face. In *Rethinking Synagogues*, Rabbi Larry Hoffman tells the story of a synagogue that labeled its car lanes one-way, making the first sign a person sees as they enter the synagogue area "Do Not Enter." At CSH there were no signs informing visitors as to which entrance to use, and once they were inside, nothing was clearly marked. I recall asking a former employee why this was so, and he responded, "Because everyone knows where everything is, so what's the point?" Well, if he meant the handful of regulars who frequented our often empty halls, he was correct. However, what about all the people who might come to shul and would attend our services if only they could find their way? The only signs that were posted read, "No Smoking on Shabbat." There must have been a sale on these signs at some point because they were everywhere. Are "No Smoking" signs really something that most of us need to publicize in this day and age? Is this really the message we want to send? Wouldn't it be better to have signs pointing to the rabbi's and cantor's offices and a sign listing the times for Shabbat services? If someone were looking for any of those things in this shul he would be lost, but the one thing he would know for sure was that smoking was prohibited on Shabbat.

So I asked the executive director if he would please remove the "No Smoking on Shabbat" signs, replacing them with messages of welcome and direction, creating a positive vibe. His answer was clear and unequivocal: "No, not until it has been approved by the board; I answer to the board." "Okay," I said. So I found a screwdriver and removed every single one of those signs the first day on the job.

"How could you do that?" he asked after I had taken the last one down.

"Have you seen Hebrew National's commercials?" I replied.

"Yes," he said, "but what does that have to do with this?"

"Because you answer to the board but I answer to a Higher Authority."

Eventually, we replaced those "No Smoking" signs with signs of welcome, of direction, and of blessing. We've added electronic signs, plasma television screens announcing schedules and events, and even a virtual *yizkor* memorial section accessible to all. Every Friday night, as we sing *L'cha Dodi*, we open the door to greet the Sabbath Bride. At CSH, our intention is to open our doors for all, inviting them in and pointing the way to places, spaces, and *Ruakh.*

Edifice Complex: Build It and They Won't Come

One of the great movies of recent memory was *Field of Dreams*, starring Kevin Costner. It gave us an iconic line that I've heard over and over again in regard to Jewish communities: "Build it and they will come." Though this worked in the movie, it has not worked in Jewish communal life. There are many beautiful, ornate Jewish structures today that sit empty and are struggling to survive. It is not just about building buildings, but about building the *right* buildings. Today we need synagogues that reflect our modern ideologies and needs. No matter how beautiful a synagogue may be, if the physical structure merely resonates with our collective nostalgia, it will more closely resemble a museum than a shul, storing our past and ignoring our future.

There was a period in American Jewish history when buildings were so central that they were deemed even more significant than core Jewish values. For instance, our synagogue, built in the late 1960s, has a fundamental problem. The main sanctuary does not face east toward Israel, the direction Jewish communities this side of the Mediterranean have been orienting themselves for generations. To make matters worse, there are two sanctuaries and neither of them faces east! The chapel faces north and the sanctuary faces due west. While this might be understandable in a congregation that, let's say, had a brick wall on its eastern side, that is not the case here at CSH. Not only are we on the East Coast, in a beach community, but we are Congregation Shirat *Hayam*, the *yam* meaning "ocean." The Atlantic is literally on our eastern side. The founders of this congregation made a clear and conscious choice not only to face away from Israel but to face away from one of the most glorious sights on God's green, or in this case, blue, earth.

Why would Conservative Jews in the 1960s turn away from the Jewish direction? Here's a hypothesis. At that time Jews here and elsewhere were trying to make a statement. They were unwanted or unwelcome in the beach clubs, yacht clubs, and country clubs. They weren't even allowed to buy real estate in certain neighborhoods just down the street. So, when forced to choose between building a synagogue that reflected Jewish values by facing eastward versus facing the street, the main thoroughfare, the place that "the goyim" would see their high-dollar space, the choice, at least to them, was clear. Building was everything. Size mattered. Impressive, awe-inspiring architecture mattered. It is what drove this temple and it is what continues to drive many temples well beyond the 1960s. The problem is that while it may have served a purpose then, it no longer does today. If we adhere to a Judaism that is externally oriented, determined to prove something to the outside world, we will continue to move away from the spirit of Judaism.

Shock and Awe: An Era of Awesome Architecture

There was a time, just a few generations ago, when synagogue membership for the majority of Jews was a given. Even if their world was not defined by religiosity, average Jews placed Judaism front and center in their lives. Their spouse was Jewish. Their friends were Jewish. Their neighborhoods were Jewish, and their lives revolved around various Jewish institutions in general and the synagogue in particular. Because of this comfort and familiarity, they wanted and needed something specific within those temple walls.

At the outset of the Iraq War, President Bush declared that "shock and awe" would put an end to the conflict. What the Jews of a previous generation wanted was "shock and awe Judaism." Whether or not "shock and awe" has its place in warfare, it certainly no longer has its place in religion. When those Jews of a different era pulled up to their synagogues, they wanted to see imposing structures. When they approached the front doors, they wanted to see impregnable entrances sending a clear message to the non-Jewish world. Inside their sanctuaries, they wanted high bimahs, distant clergy towering over them and looking down at the congregants as they sat looking up in reverence. It was frontal-facing, rapt-attention, shock and awe Judaism reflected in the temples that were built. Bigger meant better, and more imposing meant more inspirational.

Beyond spiritual masochism, such buildings served another function as well. Spaces were large, built not so much for daily or even weekly use, but primarily to accommodate the throngs of shul-goers on any given Rosh Hashanah and Yom Kippur. It didn't matter if the massive space sat empty for the other 362 days; for those three days it did its job. Such spaces reflected yet another reality of the time by making it easy to corral everyone into one space for one experience. It was a one-size-fits-all era. The only other option took place down the hall, where the children were outsourced. If kids were to be a part of the main service, they were to be seen but not heard. More likely, however, they were shipped down to the pediatric Judaism wing, clearly separated from the adults. Although all this may have worked for a previous generation, this post–World War II temple's architecture is simply not working for us today.

In our weekly staff meetings at CSH, we spend a good portion of our time talking about how to fit a square peg, Synaplex, into a round hole, a post–World War II–designed synagogue. Congregation Shirat Hayam has two classic, massive spaces—in the social hall and the sanctuary. Somehow, we make it work, but just barely, and not as smoothly and robustly as it could and should. There are so many things we simply can't do because of space constraints. Still, we pull it off. We make it work, but our old building, and the vast majority of synagogues and Jewish institutional buildings today, no longer serve our vision and they ultimately inhibit our *Ruakh*.

Removing Pews for the Jews

One of the most obvious ways this translates is through our pews, and, really, was there ever a more appropriate name for what they represent? Pews are static, oftentimes literally bolted to the ground. If they are movable at all, there's little that can be done with them to create the right feel for the space. Again, whereas the Judaism of yesterday was a one-size-fits-all model, the Judaism of today and tomorrow must be flexible. It begins with the seats.

I'm certain that getting rid of the pews and replacing them with movable seats sounds inconsequential, and there was a time when I thought so myself. But I assure you it is not. In fact, one of the most contentious issues I have ever had to navigate was unbolting the pews in my prior shul or replacing the pews in my current congregation, trying to figure out exactly which kind of seat would be best. But once we

agreed, every single person who sat in them realized just how important a shift it was. While comfort was part of the equation, the shift
was really a function of flexibility. With limited space and a myriad of
experiences taking place in our facility on any given day and on each
and every Shabbat, we needed seats that moved and configurations
that supported what we were trying to do. Our davening is done in
the round. Our funerals are set up facing forward. Weddings require
a center aisle, and High Holy Days require seven hundred aisles. Let's
face it, on airplanes and High Holy Days, aisle seats are in demand.

Accessibility

Beyond flexibility, what our synagogues today need is accessibility.
Our old facility, for instance, had a five-foot-high bimah made of
solid, poured concrete. It was grandiose, alienating, and inaccessible
in more ways than one. Some seniors and those with disabilities used
to struggle to get up those stairs, if they could get up there at all. On
numerous occasions, people were literally forced to choose between
the honor of an *aliyah* or the safety of remaining in their seats. Though
it came at a considerable financial cost, we jackhammered that bimah
right out of existence and now read our Torah down on the floor with
everyone else.

> This commandment that I set before you today is neither
> remote nor inaccessible from you. It is not in heaven, so that
> you should say, "Who shall ascend to the heavens and bring it
> down to us so that we can understand it and keep it?" It is not
> beyond the sea, so that you should ask, "Who will cross the sea
> and bring it back for us so that we can understand and keep
> it?" Indeed, it is very close to you—it is in your mouth and in
> your heart, so that you can keep it.
>
> —Deuteronomy 30:11–14

Wheelchairs can pull right alongside the Torah. Seniors need to walk
all of two feet to be a part of what's going on. As we center our chairs
around a bimah in the middle of the congregation, not up on high

but in community with people, we center ourselves around Judaism in ways that have been forgotten for far too long.

Accessibility is not simply an imperative in accessing the scrolls in our ark. Our synagogues and institutions also have an imperative to create bathrooms that are handicap-accessible, toddler-friendly, and family-oriented, too. If we are inviting people into our midst in word but not in deed, we have failed in our mission. Bathroom stall theology, being able to relieve oneself and clean oneself up afterwards, is not a luxury but a necessity. If we do not afford this dignity to our two-foot-tall toddlers or those in wheelchairs, then we can hardly call ourselves welcoming. God is found not just on the bimah but in the bathroom, too, and everywhere in between.

A Child-Friendly Congregation

Accessibility also speaks to the need for options for families with young children. For instance, parents should not have to decide whether or not their child can make it through services quietly. No child can—heck, in far too many synagogues most of their parents are hanging on for dear life. God forbid, we should ever "shush" a child when she is speaking or crying in our shul or during our services. Frankly, we have shushed an entire generation of Jews right out the door. Rather, we should heed the advice of the Talmud, which relates that when Rabbi Yehoshua ben Chananya was a small child, "his mother would take him in his cradle to the synagogue, in order that the child's ears should be connected with the words of Torah."[1] Inspired by this notion, CSH has instituted what we call a "no shush policy" in all our holy spaces. Babies, toddlers, and young children are allowed to make noise, and it is a transgression to shush them. After all, would we dare interrupt a holy mystic if she were in the midst of deep prayer as she conversed with the Divine? This is simply their way of speaking with God. Instead of being annoyed by their cries, we should revel in their piety and heed their example.

Still, oftentimes it is appropriate for a parent to excuse himself and his restless child because he chooses to, not because he is expected to leave. Perhaps he would prefer to be part of the service, but neither seen nor heard. That is why churches often build "cry rooms," rooms adjacent to the sanctuary where parents can look through soundproof, one-way glass with the sound pumped in through a speaker. At CSH, we couldn't make an adjacent "cry room" work architecturally. Instead, we opted for transforming our lobby into this space with plasma-screen televisions broadcasting our various services. There's a coffee bar, muffins, and fruit, along with comfy chairs and toys for the kids to play with. Family bathrooms, toddler toilets, and age-appropriate toys and books are also essential as we move forward with our mission to reach out to this constituency.

Third-Place Judaism

Jews today don't need shock and awe Judaism. Instead, we need gentle invitations and an atmosphere that cultivates a sense of wonder. We need buildings that say, Come on in, you are wanted, you are welcome. We need to think through the messages our spaces send, the philosophies, even theologies that they embody. And if we do this, perhaps we will have created what Starbucks founder Howard Schultz has termed "a third place."

Do you know the real power of Starbucks? Regardless of whether or not you drink coffee, independent of whether or not you like theirs, Starbucks has redefined the way many of us live. Part of its core mission was not simply to be a coffeehouse. Rather, it was to become what the company calls "a third place." You have a home, you have an office, and you have a Starbucks that can serve as a home away from home, and an office away from the office. It is a place to carve out both quiet and alone time, and connecting and conversation time.

Whereas synagogues of yesteryear were built around being a destination where you loaded up the car and headed off for a High Holy Day show at the temple, today's congregations must become lifestyle experiences. They need to be built for prayer as well as simply spaces to congregate and hang out. Judaism today needs to be part of our daily, or at least weekly, lives if it is going to thrive. If we want families to join our synagogues, and more importantly attend them, we are going to have to insert ourselves into their lives, responding to their needs and their wants. Torah is not boring. Synagogues don't have to be solemn and serious "houses of worship." They should be joyous. They should be fun. They should be places to pray but equally places to play. Until we start building our spaces with this in mind, we may say that people are welcome, but our synagogues will say otherwise.

Shopping malls today understand this. That is why they build state-of-the-art play areas at the center of their facility. What does playing on high-tech, cushiony, fake animals have to do with shopping? Everything. It makes the kids want to go to the mall and that makes it a pleasant experience for the parents, who will in turn spend their money there. They are happy. Their kids are happy. They love spending their time, their money, and their lives at the mall. Would it be so bad if families felt this way about their shul? At the center of our synagogues, we should have gathering places and play spaces.

> If your Torah had not been my plaything, I should have perished in my affliction.
>
> —Psalm 119:92

As part of our lifestyle shift, the synagogue must become a one-stop shop. It wouldn't hurt if at the center, immediately upon walking in, we had a coffee bar. Maybe a Starbucks or a Dunkin' Donuts. Why? Because in addition to a radically different kind of "whiff" that would drift into our nostrils, most of all it would send a different message to those who enter. It would say to the congregation, to the Jews in the community who aren't yet members, to the semi- and non-Jews in our neighborhoods that this is a place of gathering, this can serve as a daily stop in their busy lives.

The Jewish institutions of tomorrow must compel Jews from around the community to come and spend time within the synagogue and, yes, have a fine cup of coffee in our café. Whether it be Starbucks, Dunkin' Donuts, or an in-house production like "Elijah's Mug," imagine housing a first-rate, professionally run café where people can sip their double tall soy latte as they read their newspapers, check e-mail, or surf the web. People can drop their kids off in day care or class and stay in the shul to do their work, schmooze, or simply relax before moving on in their day. And why stop there? What if we went beyond a coffee bar and opened a café serving kosher sandwiches and baked goods, where friends, parents, and children could meet and eat? Rather than holding a meeting at an outside venue, people could meet in the synagogue café to discuss their work; parents could plan playdates for their kids at the shul. The point is, the synagogue could serve as a central point and place in the lives of congregants, offering a beautiful, modern space with relevant amenities, quality products, and an inviting, nurturing atmosphere. Not only can we generate revenue in the process, we can simultaneously generate community.

From Libraries to Bookstores

When I arrived at CSH, much of the library was dedicated to the modern history of Israel, which, of course, is important. However, the problem was that, for them, "modern" meant roughly the time the shul was built, which ended before the Yom Kippur War even began! Gone are the days of the synagogue providing 1970s books on the State of Israel or broken collections of all Hebrew talmudic commentary. In an era when large bookstore chains are going bankrupt, resulting in fewer places for people to wander about and see what books pique their interest, wouldn't it make sense to have books for sale in the shul? There are many new books on everything Jewish, but most of our Jewish institutions currently house virtually none of them. Barnes & Noble offers better, newer, and greater choices of Judaic books than synagogues, and this makes little sense. We want people to sit in our synagogue lobbies and spaces, reading hot-off-the-press Jewish books, as well as ancient texts. Imagine how compelling it would be to invite people to come sit in our café, read our books, and make a day of being in the synagogue.

From *Mikvah* Mayhem to *Mikvah* Magic

One of the great renaissances in modern Jewish life is the rise in popularity of the *mikvah*. Although Orthodox Jews—Jewish women in particular—have always frequented the *mikvah*, in non-Orthodox Jewish life, except for conversion, it had all but disappeared. But today, many women and men are returning to the *mikvah* for traditional reasons like "family purity" and spiritual preparation for the High Holy Days among a myriad of other creative reasons and rituals as well.

My wife, far from being Orthodox, began using the *mikvah* after our marriage. In time it became a centerpiece of her spiritual path, and each month she looks forward to it longingly and with anticipation. Then we moved from Los Angeles, with its plethora of *mikva'ot*, out into various communities that technically might have had a *mikvah* but it certainly was not the *mikvah* experience to which she or I had become accustomed.

In one such place, my wife was horrified at what she found. On her first visit to a nearby *mikvah*, she was expecting some version of the beautiful, ornate, or at least clean *mikva'ot* that she had frequented in the past. What she found, however, almost turned her off the *mikvah* path entirely. Instead of beauty, this particular *mikvah* was in a dark, dank, and frankly terrifying basement.

There was no water in the *mikvah*. "The *mikvah* lady" told her she'd have to wait half an hour for the water to warm up and the tub to fill. "Fine," my wife thought. "So radical hospitality wasn't their thing." She could wait. But then, as she looked down, not only were there spiderwebs in the *mikvah*, but at the center of one of those webs sat a giant, hairy, creepy spider crawling up the dry water spout. My wife pointed it out. The *mikvah*, lady was oblivious and had the audacity to tell my wife to undress. She told my wife she would be back to inspect her thoroughly to make sure she was clean, which was ironic given the "impurity" of the space. Between the state of the *mikvah* and the attitude of the *mikvah* lady, my wife made a beeline for the exit, never to return to that *mikvah* again.

Contrast that *mikvah* with the one we currently frequent in Newton, Massachusetts, called Mayyim Hayyim. Mayyim Hayyim was created a few years back by Jews who wanted to reclaim *mikvah* as a spiritual practice, an art, a deep and meaningful experience from start to finish. Mayyim Hayyim is a glorious facility that, architecturally alone, is inspirational. It is in constant use for all kinds of purposes—traditional as well as creative—both as a *mikvah* and as a cultural arts center. The professionals and volunteers at Mayyim Hayyim, called *mikvah* guides rather than *mikvah* ladies, are trained in the art of radical hospitality, treating everyone who enters their doors as royalty. The atmosphere and attitude is one of nonjudgment, warmth, and graciousness. Everyone to whom I have spoken, mostly first-time *mikvah*-goers, literally kvell over their experience. The *mikvah* at Mayyim Hayyim is simply the embodiment of *Ruakh*, the way it was always meant to be.[2]

One of the hallmarks of every authentic Jewish community for thousands of years has been the *mikvah*, but too few communities offer this any longer. And the question is, even if a *mikvah* does exist, is it a Mayyim Hayyim experience or a hairy, scary spider *mikvah* that causes post-traumatic stress disorder? As we rethink the future of our shuls, why not imagine building such an inspirational *mikvah*? It is time to go beyond the letter of the law, building bare minimum *mikva'ot* and assuming that this will be enough to attract a lost generation back. Rather, we need to reclaim the spirit of the law, reinforcing the idea that God is not only "out there" but God is "in here" as well. As we recite every morning from the siddur:

> You are the Source of blessing, Adonai our God, Sovereign of the universe, who has fashioned the human body with sublime wisdom, creating an intricate network of veins, arteries, structures, and organs, each of which must function properly for our survival. You are the Source of blessing, Adonai, who heals all creatures and performs wonders.

Jews have been pining for opportunities to connect to their community and their Creator for decades. Many are tired of frontal-facing prayer opportunities or hearing the rabbi declare tirelessly, "Please rise;... please sit" as if this were Jewish calisthenics. God can be found in all aspects of our lives, out in the physical world and right here, within our bodies as well.

Virtual Makeover: Time to Talk Tech in Our Shuls

Technology in the Jewish nonprofit world is generally years behind the secular marketplace. If we are going to reposition our institutions and organizations at the center of our constituents' lives, we are going to need a virtual makeover. There are too few synagogues around the world webcasting their services. At CSH, however, we are webcasting, or, as we call it, "shulcasting," on multiple channels. There are so many homebound seniors who benefit from joining in on a shulcast. We are connected to Jewish nursing homes, bringing a sense of vitality and hope into the residents' lives. Moreover, there are always families or friends who want to attend a family *simcha* but in this complicated world are unable to make the trip. Beyond Shabbat services, there are weekday services, *Havdalah*s, classes, funerals, weddings, brises and baby namings, and events of all kinds we could and should share with friends and family across the world. Not only is this a gift to our membership, extended families, and friends, but it is a mitzvah.

Here's an example of the way technology can brighten our lives and community: Before I was a congregant at CSH, I heard about the way Rabbi B was using technology to bring people together. As a hospice volunteer, I was working with a wonderful man who, due to his failing health, was homebound. Every week, for nearly a year, we would spend a few hours in the family room together, where his hospital bed was set up, talking and sharing our lives. One of the stories he loved to tell me was how even though he was unable to go to the synagogue for his granddaughter's bat mitzvah, he was able to virtually be with her thanks to the innovative thinking at the synagogue. Through the technology used at CSH, this grandfather was introduced to Skype and was able to kvell along with his granddaughter, family, and community. It was a gift that brought both his family and him great joy, and one that continued to bring a smile to his face whenever he spoke of the event. Together, we marveled at how technology had the ability to bring people together and the incredible opportunities it invited.

Technology certainly has the power to disrupt our lives, disconnect our communities, and wreak havoc on our spirits. However, it equally has the power to connect us, to expand us, and to sustain us in ways never imaginable until this very moment in history. When our synagogues and Jewish institutions don't shy away from this technological revolution, but embrace it and expand on it within our modern *mikdash*, *Ruakh* will return. The Jewish mission, after all, is to be a "light unto nations" (Isaiah 49:6), and in the twenty-first century the virtual light needs to shine through the window of every laptop, television, tablet, and smartphone across the world.

The shuls of today and tomorrow must offer numerous pathways for people to connect with themselves, with community, and with God. But such opportunities will require money and we must continually seek creative ways to generate revenue. As it says in the Talmud, "*Ayn kemach; ayn Torah*—If there is no bread [material sustenance], there is no opportunity to study Torah, engage Judaism, or fully participate in Jewish life."[3] Simply put, we need dough to rise to the challenge of reimagining our Jewish spaces and reenergizing our communal places. We need financial viability and sustainability. We need new revenue streams. We need a new financial model. We need a revenue revolution.

9

Revenue
Revolution

Cut Flowers: American Judaism Dying on the Vine

Jews in America in the early twenty-first century are among the most successful, educated, influential, and wealthy sociocultural-religious group today. We have succeeded in so many areas and in so many ways.

And yet, somehow we have lost sight that our inherited pioneering spirit has come with a price paid by our immigrant forebears. These were the men and women who sold *shmatas* so we wouldn't have to; these were our warrior predecessors who took up arms and sacrificed their lives for our freedoms; these were our visionary ancestors who held Judaism and Jewish community together, allowing us to grow up within its rich soil, like strong rooted trees with far-reaching branches, ultimately enabling us to bloom.

But our successes are not ours alone, and without a concerted effort, they will not survive collectively for the next generation. We are simply experiencing what the great American Jewish thinker Will Herberg called "cut flower culture." When someone cuts flowers and transfers them elsewhere to be displayed in a vase, it is tempting to believe those flowers are alive and well. From the moment they are uprooted from the soil that gave them life, however, they are no longer living, not really. They may look fine, they may still smell good, but it's only a matter of time before they wither, die, and begin to stink.

In short, the soil of preceding generations, a soil once rich, fertile, and filled with promise, has gone unattended and undernourished. Ours is a generation of "cut flowers" and unless we tend to our institutions, communities, and, specifically, our synagogues, investing in them and replenishing the soil from which we have come, Judaism, Jewish communities, and the Jewish people will continue to wither and eventually die.

Bake Sales and Other Half-Baked Ideas

Let me tell you about a synagogue I was invited to consult with. We'll call it Congregation Rodef Kesef. This was a decent-sized synagogue in a well-to-do, though not over-the-top wealthy suburb. The lay leadership were entrepreneurs, business owners, and professionals who were obviously educated, successful, and financially well off. They were open to and excited by many of the *Ruakh* ideas we discussed and wanted to implement them but didn't think they could pull it off.

"There is simply no money in the budget, no way we can pass on the costs to our congregants," they told me.

They wanted to reimagine their stagnating, lackluster synagogue into a vibrant community reflective of their energetic, successful, and polished lives but didn't feel they had the resources to make it happen. At the end of that first meeting, we decided they would brainstorm alternative ways of generating revenue to pay for the *Ruakh* initiatives and we would discuss them the next time we met.

A week went by and I hadn't yet heard back from them. I had assumed they were busily working away, coming up with some interesting, aggressive, and—knowing this bunch of successful minds— revolutionary ways to generate revenue and pay for the new direction in which they were so eager to head. When we met again, I learned just how wrong I was. Instead of rethinking their financial model, they simply resorted to the same old, same old: a phone-a-thon, a pancake breakfast, a gala, a bake sale, solicit donors for larger gifts, or, if all else fails, raise dues.

These were Ivy League graduates. These were business-minded professionals who would never have the chutzpah to bring such low-level ideas or thinking to their corporate boardrooms. And yet somehow, for some reason, they mentally checked out when it came to their shul. If all else failed they were comfortable with resorting to begging to pay their synagogue's bills.

How is it that successful, well-to-do, educated, American Jews approach the secular world with great expectations, vision, and know-how and all that falls by the wayside when they enter the temple doors? Why is it that such a group of modern thinkers would generate such a tired vision? Whereas their lifestyles may have been worlds apart from those of their grandparents, in the end the 1960s were alive and well in that synagogue boardroom, where they were serving the same weak coffee and the same weak ideas that got them into this predicament a generation or two earlier. Bake sales, car washes, and cutting out box tops are no longer enough. Our old financial models are failing us and pricing far too many Jews out of their own religion.

Rabbi B's Story: I Can't Afford to Be Jewish

If I were to think of the most *Ruakh*-shattering things I hear in synagogue life, it would be this: "Rabbi, I want to be Jewish, I want to come to shul, I want to participate. However, I simply can't afford it."

It doesn't matter how much I reach out to these people or how kind and considerate our synagogue abatement process may be. It doesn't even matter if I tell them not to worry about dues—just come, join us, and make yourselves at home. They do not feel at home if they feel like they have been priced out of Judaism or if they feel as if they are not paying their share.

Let me tell you a story about Beth. Beth was a single mom, raising two kids. Beth made a good living, but just good enough to make ends meet. She wasn't rich. She wasn't poor. She was financially okay, but with no wiggle room for anything more. So when it came time for her children to receive a Jewish education, Beth, like so many young Jews today, went shul shopping to see what she could find. First, Beth went to the "name brand" temples in the big city, for no other reason than they were close, they were familiar, and they were considered the place to be.

Beth inquired about membership. Sadly, Beth wasn't greeted with radical hospitality, not even with a hello. No one asked about her story, where she was from, what inspired her to seek them out, or even her name. Instead, she was asked for a copy of her tax returns; that's what they wanted to know.

Needless to say, Beth was taken aback. She put off membership, too embarrassed to turn in her modest returns, and frankly too offended to continue exploring that shul. However, the High Holy Days were approaching and Beth felt that at the very least she and her children needed a place to attend. So she sought out a much smaller, seemingly less pretentious shul. Coming from the Midwest, she had no idea that you couldn't just show up, that you needed tickets to pray. And so, on Rosh Hashanah, as the sun was setting, as the Jews were entering that shul with tickets in hand, Beth and her children walked right up to the front door where they were barred from entering. Beth was literally told, "No ticket, no *tefilah*," and for the next few years Beth and her children had neither membership, tickets, *tefilah*, nor Jewish community. Beth and her children were on their own.

Dues and Don'ts: Making Judaism Affordable

Let's face it, Jews like to argue and debate. As it's been said, "Two Jews, three opinions." But one area where Jews overwhelmingly agree is that High Holy Day tickets are an embarrassment and that the structure of current synagogue dues is uninspired. I have yet to meet anyone who is passionate about synagogue revenue models, and certainly no one is jumping up and down praising our ticketing system. Not only is it uninspired, the consensus is that it is offensive, if not outright absurd. We have to buy a ticket to be part of a spiritual community? We have to pay an admission price to talk to God? We have to fork over extra dollars for premier seating? From rabbis to cantors, board members to congregants, nearly everyone agrees that tickets and current dues models need to be rethought. We are fortunate that there are already trailblazing, visionary, courageous synagogues leading the way. For example, Temple Israel of Sharon, Massachusetts, and Temple Ahavat Achim of Gloucester, Massachusetts, have both done away with mandatory dues. In its place, they have implemented a flexible membership where a minimum dues dollar amount is suggested, while congregants pay what they feel they can afford.

It's time to break free from our uninspired financial rut. It's time for a new revenue model, one that is less expensive to congregants, one that doesn't feel contrary to spirituality and radical hospitality, and, frankly, one that works. No more dues, no more tickets, and no more turning away Jews and guests, pricing them out and sending them away from their spiritual home because they didn't realize you had to pay to pray!

The Half-Shekel versus the Whole Heart: Two Models of Gift Giving

It is truly a remarkable thing that the Torah, our central spiritual document as Jews, doesn't revolve around what we might term "spiritual" activities or endeavors. Rather, it primarily revolves around the building, functioning, and sustaining of the *Mishkan* (Tabernacle), later to become the *Beit Mikdash* (Temple), which was ultimately transformed into the synagogues that we operate today. More ink was put down on the parchment of our Torah pertaining to this subject than any other topic.

The Torah and Judaism simply do not delineate between the physical and the spiritual. Spirituality is not something that happens beyond our synagogue walls; it is bound up within them, in the way that our synagogues are erected, in what they look like, and in how they are run. The Torah puts forth two primary ways to generate revenue to build and maintain that Temple and their community and, by extension, ours today as well.

> And the Lord spoke to Moses, saying: When you take the census of the people of Israel according to their number, then shall they give every man a ransom for his soul to the Lord, when

you count them.... This they shall give, everyone who passes among those who are counted, half a shekel according to the shekel of the sanctuary.... The rich shall not give more, and the poor shall not give less than half a shekel, when they give an offering to the Lord, to make an atonement for your souls.

—Exodus 30:11–15

The half-shekel served multiple functions, not the least of which was the biblical notion of minimum dues or, better yet, affordable minimum dues. Everyone could afford to belong and participate within that community. Judaism is egalitarian in that every (male) Jew had a seat at the table with a payment of a half-shekel. Then as now, it was important to have some type of dues structure. But make no mistake about it: the half-shekel never did and never will sustain the community or Temple or any of our communities or temples today.

We have equated "minimum dues" with what it means to "pay our dues," when there is so much more to be done. We need to give more, to invest more, and to seed the Jewish soil as never before. However, more of the same High Holy Day appeals, fund-raisers, and pleas are not enough. Rather, this is about rethinking the model of how our money is inspired, raised, and generated. It will be one of our greatest and most enduring contributions to world Jewry and future generations once we solve this with pioneering vision and spirit.

The *Lev* Initiative: Giving from the Heart

And the Lord spoke to Moses, saying, "Speak to the people of Israel, that they bring Me an offering; from every man that gives it willingly with his heart you shall take My offering."

—Exodus 25:1–2

So Moses called on his fellow Israelites to bring forth gifts that were inspired, gifts given not from a sense of obligation but from a place of desire, from their heart. Indeed, the Israelites brought so many gifts that Moses had to ask them to stop. These gifts weren't only financial in nature. Some brought money, while others brought silk, linen, or dolphin skins, reminiscent of fish in the desert.

When we participate, when we build and invest our resources in Jewish community, we seed the soil for others—for our children and for our progeny. We become partners in creation, allowing for the next generation to take hold of this ancient, worthy, and life-sustaining chain. You want to find God? We read in the Torah: *Asu li mikdash v'shakhanti b'tocham*—Make a sacred space, build a sacred place, give, donate, provide, and create it, and that's where I shall be found (Exodus 25:8).

This is exactly what has happened at CSH. Where once we used to run a generic, High Holy Day, presidential appeal, today we have replaced that with the *Lev* (heart) Initiative. The *Lev* Initiative is designated or directed giving. It's not new. It is, however, effective. Instead of asking our membership for donations in an impersonal appeal from the bimah on Yom Kippur and generically asking them to give in order to offset the deficit, today we make phone calls and sit down with people face-to-face. We discuss investing in areas within synagogue life that they are connected to, utilize, and want to see flourish.

For those connected to the Yoga Minyan, we have our Yoga *Lev* Leaders (liaisons) who know the participants, are passionate about this particular program, and therefore feel inspired asking their peers to invest. They know that it is not a "donation" per se. This isn't charity in the sense of giving something for "nothing" in return. Rather, the people they solicit are already participants, obviously sold on the product, and invariably all too happy to give. Many of these individuals pay their half-shekel already and see this as an investment in maintaining and growing a strong spiritual community, not only a charitable cause. Many participants, however, are not formal members. Perhaps they are "spiritual friends" of CSH, maybe they just come for Torah Yoga or Nosh and *Drash*, they may even be members at other shuls. And there are those who never step foot in the building but are with us every week, eagerly following us online. They are not only open to giving but eager to give. For a myriad of reasons, they haven't joined the congregation. But equally, for a myriad of reasons, they want us to continue so they invest in our mission.

With the *Lev* Initiative, we have far surpassed previous fund-raising efforts. We have done so in a way that makes it personal, that connects people with what they use and with what they love. Perhaps most of all we have gotten our lay leadership involved in a way that energizes them, rather than depleting or embarrassing them. It is more work, but it is also more effective. Still, no matter how much we can inspire people to give, it will most likely fall short of what's needed. As important as this shift toward directed giving might be, it's not a revenue revolution.

A Revenue Revolution: Redefining Our Financial Model

As we challenge long-held assumptions in our efforts to build a vibrant and sustainable Jewish community for the twenty-first century, we also need to challenge the notion of our financial model: Are dues, tickets, and donations the only way to pay? Are we really committed to this label "nonprofit"? *Nonprofit*, after all, says it all: in no way, shape, or form do we expect to turn a profit, see a profit, or move forward as profitable. We must move beyond this defeatist sentiment. Our Jewish institutions in general, and synagogues in particular, need to start turning a profit if we are going to move from merely surviving to truly thriving.

"But Rabbi," concerned congregants, community members, and colleagues tell me, "we can't become corporate in our thinking, cold and calculated in our decision making, or come across as looking to make a buck." Of course we don't want to be cold or corporate. However, why can't we be profitable? From a Jewish perspective, money is not the root of all evil. Money is not inherently corrosive, corrupting, or bad. Money, like all material things in this world, is amoral. Its meaning is determined by what we do with it, how we choose to engage it, and how we are affected by it. Hoarding resources is a sin, but there is nothing inherently holy about poverty. From a Jewish perspective, financial resources can help in addressing that which is broken. In the spirit of our tradition of *tikkum olam*, money can be part of the process in helping to repair the world and our spiritual homes as well.

Reading, Writing, and Revenue:
A Wealth of Educational Opportunities

One of the revenue sources many synagogues and Jewish Community Centers rely on are their preschool programs. We expect to make money in this area and yet that is often where our expectations end. Increasingly, we are exploring ways to help our youth find their way through synagogue doors and into numerous alternative activities. As budget cuts threaten the arts programs in many schools, CSH is seeking ways to fill the gaps. We know how busy and overscheduled kids are these days, and their parents are hectically trying to keep up with those schedules, driving through a maze of activities that often leave both parent and child exhausted. The way we have begun to think about our space and our mission has opened up a world of educational as well as financial possibilities. For example, during the week we have a large school wing that goes unused except for two days of Hebrew school. A local piano teacher approached CSH seeking to provide individual fee-based piano lessons. This idea inspired a conversation about ways to offer creative arts in a synagogue setting. We have set out to provide a service to our constituents and community, further our core mission on many fronts, as well as generate substantial revenue through an initiative we call the Betzalel Academy.

The Betzalel Academy

In the Torah, Betzalel was the chief architect and designer chosen by God to erect the Tabernacle. The Betzalel Academy in Jerusalem is Israel's premier arts school. At CSH we are designing an after-school, one-stop shop for youth to study and explore a myriad of arts-related offerings—musical arts, including piano, guitar, percussion, violin, vocals, and choir; visual arts, including drawing, painting, and sculpture; dance, including Israeli folk, African, Latin, modern, and ballet; along with creative writing and public speaking courses. The list is long. The opportunities abound.

We are designing a multitiered business where our youth can take private or group lessons and participate in Jewish or secular tracks as well. It is open to Jews and non-Jews, to any families who want to expose their children to the arts. It furthers our mission to reclaim a more robust sense of spirituality while preparing our children to get further involved in synagogue life, such as youth choirs, the *Ruakh* Rally dance troupe, and a Jewish drumming circle. Jews have always expressed their souls through the arts, as yet one more access point into the conversation with God. The performing and visual arts are an essential part of any authentic notion of spirituality and Judaism.

The University of Judaism

> Turn the Torah, turn it again and again, for everything you want to know is found within it.
>
> —PIRKE AVOT 2:25

Rabbi Ben Bag Bag captured the truth of Torah in this pithy statement. Congregation Shirat Hayam continues to grapple with and explore ways of connecting Torah to people's increasingly busy and complicated lives. It is getting ever more difficult to compel Jews to attend a class, with so many competing demands on their time. This is part of the impetus behind a project we are just creating, called the University of Judaism. The UJ (not to be confused with the former University of Judaism in Los Angeles, now known as American Jewish University, where I attended rabbinical school) is our newly forming evening educational forum.

Essentially, the UJ will be a profusion of educational opportunities during the week for teens and adults. We are in the early planning stages, but once we launch it, we intend to back it up to our weekday Hebrew school. From 4 to 6 p.m. our children are in the building busily engaged in a classroom Hebrew school expereince. At 6 p.m., when Hebrew school ends, they will be invited to join their parents for dinner. In the hustle and bustle of our busy weekday lives, there's hardly enough time to dine, and rarely enough family dining moments. Certainly it is not a Jewish value to have to choose between Judaism or family. Having dinner together and with community is a worthy, stand-alone opportunity and a mitzvah unto itself.

After dinner there will be youth-group activities while adults partake in a myriad of course offerings. We are currently engaged in dialogue with a local university about the requirements for accreditation. At the UJ, some might choose a basic Hebrew literacy course, whereas others might choose an in-depth exploration of Kabbalah. There will be cultural arts courses, Introduction to Judaism classes, and ideally, university extension courses as well. Whereas one size does not fit all in regard to worship, the same holds true in regard to education. As we move into the future, we have begun to build on our mission to be a third place not just on Shabbat, not just in terms of consumer offerings, but adding depth, value, camaraderie, and a nice meal as well.

Our synagogues, JCCs, and Jewish educational institutions should continue to exist independently. However, in this area perhaps we should join forces. Rabbi David Hartman, a modern Orthodox theologian, explains that we Jews may not be able to eat together or daven together, but Torah is Torah and we should be able to study together. From good to great, what Jews demand today in their secular academic lives is excellence, and when it comes to Jewish education, we should collaborate in offering great, dynamic, top-notch experiences as we begin to generate revenue.

Funerals: Gathering in Grief

Synagogues have always been at the center of Jewish life, revolving around life-cycle events. However, today too many of these events are missed opportunities because they are outsourced to hotels, country clubs, and function halls. Take funerals, for instance. Jews have been convinced that death is something that should be handled by funeral parlors. In fact, when I arrived at CSH there were a good number of people who believed that having a funeral at a synagogue was forbidden.

Of course, funerals are not forbidden from taking place in synagogues. Jews may be uncomfortable with death, but Judaism is not. Indeed, this is yet another reason why we should bring funerals back to our synagogues. It is important to send a message that all the stops along the life-cycle journey are meaningful and holy. There is nothing outside the purview of Jewish spirituality that doesn't have a place within synagogue walls.

From a practical standpoint, it makes no sense that so many of our facilities sit empty the vast majority of the time. From a business perspective, it is a wasted opportunity for funeral homes to be booked while our sanctuaries gather dust. We should be conducting funerals out of our spaces as we provide for all aspects of our congregants' and community needs. How many not-yet-members do we miss out on when mourners pass through the doors of a funeral home, rather than a shul, after the loss of a loved one? Then there are all the other amenities we can provide to the bereaved that are meaningful and sustaining to them and financially wise for us to offer as well.

Take the notion of shulcasting, the term we coined at CSH for webcasting our services. Do you know how often I suggest to a family that they Skype their loved one's funeral to a family member who is ill and cannot travel or to a loved one who is unable to attend? Of course the first reaction is disbelief, if not shock and even horror by some. "Is nothing sacred, safe from the evils of technology?" some might be thinking. But the truth of the matter is that this is indeed a sacred gift. Each and every time we shulcast a funeral service, the family and those connected who would have otherwise been absent are so profoundly grateful it's enough to bring tears to your eyes. They are so appreciative that technology could connect them to their loved ones, that technology could allow them to say their good-byes. The mourners are united whether they are physically or virtually present, and the synagogue becomes the place and space to honor and hold that occasion. And do you know how many funeral homes I have worked with that offer this service? Of the dozens of them, many of which are multimillion-dollar businesses, the answer is *none*! In addition, every single week perhaps hundreds of mourners, their family members, and friends return from the cemetery to eat a meal of condolence. Rarely does it take place in a home and rarely with food cooked by the community. Either it is at a restaurant or it is food catered by someone from the outside. Although many of the larger synagogues in the bigger cities already do this, there are not enough of us that offer these services and provide these opportunities. Our synagogues should be the center for our mourners in every respect. We should be cooking for our mourners and preparing their meals for the coming weeks. So many people want to help and provide food but aren't sure how to facilitate it so that the family doesn't get fifty meals the first week and none thereafter. The synagogue should be at the forefront of fostering a deeper sense of community, and in the process, we would generate revenue for a meaningful and important set of services as well.

Leaving a Legacy:
Virtual *Yizkor* and Video Testimonials

As a Jewish community, we have a duty to tend to our mourners. We also have an obligation to tend to our dead. As it has been said, a person dies two deaths, once when her body dies and again when her story is forgotten. This is why we have *yizkor* plaques in so many of our synagogues. What exactly is so timeless and holy about little bronze plaques? The answer is nothing. They are fine. They serve a purpose of getting a loved one's name up on a wall in most of our synagogues. However, at CSH, the result of a merger of two congregations, we have inherited all their plaques plus numerous others from now-defunct shuls. We don't have enough space for all those plaques, and there are so many shapes and styles from those previous synagogues that the price of making them uniform is simply prohibitive. These challenges demanded an alternative solution.

As a response we have purchased a virtual *yizkor* memorial system. "Virtual *yizkor* memorials!" we often hear people respond. Granted, it sounds cold, but it is not. There have been so many times that families have come looking for *Bubbe*'s name on that plaque and simply couldn't find it amid the sea of names strewn across our walls. Even if they could find it, they would stand there for a minute, craning their neck up to merely catch a glimpse of *Bubbe*'s memorial.

But virtual *yikzor* memorials are a totally different experience. At CSH we have replaced our plaques with a plasma-screen system that shows the *yahrtzeits* of the day or offers a database for one to pull up *Bubbe*'s or *Zayde*'s plaque and so much more. Our plans are to build a beautiful, contemplative space to house this technology, as well as to create a database that can house *Bubbe*'s favorite recipes, letters *Zayde* wrote during the war, and play their favorite music. Loved ones can look at their pictures and archive the memories of their lives. *Yizkor* means "memory," and a virtual *yizkor* memorial fulfills the essence of this ancient rite in ways our plaques never could. This is not only a paid service we provide to our congregants, but a service we offer the larger community as well. Through this service we generate revenue, memories, and a priceless legacy.

Taking it a step further, CSH is at the beginning stages of developing a virtual memorial business. Why wait until our loved ones are gone to record their precious life stories and memories? We should have them recorded through video now, while our loved ones are alive, and archived on our virtual *yizkor* site. We have started to do just that. We are building a business creating "legacy videos" and charging a fee for the service.

The costs involved in all these endeavors are well worth the investment, adding to a growing revenue stream. "*L'dor vador*—from generation to generation," we say time and again. The revenue generated in honoring the past is a source of fertile soil for the present, for the generation that follows in *Bubbe* and *Zayde*'s footsteps.

Generating New Business from an Old-World Model

Although these new, marketplace-driven initiatives may prove fruitful, in the end they will probably never be enough. To compete in the marketplace, vast sums are required to offset the rising costs of inspirational Judaism. We need a radical revenue revolution, and that is why we have launched Zuzzim, an independently operated business-to-business and consumer collaboration. Zuzzim is our next step in reimagining revenue sources and reconnecting Jewish community. Zuzzim is first and foremost a think tank that exists independently of CSH. It is made up of a group of entrepreneurs and business owners, inspired by CSH, who are committed to reenvisioning the way CSH, Jewish communities, and nonprofits operate. It is important to note that Zuzzim is in the experimental stage. While we have great hopes for this model, as with all start-up endeavors, the outcome is unknown. Although the specifics of Zuzzim will undoubtedly evolve in vision and direction, the goal of reimagining Jewish nonprofits will remain the same. Regardless of success, Zuzzim is one potential response to a needed revenue revolution in the Jewish marketplace today.

Zuzzim's current effort is to operate as an independent business that will help create and implement business-to-business (B2B) and business-to-consumer (B2C) networking groups for all Zuzzim member institutions. It will operate as both a physical and a virtual platform to reconnect Jews and to reestablish lines of connection and commerce between the community and our Jewish institutions—connections much like the ones in the shtetl.

Not too many years ago, Jewish communities in this country were far closer in appearance to shtetls in the Old Country than they are to our modern Jewish communities today. They may have been situated in places called the Lower East Side in New York, Chelsea in Massachusetts, and the Fairfax district in LA, but they were hardly different than their forebears' shtetls of Chelm, Lodz, or Anatevke across the seas, back in time.

Whether it be the shtetl in the Old Country or the American shtetls of yesteryear, Saul the tailor would only ever patronize Sam the kosher butcher. They lived in the same community, they belonged to the same shul. Sam's parents and family had always given Saul a lot of business. When Saul's wife, Sadie, was sick, it was Sam's sister, Feigele, who cooked for her, cleaned for her, and helped nurse her back to health. It would be inconceivable not to patronize Sam; this was community, this was *mishpacha* (family), and family takes care of their own.

The ancient and modern shtetls were defined by geographical proximity. Jews lived within walking distance of their shul, their businesses, their centers of commerce, and the daily activities and lives of their fellow Jews. Most of all, Jews primarily interacted with other Jews. The Jewish community was tightly knit and self-sustaining, as Jewish lives were bound up with one another. They patronized one another's businesses and utilized each others' services, creating a community of reciprocity. We need to caution ourselves not to over-romanticize the shtetl, as persecution, anti-Semitism, xenophobia, and a whole host of social dysfunctions made life perilous in these communities. Rather, it's about living out the Jewish maxim *Kol Yisrael areivim zeh bazeh*— All Jews are responsible for one another. In these tight-knit Jewish communities, on multiple levels, Jews were inextricably bound up in one another's lives.

Over the past few decades, outside of a handful of Jewish enclaves around the country, the self-imposed shtetl has disappeared. Like other ethnic groups, Jews have moved out to the suburbs, out into the world, and, by and large, out of one another's lives. Add to this the radical shift toward an ever-growing global, and now virtual, economy, and the notion of Jews doing business with other Jews, patronizing one another's shops and services, and even taking care of their own is increasingly becoming a thing of the past.

With this dispersal of Jewish community has come a sense of disconnection and loneliness perhaps never before experienced to this degree in Jewish communities and in Jewish lives. Although it is the purview and responsibility of synagogues, JCCs, Jewish Federations, and other Jewish nonprofits to function as the spiritual, social, and even financial glue that binds Jews together, clearly something is missing. Jewish communities are unraveling, and it is imperative that we reclaim our lines of connection in a myriad of ways, including the financial realm. We should do business with one another. Members of our institutions should patronize those who are in our community or support our Jewish causes. Zuzzim is the organization that makes these connections and brokers these relationships. Revenue is created and the spirit of community is reclaimed.

From Saul to Paul: How Zuzzim Works

Instead of Saul, today we have Paul, who is new to Judaism and new to the community. Paul is also a successful entrepreneur who runs a clean-tech start-up. Instead of Dov, we have Dave. Dave is an established businessman. He owns over a dozen car dealerships and is known for his philanthropy to the synagogue and Jewish community. Although these two belong to CSH, they had never met. Paul had purchased his car previously from a dealer who has never given a dime to the Jewish community. And with Paul's help, Dave's business was potentially sitting on a cost-savings opportunity, an opportunity he didn't even know he had.

Zuzzim brought these two men together. Dave retrofitted his dealerships with Paul's energy-cost-reduction services. Dave has realized substantial savings and 10 percent of those savings have flowed through Zuzzim to Dave's elected nonprofit, CSH. Paul has since purchased a car from Dave, who in turn has directed a percentage of that sale through Dave to Paul's elected nonprofit, once again CSH. Business relations are fostered. Cost savings are found. Substantial revenue flows. But most of all real-life human relationships have been created: Paul and Dave are now friends.

Again, although Zuzzim was inspired by CSH, it is an independent start-up in the business of working with all Jewish nonprofits. Any Jewish nonprofit can become a "partner institution." All it takes is for the institution to formally join Zuzzim, bringing their membership list to the table and their business owners, professionals, and consumer base into the conversation. Each and every one of those people who belong to that "partner institution," for example, a synagogue, JCC, Federation, or Hillel, is therefore a member of Zuzzim and has a right to offer their goods or services to anyone within the larger Zuzzim network, locally or abroad, in person or online. All members, regardless of whether or not they are business owners or service providers, are consumers. Now, however, their consumption of goods and services can serve a greater good, or what we at Zuzzim call "purpose purchasing." Each and every time they shop and consume through Zuzzim, they will be sustaining their "partner institution," their beloved JCC or Federation or synagogue.

Beyond our respective institutions, we can then link our institutions together so that synagogue constituents can patronize JCC business owners, who can use the professional services of those in the Federation's roster. And then our network can begin to grow. We will expand beyond our geographic communities to other Jewish communities around the country, to Israel and around the world. Through a virtual, web platform, we will bring business owners, professionals, and consumers together. Here within our twenty-first-century shtetl, as we find one another, do business together, and get to know each other, we will generate a revenue revolution.

Zuzzim in no way seeks to return to the shtetl shadows of xenophobia, an "us versus them" mentality or exclusivity. This is not exclusive to Jews or Jewish communities. On the contrary, Zuzzim is poised to tear down such walls, eliminating barriers. One need not be Jewish to participate. A business or service provider need not be a Jew to belong. This is about supporting our Jewish institutions, institutions that anyone and everyone are welcome to belong to, participate in, and sustain.

Fishing for Solutions

Without a profitable economic arm within the Jewish community today, one whose sole purpose is to generate revenue for the Jewish community, Judaism as we know it will be incomplete, certainly uninspired, and ultimately unsustainable. Sure, we can indefinitely sustain *Ruakh*-less, cheap synagogue operations, but is this what we want for our future? Sooner or later, even these inexpensive offerings will collapse. Zuzzim is simply one response—our response—to becoming part of the solution through reenvisioning the landscape of the Jewish communities in which we live. So if it isn't Zuzzim, then it will need to be something else, or many something elses. Perhaps you have created your own models for a revenue revolution, which you can share with us at www.revolutionofjewishspirit.com.There is no one answer, no one be-all-end-all solution, no one catchall system that our future Jewish communities can or should turn to. Gone are the days of "one size fits all" in any area of our lives or Jewish practices. This certainly holds true when it comes to our finances. We need to start thinking outside the box, start imagining new ways of functioning, and have the courage to fail, if need be, knowing that this is the pathway toward real breakthrough in secular business and in inspirational Judaism, too.

If we do not address this last area of finances and dues, no matter how much we thrive in other areas, ultimately we will fail. But if we address it with our *chalutzim* (pioneering) vision and spirit, we will thrive. More importantly, we will have offered a lasting contribution to the Jewish world and to our children's children. We will not simply have fulfilled an ancient Chinese maxim and ideal: "Give a man a fish and you feed him for a day. Teach a man to fish and you feed him for a lifetime." In our Jewish version, we will teach our children to fish not only in lakes, rivers, and oceans; we will teach them how to catch fish, in, of all places, the desert.

Conclusion

And You Shall Be a Blessing

L'dor Vador: From Generation to Generation

Who could have imagined the changes we've seen in our lifetime? Twenty years ago, the words *Google* or *Facebook* or *Twitter* would have made no sense to us. No one knew about iPads and smartphones and laptops. The world is moving fast. How fortunate we are that both Torah and Talmud are alive with opportunities to guide us in our current predicaments and challenges if we return to them with fresh eyes and open hearts and minds. The wisdom of our tradition is both timeless and timely. As we move forward into the twenty-first century, we must carry with us the lessons of the past and the vision of our future, with *Ruakh* as our guiding force.

Imagine a snapshot, a moment in time, where a Bar or Bat Mitzvah family is on the bimah. Maybe it is your family, or maybe it is a family close to you. It may be recent or decades old. Regardless, the image shares a constant, a grouping of grandparents and parents and a thirteen-year old at the threshold of Jewish adulthood passing the Torah down from one generation to another. In that passing our Jewish ancestors are also present, all who have taken part in this great lineage of *l'dor vador*, "from generation to generation." The questions

171

that beg to be asked today are these: What are we truly passing down? How do we keep Torah alive? How do we honor the past while we serve the future? Each snapshot of family passing down the Torah through the ages represents both a shared collective history and value system and also a unique history that speaks to that very moment in time. While we are passing down our tradition, we are also passing down our understanding that the future is unknown. Yes, the past can guide us, but it is our new perspectives, interpretations, and ideas that will keep the tradition thriving, keep it a living and breathing practice. If we simply live in the past, attempting to press rewind and insisting that our children practice their Judaism in a one-size-fits-all model from the days of yesteryear, both individually and collectively we will fail.

There's a well-known story, attributed to different nineteenth-century rabbis, about a man who boasts that he's been through the Talmud many times. "Fine," replies the rabbi, "but how many times has the Talmud been through you?" Judaism isn't about perpetuating a meaningless loop of repetition and passing that down to the next generation, expecting them to simply repeat this process. What we must pass down is the spark that kindles the heart and spirit and touches the soul; what we must pass down is the invitation to let the Talmud course through each person. As we pass on the beauty of the traditions, values, and rituals of Judaism, what is also crucial to pass along is a blessing to the next generation to move into their Torah and spirit in a way that is authentic to their lives.

Fostering Fearlessness

Remember the "2,000-Year-Old Man," played by Mel Brooks, with Carl Reiner as the interviewer? That classic and comedic routine had some great pearls of wisdom. At one point, Reiner asks the 2,000-year-old man, "What was your means of transportation back then?"

The 2,000-year-old man replies, "Uhh, mostly fear."

"Fear transported you?" the interviewer asks.

"Fear, yes. You see, an animal would growl, you would go two miles in a minute."

In some ways, we are still responding from a place of fear. But it is our duty to face our future, and the future of our children, not running away in fear, but running forward with fearlessness.

No longer is it enough to insist upon continuity for the sake of continuity from an insular, victimized, and frightened place. Rabindranath Tagore, the Indian teacher and poet, wrote, "Let me not pray to be sheltered from dangers, but to be fearless in facing them."[1] That is the mantra we must take with us into the future. If Jewish history has taught us anything, it has taught us this: no matter how successfully we navigate these turbulent times, tomorrow will hold a new set of challenges. Today's changes will be tomorrow's assumptions. The greatest gift we can give our children and grandchildren is not merely the ancient, timeless, rooted values and practices of our tradition. We must also give our progeny the tools to navigate change, adapt to uncertainty, and move forward with vision and fearlessness. This is what *Revolution of Jewish Spirit* is all about.

A Hebrew proverb says, "Whoever teaches his son teaches not just his son but also his son's son, and so on to the end of generations."[2] If we teach our sons and our daughters to be truly awake to the world—both the beauty and the challenges—we will have taught them well. Like Jacob who becomes Israel, one who wrestles with God and humanity and is able to remain present in the struggle, we, too, must teach our children to be fearless explorers, working toward greater connection with themselves, with one another, and with God, regardless of the demands and challenges of the day.

We must exemplify the courage to hear and respond to our own calls in the moment and to journey forward. In this way, we will have opened the gate for our children's future, one that they will walk through themselves in their own unique ways, to the calls of their time, with our blessing.

Both individually and communally, we must declare: *Hineni*, I am here, and *hinenu*, we are here. We must make room in our tents, as Abraham and Sarah did, for our brothers and sisters; we must make room in our synagogues for diversity in our community and for choices in how people express their Jewish identities and their spiritual paths.

Congregation Shirat Hayam is one example of how synagogues can once again flourish by embracing a willingness to let go of what is no longer serving the community, to take risks regardless of the chorus of voices that shout out, *"No!"* and to take a vision and turn that into reality. Is it sometimes scary? Sure. Most things worth doing move us out of our comfort zone. Do we sometimes fail in our attempts at change? Absolutely. Or in the words of the Kotzker Rebbe:

> One who seeks to be a rebbe must ascend mountains and descend valleys, to seek hidden treasures, to knock on the gates, many gates, until the heart breaks, until the body crumbles, until heaven and earth collapse, while he maintains his way.[3]

What a wonderful lesson to teach the next generation: we can be scared, we can fail, but like the matriarchs and patriarchs in our Torah, we get up, dust ourselves off, and try again. Moses smashed the Ten Commandments. He went right back up the mountain to reclaim a new set. The Torah is a book about resilience of spirit and moving toward wholeness, of falling down and picking oneself up again. Every Jewish community, synagogue, and institution faces both shared and unique challenges. *Revolution of Jewish Spirit* puts *Ruakh* front and center in repairing the brokenness within us individually and collectively. How we choose to get back up again and how we mend our brokenness might look different depending on each community's needs, but the central force in lightening our load is *Ruakh*. What makes our work and the work of the next generation a blessing rather than a burden? *Ruakh!* With *Ruakh* we radiate both light and lightness of being. With *Ruakh*, anything is possible. With *Ruakh* we will never lose our way.

Seeds of the Future

Theodor Herzl said, "It is true that we aspire to our ancient land. But what we want in that ancient land is a new blossoming of the Jewish spirit."[4] Grounded in Torah, rooted in the richness of our traditions is a flowering bud that is growing toward the warmth and light of today. Far from being pulled off the tree or suffering from "cut flower culture," it is being watered with *Ruakh* and blossoming as a result of our collective past and all that the future holds. We need to teach our children how to continually nourish Judaism by planting the seeds of ongoing learning and love for our heritage and by showing them how Torah can speak to each person and community in the present moment.

Elie Wiesel reflects, "I marvel at the resilience of the Jewish people. Their best characteristic is their desire to remember. No other people has such an obsession with memory." So how will this generation be remembered? Will we be seen for our fearfulness, resorting to the old, tired arguments of continuity for the sake of continuity? Will we be remembered for being insular in determining who is part of the tribe and for being wed to a Jewish practice that offers just one door to walk through and one way to walk through it? Or will we be remembered for opening our tent flaps and inviting people in, offering different doors and different ways to walk through and into our spiritual community? Will we exemplify fearlessness in moving forward into the future with *Ruakh* lighting our path? Each generation has both an opportunity and a responsibility to carry the precious gifts of our tradition and to move our story forward.

> And the Divine called to Abram: Journey forth, from the known [from your land, from your birthplace, from your father's house] to the unknown [the land that I will show you]. And I will make you into a great nation, and I will bless you, and I will increase your name, and you shall be a blessing.
>
> —GENESIS 12:1–2

Acknowledgments

The creation of the world would not have been possible without the *Ruakh* of God. The creation of this book would not have been possible without the support and contributions of so many wonderful, illuminating, and *Ruakh*-filled souls.

Baruch's Thank-Yous

First and foremost, thank you to Congregation Shirat Hayam (CSH). CSH is quite literally the embodiment of the values and spirit found within this book. You have been so open to and supportive of me and this revolution of Jewish spirit. You have been gracious in allowing me to do this work, write this book, and shine this spirit out into the world. It's one thing to say it. It's another to embody it. Thank you for sustaining and supporting my family and me.

And thank you from the bottom of my heart to all of the hardworking souls who have made CSH possible: Cantor Emil Berkovits, Cantor Elana Rozenfeld, Marla Gay, Jed Filler, Bob Krentzman, Barri Stein, Marylou Barry, Leslie Sack, Debbie Liebowitz, Ann Navon, Marcy Yellin, the *Ruakh* Rally Band, all of the wonderful teachers, our maintenance team, Gus Ventura and Robert Monegro, and our lay leadership. You are part and parcel of CSH, our success, and a revolution of Jewish spirit.

A special thanks to my personal IT specialist, congregant, and friend Chris Hockert. Chris, the countless hours you have put into making my website, podcasts, webcasts, and anything with a lens, screen, or battery work are beyond measure. Thank you.

To the guys of Zuzzim: Joe Selby, Hal Schwartz, David Rosenberg, Mark Friedman, and Paul Gregory, it has been an honor to work with you on implementing this bold new idea of Zuzzim in an attempt to make Judaism affordable for all.

Thank you to Phyllis Karas and Doug Reeves. Both of you believed in me and encouraged me to write. Phyllis, your early comments truly shaped this book. Thanks for inspiring me and believing in me.

Thank you to all of the CSH benefactors and Prime Motor Group. Your generosity and support have allowed CSH to expand our innovative programming, enriching the life of our synagogue and spiritual community. A special thank you to David Rosenberg. David, you have been like a brother, your support unwavering. Thank you.

Thank you to Tifereth Israel Synagogue in Des Moines, Iowa. Particularly, my gratitude to Don Schoen, Alice Friedgood, and Marvin Pomerantz (z"l). I will never forget the early years of my rabbinate, the successes and the mistakes, but most of all, the friendships that were formed along the way.

To my teachers and mentors at American Jewish University, particularly Rabbis Brad Artson and Elliot Dorff: I have acquired so much knowledge and drawn so much inspiration not only from your words of Torah, but from the way you embody all that you preach and teach.

Thank you to Rabbi Mordecai and Meirav Finley and the holy people of congregation Ohr HaTorah in Los Angeles. It was there that I found not only my wife, but also my rabbinic voice. Mordecai, you took me in and mentored me. I will be forever grateful to you for showing me the path.

To my *chevrutot* (study partners): Beginning the journey with you in rabbinical school was among the highlights of my life. Rabbis Daniel Greyber, Mark Ankcorn, Brian Strauss, and Ranon Teller, you are my spiritual brothers and I thank you for reading and commenting on the earlier versions of this book.

To my mentor, friend, and spiritual father, Larry Robinson: You have helped me become a better husband, father, and man. I love you.

To Steve Frankel: Thank you for all of your tech support and guidance. But most of all, thank you for putting up with all of the hours Ellen and I spent writing this book. You are a good man and a good friend.

To my beloved grandparents, Florence Brody and Jack Brody (z"l), and Harold and Babe Perelman (z"l): "It is easy to look down upon giants when you are standing upon their shoulders." Thank you for the giant sacrifices you have made for me.

To my sister, Rebecca Rosen; brother-in-law, Brian; nephews, Jakob and Sam; brother, Zachary; and my lifelong friend and blood brother, Mark Erman: I love you all. You are part and parcel of my soul and my life.

To all of my in-laws, Rob and Linda Kaufman, Jim and Gail Kelch, Ann Dach and Jenny Kelch: Thank you for giving me your daughter and sister, for your love, and for your support.

And a special thank you to my mother, Jan Goldstein; stepfather, Howard Goldstein; and father of blessed memory, Sheldon Perelman (z"l). Mom, there isn't a day that goes by that I don't live out the Jewish values you instilled in me and embody in your tireless work on behalf of the Jewish people and the Jewish homeland. Dad, there isn't a day that goes by that I don't think of you, miss you, and draw upon your memory to carry me and my mission forward.

Thank you to my great writing partner and even better friend. Ellen, you have not only kept me on track with this book, but your joyful spirit has lifted my spirits, keeping me on track with my life. This endeavor is among the most precious journeys I have ever made. Thank you for making it with me. I am already anticipating our next project together.

And above all else, thank you to my beloved wife, Ariela. You are part of me. You are my other half, my better half, my soul mate, and the love of my life. Thank you for your patience, all of the growing pains, practice sermons, and everything else you have to put up with as both my wife and the *rebbetzin*. You are my one true love.

And to the four precious souls we have been graced with and given the opportunity to parent, protect, and love: Yehuda, Maya, Shoshana, and Aviv. Words will never convey just how much I adore you. This book is ultimately about you and my prayer that you live a life inspired by *Ruakh*. *Ruakh* is exactly what you have brought to my life.

Ellen's Thank-Yous

While my Jewish roots grounded me in the soil of my ancestors, my branches stretched toward the teachings of the East. My Jewish roots were watered and nurtured when I met Rabbi Alan Ullman over a decade ago, and I have been studying with him ever since. A traveling rabbi who teaches Torah as a spiritual path, Rabbi Alan opened a door for me that led deep into the heart of a Jewish spiritual path. Whether diving into a Torah passage or a Zen parable, studying with Rabbi Alan is to be in a sacred space where ancient teachings speak to the heart and soul of life today. Thank you, Rabbi Alan, for being both my great teacher and friend and for supporting both my roots and my branches.

To Shelley Poulsen and Hanna Sherman, my Torah companions and Dharma buddies: Your wisdom, compassion, and love have enriched my life in ways that are truly beyond measure. As we study together with Rabbi Alan, the world opens to new possibilities again and again.

Thank you also to the members of my other Torah study group on the North Shore of Boston: Steve Frankel, Ann Laff, Miriam Pollack, Wendy Wicks, Pat Kravtin, Carole Schutzer, Debbie Ankeles, Bob Friedman, and Ina-Lee Hoffman. Your insights, friendships, and love of Torah have been an inspiration in my life.

As always, my gratitude to Barbara McCollough, my ferrywoman extraordinaire, who sailed with me from shore to shore and taught me to embrace both the calm waters and to ride the inevitable waves. What a gift you are in my life.

My deepest gratitude to Congregation Shirat Hayam (CSH), for being a shining example of a synagogue that puts *Ruakh* front and center and everywhere in between. Whether walking through the open doors (literally and figuratively) weekly on Shabbat, during the High Holy Days, or simply for the various reasons that bring me to CSH so often during the week, I feel a deep sense of "coming home" and the love of this spiritual family. Thank you to MaryLou Barry, for greeting all who enter CSH with her wonderful smile and graciousness, and to Marla Gay, for her enthusiastic support of new ideas and projects and for always having time for a quick chat regardless of how busy she is. My thanks also to Jed Filler, Barri Stein, Bob Krentzmen, and Cantors Emil Berkovits and Elana Rosenfeld for their ongoing work in creating such a spirited synagogue and for their ongoing support of our work on this book.

When I joined CSH, I was introduced to a group of women called "The Spirited Sisters," and that name says it all. Whether jumping out of our seats during Shabbat to dance together around the sanctuary, meeting together in support of a sister facing a challenge, or setting aside time to study together with the spirit of the Divine feminine, these sisters, my spirited sisters, have welcomed me, supported me, and invited me to experience the power of sisterhood. I offer my gratitude to this amazing community.

A special thank you to Michele Tamaren, fellow writer and seeker, whom I met only a few years ago at CSH but feel I've known for many lifetimes. Your friendship is a treasure.

Thank you to my dear friends: Phyllis Eidelman, Ellen Reifler, Mark Messenger, Gail Goldstein, Wendy Webber, Judy Toner, Lisa Weisman, Amy Forman, Marjorie Patkin, Susan Yorks, Rosalie and Todd Miller, Fanny and Irv Danesh, and my brother- and sister-in-law, Jeff and Dara Frankel, for your ongoing support as I wrote this book and for all the support you've shown me in my other writing endeavors.

My gratitude goes out to Peggy Elam of Pearlsong Press, for her continued support of my work and books wherever they call home. You, my friend, are a woman of vision, tremendous energy, and inspiration.

My family has loved and supported me every step of the way. Thank you to my wonderful parents, Lorraine and Joe Matz. You have stood by me as my spiritual search has taken me from Israel to the Himalayas and back again (and again). You are always there to listen to me, to ponder with me, and to laugh with me. You have given me life, and you sustain that life with your love. Great thanks also to my mother-in-law, Maxine Frankel, for your ever-present love and support.

Thank you, thank you, and thank you to my sister, Judith Matz, who shares with me the writing life. Over endless conversations, you have supported me while I wrote, and willingly gave of your time and insight to help me during the challenges, along with your enthusiasm and joy when celebrating a breakthrough and milestone. Also, much gratitude to my brother, Robert Matz, for his ongoing support, love, and encouragement. As both an English professor and writer, your love of the written word has inspired me through the years. My gratitude also to my wonderful brother-in-law, Dave Barhydt, and sister-in-law, Teresa Michals.

It has been my great fortune, honor, and pleasure to write this book with Rabbi B. When you throw a pebble into a pond, you can watch the concentric circles that the ripple creates. To me, Rabbi B is like that pebble; his great *Ruakh*-filled vision inspires ongoing creative impulses that flow outward in ever more ways. You are both a wonderful writing partner and a dear friend whose kindness, humor, and wisdom continue to enrich my life in countless ways. It's amazing how you can make working on the book at Starbucks for a long stretch of time feel like a piece of (coffee) cake.

Thank you also to Ariela HaLevi. There were times when Baruch and I were in a writing marathon of sorts, and your ongoing support of our work and the gift of your friendship have meant so much to me.

My children, Allie and Matt, continue to inspire me every day. You are the greatest gifts in my life, and it is an honor to be your mother and to watch you both move into the world with your passions, convictions, dreams, and above all, the kindest of hearts. Thank you for the love, support, and joy you bring to my life.

And finally, to Steve: For over thirty years you have been by my side with endless love and support. Who could have foreseen all that we would share in our lives? And to think, I fell in love with you long before the digital age, and long before I knew that you would be coming to my rescue with your computer know-how, saving me from myself when I thought I'd lost yet another document or needed help setting up yet another website. You are my light, my love, my past, present, and future. Thank you for sharing your life with me.

Together, we would like to thank Jewish Lights Publishing and the wonderful people who worked together to bring *Revolution of Jewish Spirit* out into the world. Our gratitude to Stuart M. Matlins, founder, editor-in-chief, and publisher of Jewish Lights, who saw the potential in our book and, with keen insight, patience, and wisdom, helped us to create a stronger book by guiding us in what the pages needed more and less of. Great thanks to Editorial Vice President Emily Wichland, for helping to make the *Ruakh* of *Revolution of Jewish Spirit* shine through the pages. Thanks also to Kaitlin Johnstone, editorial assistant; Tim Holtz, interior designer; Jennifer Rataj, publicity manager; and Jenny Buono, who created the wonderful cover design that dances with *Ruakh*. Working with all of you has truly been a pleasure.

We would be remiss if we didn't give a big thank-you to our local Starbucks in Marblehead and Swampscott, Massachusetts. We have sat at your tables for hours with laptops open and coffee cups full, morning, noon, and night. Though typically a toast of *L'chayim* (to life) is made with wine, to you, and Howard Schultz's vision of creating a "third place" of being a home away from home, and an office away from the office, we raise our *grande* lattes and say *L'chayim* and thank you!

Notes

Introduction

1. This term was coined by Dr. Ron Wolfson and eloquently defined in his book *The Spirituality of Welcoming: How to Transform Your Congregation into a Sacred Community* (Woodstock, VT: Jewish Lights Publishing, 2006).
2. CSH is a member of United Synagogue of Conservative Judaism. We abide by the USCJ's laws and standards for Conservative Judaism and synagogues.
3. Stewart Ain, "United Synagogue Turns Inward," *The Jewish Week* (February 8, 2011), http://www.thejewishweek.com/news/new_york/united_synagogue_turns_inward (accessed March 1, 2012).
4. Paul Vitello, "Synagogues Are Merging, Delicately, as Jews Move," *New York Times* (September 11, 2007), http://www.nytimes.com/2007/09/11/nyregion/11jews.html?pagewanted=all (accessed February 26, 2012).
5. Ira M. Sheskin, "Elderly Jews: An Increasing Priority for the American Jewish Community?" *Institute for Global Jewish Affairs* (July 15, 2010): 15, 58.
6. Carla Rivera, "Jewish Day Schools Facing an Economic Crisis," *Los Angeles Times* (May 18, 2009), http://articles.latimes.com/2009/may/18/local/me-schools18 (accessed February 27, 2012).
7. Stacey Palevsky, "Religious School Dropout? Initiative Aims to Curb Post–Bar Mitzvah Exodus," *J: The Jewish News Weekly of Northern California* (May 30, 2008), http://www.jweekly.com/article/full/35048/religious-school-dropout-initiative-aims-to-curb-post-bar-mitzvah-exodus (accessed February 15, 2012).
8. Jack Wertheimer, "Vital Signs: Hebrew, Nature's Way," *Jewish Ideas Daily* (March 8, 2010), http://www.jewishideasdaily.com/content/detail/continue-reading-vital-signs-hebrew-natures-way (accessed February 17, 2012).
9. Steven M. Cohen and Ari Y. Yelman, "Beyond Distancing: Young Adult American Jews and Their Alienation from Israel," *Berman Jewish Policy Archive*, Jewish Identity Project of Reboot, 2007, http://www.bjpa.org/Publications/details.cfm?PublicationID=326 (accessed February 18, 2012).
10. Joe Berkofsky, "Poll: Richest U.S. Jews Give Mostly to Non-Jewish Causes," *J: The Jewish News Weekly of Northern California* (April 4, 2003), http://www.jweekly.com/article/full/19608/poll-richest-u-s-jews-give-mostly-to-non-jewish-causes/ (accessed February 15, 2012).

11. Fern Chertok, Joshua Tobias, Shirah Rosin, and Matthew Boxer, "Volunteering + Values: A Repair the World Report on Jewish Young Adults," Cohen Center for Modern Jewish Studies (June 2011), http://werepair.org/blog/volunteering-values-a-repair-the-world-report-on-jewish-young-adults/7018, p. 8 (accessed February 12, 2012).

12. For a detailed account of the work of S3K, refer to Ron Wolfson, *The Spirituality of Welcoming: How to Transform Your Congregation into a Sacred Community* (Jewish Lights Publishing, 2006); Lawrence A. Hoffman, *Rethinking Synagogues: A New Vocabulary for Congregational Life* (Jewish Lights Publishing, 2006)

Chapter 1

1. Talmud, Sanhedrin 106b.

2. Gila Gevirtz, *Partners with God* (West Orange, NJ: Behrman House, 1995), 82.

3. Julie Gruenbaum Fax, "How Different Is IKAR? Rabbi Sharon Brous Inspires Change ... and Controversy," Jewish Journal June 22, 2010, accessed May 27, 2012, http://www.jewishjournal.com/community/article/how_different_is_ikar_rabbi_sharon_brous_inspires_change_and_controversy_20/ http://.

Chapter 2

1. Talmud, Shevout 39a.

2. Pirke Avot 1:14.

3. Albert Einstein, *Living Philosophies*. (New York: Simon and Schuster, 1931).

4. William Safire, "Zim Serves Africa," *The Israel Export and Trade Journal*. Tel Aviv, July 1963, 15:25.

Chapter 3

1. Midrash Tanchuma, Nitzavim 3.

2. Mark Gafni, "Soul Prints and Parenting," February 2, 2008. http://www.marcgafni.com/?p=123

Chapter 4

1. Adopted from Mark Dov Shapiro, *Gates of Shabbat* (New York: CCAR Press, 1991), 1–2.

2. Viktor E. Frankl, *Man's Search for Meaning* (Boston: Beacon Press, 2006), 65–66.

3. Elie Wiesel, interview with Alvin P. Sanoff, "One Must Not Forget," *U.S. News & World Report*, October 27, 1986, 68.

4. Talmud, Sotah 11a.

5. Avivah Gottlieb Zornberg, *The Particulars of Rapture: Reflections on Exodus* (New York: Doubleday, 2001), 24.

6. Avivah Gottlieb Zornberg, *The Particulars of Rapture: Reflections of the Exodus* (Prague: Schocken, 2011), Kindle edition, 57–58.

Chapter 5

1. *Tzava'at ha-Rivash* (sec. 133)
2. Kalonymus Kalman Shapira, *Conscious Community: A Guide to Inner Work* (Northvale, NJ: Jason Aronson, 1999), 65–66.
3. Rabbi Abraham Isaac Hakohen Kook, *Orot* (Jerusalem: 1950), 80; *Orot: The Original 1920 Version*, translated by Bezalel Naor (Spring Valley, NY: Orot, 2004), 189.
4. Pirke Avot 2:6.
5. Talmud, Eruvin 13b.
6. Lawrence A. Hoffman, *Rethinking Synagogues: A New Vocabulary for Congregational Life* (Woodstock, VT: Jewish Lights, 2006), 46.

Chapter 6

1. Midrash, Leviticus Rabbah 2:9.
2. Midrash, Avot D'Rabbi Natan, chap. 12.
3. Pesachim 87b.

Chapter 7

1. Talmud, Ta'anit 23a.
2. Avot D'Rabbi Natan, 31b.
3. Dan Senor and Saul Singer, *Start-Up Nation: The Story of Israel's Economic Miracle* (New York: Twelve Hachette Book Group, 2011), Kindle edition, 1708.
4. Talmud, Berakhot 34b.
5. Wikipedia: http://en.wikipedia.org/wiki/Ant_mill.
6. Randy Alcorn, *Heaven.* (Carol Stream, IL: Tyndale House Publishers, Inc., 2004).
7. http://www.mahal-idf-volunteers.org/index.html (accessed April 17, 2012).
8. Talmud, Sanhedrin 17a.

Chapter 8

1. Jerusalem Talmud, Yevamot 1:6.
2. For more information, visit http://www.mayyimhayyim.org/.
3. Pirke Avot 3:21.

Conclusion

1. Rabindranath Tagore, *Fruit Gathering.* (New York: The Macmillian Company, 1916).
2. Talmud, Kiddushin 30a.
3. Simcha Raz, *The Sayings of Menahem Mendel of Kotzk.* (New York: Jason Aronson, Inc., 1995): 94.
4. Theodor Herzl speaking at the Second Zionist Congress in Basel, Switzerland, on August 28, 1898.

Suggestions for Further Reading

Aron, Isa. *Becoming a Congregation of Learners: Learning as a Key to Revitalizing Congregational Life*. Woodstock, VT: Jewish Lights Publishing, 2000.

————. *The Self-Renewing Congregation: Organizational Strategies for Revitalizing Congregational Life*. Woodstock, VT: Jewish Lights Publishing, 2002.

Aron, Isa, Steven M. Cohen, Lawrence A. Hoffman, and Ari Y. Kelman. *Sacred Strategies: Transforming Synagogues from Functional to Visionary*. Hendon, VA: Alban Institute, 2010.

Brown, Erica. *Spiritual Boredom: Rediscovering the Wonder of Judaism*. Woodstock, VT: Jewish Lights Publishing, 2009.

Collins, Jim. *Good to Great: Why Some Companies Make the Leap ... and Others Don't*. New York: HarperBusiness, 2001.

Godin, Seth. *Purple Cow: Transform Your Business by Being Remarkable*, new edition. New York: Portfolio, 2009.

Green, Arthur. *Radical Judaism: Rethinking God and Tradition*. New Haven, CT: Yale University Press, 2010.

Hoffman, Lawrence A. *Rethinking Synagogues: A New Vocabulary for Congregational Life*. Woodstock, VT: Jewish Lights Publishing, 2006.

Kamenetz, Rodger. *The Jew in the Lotus: A Poet's Rediscovery of Jewish Identity in Buddhist India*. New York: HarperOne, 1994.

Kula, Irwin. *Yearnings: Embracing the Sacred Messiness of Life*. New York: Hyperion, 2006.

Michaelson, Jay. *God in Your Body: Kabbalah, Mindfulness and Embodied Spiritual Practice*. Woodstock, VT: Jewish Lights Publishing, 2007.

Schwarz, Sidney. *Finding a Spiritual Home: How a New Generation of Jews Can Transform the American Synagogue*. Hoboken, NJ: Jossey-Bass, 2000.

Senor, Dan, and Saul Singer. *Start-Up Nation: The Story of Israel's Economic Miracle*. New York: Twelve Hachette Book Group, 2009.

Teutsch, David. *Spiritual Community: The Power to Restore Hope, Commitment and Joy*. Woodstock, VT: Jewish Lights Publishing, 2005.

Wolfson, Ron. *The Spirituality of Welcoming: How to Transform Your Congregation into a Sacred Community*. Woodstock, VT: Jewish Lights Publishing, 2006.

AVAILABLE FROM BETTER BOOKSTORES.
TRY YOUR BOOKSTORE FIRST.

Bible Study/Midrash

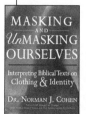

The Book of Job: Annotated & Explained
Translation and Annotation by Donald Kraus; Foreword by Dr. Marc Brettler
Clarifies for today's readers what Job is, how to overcome difficulties in the text, and what it may mean for us. Features fresh translation and probing commentary.
5½ x 8½, 256 pp, Quality PB, 978-1-59473-389-5 **$16.99**

Masking and Unmasking Ourselves: Interpreting Biblical Texts on Clothing & Identity   *By Dr. Norman J. Cohen*
Presents ten Bible stories that involve clothing in an essential way, as a means of learning about the text, its characters and their interactions.
6 x 9, 240 pp, HC, 978-1-58023-461-0 **$24.99**

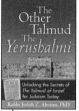

The Other Talmud—*The Yerushalmi*: Unlocking the Secrets of The Talmud of Israel for Judaism Today   *By Rabbi Judith Z. Abrams, PhD*
A fascinating—and stimulating—look at "the other Talmud" and the possibilities for Jewish life reflected there.   6 x 9, 256 pp, HC, 978-1-58023-463-4 **$24.99**

The Torah Revolution: Fourteen Truths That Changed the World
By Rabbi Reuven Hammer, PhD   A unique look at the Torah and the revolutionary teachings of Moses embedded within it that gave birth to Judaism and influenced the world.   6 x 9, 240 pp, HC, 978-1-58023-457-3 **$24.99**

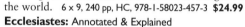

Ecclesiastes: Annotated & Explained
Translation and Annotation by Rabbi Rami Shapiro; Foreword by Rev. Barbara Cawthorne Crafton
5½ x 8½, 160 pp, Quality PB, 978-1-59473-287-4 **$16.99**

Ethics of the Sages: Pirke Avot—Annotated & Explained   *Translation and Annotation by Rabbi Rami Shapiro*   5½ x 8½, 192 pp, Quality PB, 978-1-59473-207-2 **$16.99**

The Genesis of Leadership: What the Bible Teaches Us about Vision, Values and Leading Change   *By Rabbi Nathan Laufer; Foreword by Senator Joseph I. Lieberman*
6 x 9, 288 pp, Quality PB, 978-1-58023-352-1 **$18.99**

Hineini in Our Lives: Learning How to Respond to Others through 14 Biblical Texts and Personal Stories   *By Rabbi Norman J. Cohen, PhD*   6 x 9, 240 pp, Quality PB, 978-1-58023-274-6 **$16.99**

A Man's Responsibility: A Jewish Guide to Being a Son, a Partner in Marriage, a Father and a Community Leader   *By Rabbi Joseph B. Meszler*   6 x 9, 192 pp, Quality PB, 978-1-58023-435-1 **$16.99**

The Modern Men's Torah Commentary: New Insights from Jewish Men on the 54 Weekly Torah Portions   *Edited by Rabbi Jeffrey K. Salkin*
6 x 9, 368 pp, HC, 978-1-58023-395-8 **$24.99**

Moses and the Journey to Leadership: Timeless Lessons of Effective Management from the Bible and Today's Leaders   *By Rabbi Norman J. Cohen, PhD*
6 x 9, 240 pp, Quality PB, 978-1-58023-351-4 **$18.99**; HC, 978-1-58023-227-2 **$21.99**

Proverbs: Annotated & Explained
Translation and Annotation by Rabbi Rami Shapiro
5½ x 8½, 288 pp, Quality PB, 978-1-59473-310-9 **$16.99**

Righteous Gentiles in the Hebrew Bible: Ancient Role Models for Sacred Relationships
By Rabbi Jeffrey K. Salkin; Foreword by Rabbi Harold M. Schulweis;
Preface by Phyllis Tickle   6 x 9, 192 pp, Quality PB, 978-1-58023-364-4 **$18.99**

Sage Tales: Wisdom and Wonder from the Rabbis of the Talmud
By Rabbi Burton L. Visotzky   6 x 9, 256 pp, HC, 978-1-58023-456-6 **$24.99**

The Wisdom of Judaism: An Introduction to the Values of the Talmud
By Rabbi Dov Peretz Elkins   6 x 9, 192 pp, Quality PB, 978-1-58023-327-9 **$16.99**

Or phone, fax, mail or e-mail to: **JEWISH LIGHTS Publishing**
Sunset Farm Offices, Route 4 • P.O. Box 237 • Woodstock, Vermont 05091
Tel: (802) 457-4000 • Fax: (802) 457-4004 • www.jewishlights.com
Credit card orders: **(800) 962-4544** (8:30AM–5:30PM EST Monday–Friday)
Generous discounts on quantity orders. SATISFACTION GUARANTEED. Prices subject to change.

Bar/Bat Mitzvah

The Mitzvah Project Book
Making Mitzvah Part of Your Bar/Bat Mitzvah ... and Your Life
By Liz Suneby and Diane Heiman; Foreword by Rabbi Jeffrey K. Salkin; Preface by Rabbi Sharon Brous
The go-to source for Jewish young adults and their families looking to make the
world a better place through good deeds—big or small.
6 x 9, 224 pp, Quality PB Original, 978-1-58023-458-0 **$16.99** For ages 11–13

The Bar/Bat Mitzvah Memory Book, 2nd Edition: An Album for Treasuring
the Spiritual Celebration
By Rabbi Jeffrey K. Salkin and Nina Salkin
8 x 10, 48 pp, 2-color text, Deluxe HC, ribbon marker, 978-1-58023-263-0 **$19.99**

For Kids—Putting God on Your Guest List, 2nd Edition: How to Claim the
Spiritual Meaning of Your Bar or Bat Mitzvah   *By Rabbi Jeffrey K. Salkin*
6 x 9, 144 pp, Quality PB, 978-1-58023-308-8 **$15.99** For ages 11–13

The Jewish Prophet: Visionary Words from Moses and Miriam to Henrietta Szold
and A. J. Heschel   *By Rabbi Dr. Michael J. Shire*
6½ x 8½, 128 pp, 123 full-color illus., HC, 978-1-58023-168-8 **$14.95**

Putting God on the Guest List, 3rd Edition: How to Reclaim the Spiritual
Meaning of Your Child's Bar or Bat Mitzvah   *By Rabbi Jeffrey K. Salkin*
6 x 9, 224 pp, Quality PB, 978-1-58023-222-7 **$16.99**; HC, 978-1-58023-260-9 **$24.99**

Putting God on the Guest List Teacher's Guide
8½ x 11, 48 pp, PB, 978-1-58023-226-5 **$8.99**

Teens / Young Adults

Text Messages: A Torah Commentary for Teens
Edited by Rabbi Jeffrey K. Salkin
Shows today's teens how each Torah portion contains worlds of meaning for
them, for what they are going through in their lives, and how they can shape their
Jewish identity as they enter adulthood.
6 x 9, 304 pp (est), HC, 978-1-58023-507-5 **$24.99**

Hannah Senesh: Her Life and Diary, the First Complete Edition
By Hannah Senesh; Foreword by Marge Piercy; Preface by Eitan Senesh; Afterword by Roberta Grossman
6 x 9, 368 pp, b/w photos, Quality PB, 978-1-58023-342-2 **$19.99**

I Am Jewish: Personal Reflections Inspired by the Last Words of Daniel Pearl
Edited by Judea and Ruth Pearl   6 x 9, 304 pp, Deluxe PB w/ flaps, 978-1-58023-259-3 $18.99
Download a free copy of the *I Am Jewish Teacher's Guide* at www.jewishlights.com.

The JGirl's Guide: The Young Jewish Woman's Handbook for Coming of Age
By Penina Adelman, Ali Feldman and Shulamit Reinharz
6 x 9, 240 pp, Quality PB, 978-1-58023-215-9 **$14.99** For ages 11 & up

The JGirl's Teacher's and Parent's Guide
8½ x 11, 56 pp, PB, 978-1-58023-225-8 **$8.99**

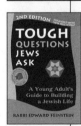

Tough Questions Jews Ask, 2nd Edition: A Young Adult's Guide to Building a
Jewish Life   *By Rabbi Edward Feinstein*
6 x 9, 160 pp, Quality PB, 978-1-58023-454-2 **$16.99** For ages 11 & up

Tough Questions Jews Ask Teacher's Guide
8½ x 11, 72 pp, PB, 978-1-58023-187-9 **$8.95**

Pre-Teens

Be Like God: God's To-Do List for Kids
By Dr. Ron Wolfson
Encourages kids ages eight through twelve to use their God-given superpowers
to find the many ways they can make a difference in the lives of others and find
meaning and purpose for their own.
7 x 9, 144 pp, Quality PB, 978-1-58023-510-5 **$15.99** For ages 8–12

The Book of Miracles: A Young Person's Guide to Jewish Spiritual Awareness
By Lawrence Kushner, with all-new illustrations by the author.
6 x 9, 96 pp, 2-color illus., HC, 978-1-879045-78-1 **$16.95** For ages 9–13

Congregation Resources

A Practical Guide to Rabbinic Counseling
Edited by Rabbi Yisrael N. Levitz, PhD, and Rabbi Abraham J. Twerski, MD
Provides rabbis with the requisite knowledge and practical guidelines for some of the most common counseling situations.
6 x 9, 432 pp, HC, 978-1-58023-562-4 **$40.00**

Professional Spiritual & Pastoral Care: A Practical Clergy and Chaplain's Handbook
Edited by Rabbi Stephen B. Roberts, MBA, MHL, BCJC
An essential resource integrating the classic foundations of pastoral care with the latest approaches to spiritual care, specifically intended for professionals who work or spend time with congregants in acute care hospitals, behavioral health facilities, rehabilitation centers and long-term care facilities.
6 x 9, 480 pp, HC, 978-1-59473-312-3 **$50.00**

Reimagining Leadership in Jewish Organizations: Ten Practical Lessons to Help You Implement Change and Achieve Your Goals
By Dr. Misha Galperin
Serves as a practical guidepost for lay and professional leaders to evaluate the current paradigm with insights from the world of business, psychology and research in Jewish demographics and sociology. Supported by vignettes from the field that illustrate the successes of the lessons as well as the consequences of not implementing them.
6 x 9, 192 pp, Quality PB, 978-1-58023-492-4 **$16.99**

Empowered Judaism: What Independent Minyanim Can Teach Us about Building Vibrant Jewish Communities
By Rabbi Elie Kaunfer; Foreword by Prof. Jonathan D. Sarna
6 x 9, 224 pp, Quality PB, 978-1-58023-412-2 **$18.99**

Building a Successful Volunteer Culture: Finding Meaning in Service in the Jewish Community
By Rabbi Charles Simon; Foreword by Shelley Lindauer; Preface by Dr. Ron Wolfson
6 x 9, 192 pp, Quality PB, 978-1-58023-408-5 **$16.99**

The Case for Jewish Peoplehood: Can We Be One?
By Dr. Erica Brown and Dr. Misha Galperin; Foreword by Rabbi Joseph Telushkin
6 x 9, 224 pp, HC, 978-1-58023-401-6 **$21.99**

Finding a Spiritual Home: How a New Generation of Jews Can Transform the American Synagogue
By Rabbi Sidney Schwarz
6 x 9, 352 pp, Quality PB, 978-1-58023-185-5 **$19.95**

Inspired Jewish Leadership: Practical Approaches to Building Strong Communities
By Dr. Erica Brown 6 x 9, 256 pp, HC, 978-1-58023-361-3 **$27.99**

Jewish Pastoral Care, 2nd Edition: A Practical Handbook from Traditional & Contemporary Sources
Edited by Rabbi Dayle A. Friedman, MSW, MAJCS, BCC
6 x 9, 528 pp, Quality PB, 978-1-58023-427-6 **$30.00**

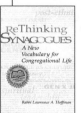

Jewish Spiritual Direction: An Innovative Guide from Traditional and Contemporary Sources
Edited by Rabbi Howard A. Addison, PhD, and Barbara Eve Breitman, MSW
6 x 9, 368 pp, HC, 978-1-58023-230-2 **$30.00**

Rethinking Synagogues: A New Vocabulary for Congregational Life
By Rabbi Lawrence A. Hoffman, PhD 6 x 9, 240 pp, Quality PB, 978-1-58023-248-7 **$19.99**

Spiritual Community: The Power to Restore Hope, Commitment and Joy
By Rabbi David A. Teutsch, PhD
5½ x 8½, 144 pp, HC, 978-1-58023-270-8 **$19.99**

Spiritual Boredom: Rediscovering the Wonder of Judaism *By Dr. Erica Brown*
6 x 9, 208 pp, HC, 978-1-58023-405-4 **$21.99**

The Spirituality of Welcoming: How to Transform Your Congregation into a Sacred Community
By Dr. Ron Wolfson 6 x 9, 224 pp, Quality PB, 978-1-58023-244-9 **$19.99**

Holidays/Holy Days

Prayers of Awe Series

An exciting new series that examines the High Holy Day liturgy to enrich the praying experience of everyone—whether experienced worshipers or guests who encounter Jewish prayer for the very first time.

We Have Sinned—Sin and Confession in Judaism: *Ashamnu* and *Al Chet*
Edited by Rabbi Lawrence A. Hoffman, PhD
A varied and fascinating look at sin, confession and pardon in Judaism, as suggested by the centrality of *Ashamnu* and *Al Chet*, two prayers that people know so well, though understand so little.   6 x 9, 304 pp, HC, 978-1-58023-612-6 **$24.99**

Who by Fire, Who by Water—*Un'taneh Tokef*
Edited by Rabbi Lawrence A. Hoffman, PhD   6 x 9, 272 pp, HC, 978-1-58023-424-5 **$24.99**

All These Vows—*Kol Nidre*
Edited by Rabbi Lawrence A. Hoffman, PhD   6 x 9, 288 pp, HC, 978-1-58023-430-6 **$24.99**

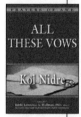

Rosh Hashanah Readings: Inspiration, Information and Contemplation
Yom Kippur Readings: Inspiration, Information and Contemplation
Edited by Rabbi Dov Peretz Elkins; Section Introductions from Arthur Green's These Are the Words
Rosh Hashanah: 6 x 9, 400 pp, Quality PB, 978-1-58023-437-5 **$19.99**
Yom Kippur: 6 x 9, 368 pp, Quality PB, 978-1-58023-438-2 **$19.99**; HC, 978-1-58023-271-5 **$24.99**

Reclaiming Judaism as a Spiritual Practice: Holy Days and Shabbat
By Rabbi Goldie Milgram   7 x 9, 272 pp, Quality PB, 978-1-58023-205-0 **$19.99**

The Sabbath Soul: Mystical Reflections on the Transformative Power of Holy Time
Selection, Translation and Commentary by Eitan Fishbane, PhD
6 x 9, 208 pp, Quality PB, 978-1-58023-459-7 **$18.99**

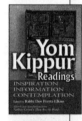

Shabbat, 2nd Edition: The Family Guide to Preparing for and Celebrating the Sabbath
By Dr. Ron Wolfson   7 x 9, 320 pp, Illus., Quality PB, 978-1-58023-164-0 **$19.99**

Hanukkah, 2nd Edition: The Family Guide to Spiritual Celebration
By Dr. Ron Wolfson   7 x 9, 240 pp, Illus., Quality PB, 978-1-58023-122-0 **$18.95**

Passover

My People's Passover Haggadah

Traditional Texts, Modern Commentaries
Edited by Rabbi Lawrence A. Hoffman, PhD, and David Arnow, PhD
A diverse and exciting collection of commentaries on the traditional Passover Haggadah—in two volumes!
Vol. 1: 7 x 10, 304 pp, HC, 978-1-58023-354-5 **$24.99**
Vol. 2: 7 x 10, 320 pp, HC, 978-1-58023-346-0 **$24.99**

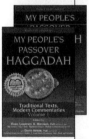

Freedom Journeys: The Tale of Exodus and Wilderness across Millennia
By Rabbi Arthur O. Waskow and Rabbi Phyllis O. Berman
Explores how the story of Exodus echoes in our own time, calling us to relearn and rethink the Passover story through social-justice, ecological, feminist and interfaith perspectives.   6 x 9, 288 pp, HC, 978-1-58023-445-0 **$24.99**

Leading the Passover Journey: The Seder's Meaning Revealed,
the Haggadah's Story Retold   *By Rabbi Nathan Laufer*
Uncovers the hidden meaning of the Seder's rituals and customs.
6 x 9, 224 pp, Quality PB, 978-1-58023-399-6 **$18.99**

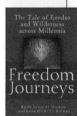

Creating Lively Passover Seders, 2nd Edition: A Sourcebook of Engaging Tales,
Texts & Activities   *By David Arnow, PhD*   7 x 9, 464 pp, Quality PB, 978-1-58023-444-3 **$24.99**

Passover, 2nd Edition: The Family Guide to Spiritual Celebration
By Dr. Ron Wolfson with Joel Lurie Grishaver   7 x 9, 416 pp, Quality PB, 978-1-58023-174-9 **$19.95**

The Women's Passover Companion: Women's Reflections on the Festival of Freedom
Edited by Rabbi Sharon Cohen Anisfeld, Tara Mohr and Catherine Spector; Foreword by Paula E. Hyman
6 x 9, 352 pp, Quality PB, 978-1-58023-231-9 **$19.99**; HC, 978-1-58023-128-2 **$24.95**

The Women's Seder Sourcebook: Rituals & Readings for Use at the Passover Seder
Edited by Rabbi Sharon Cohen Anisfeld, Tara Mohr and Catherine Spector
6 x 9, 384 pp, Quality PB, 978-1-58023-232-6 **$19.99**

Inspiration

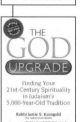

God of Me: Imagining God throughout Your Lifetime
By Rabbi David Lyon Helps you cut through preconceived ideas of God and dogmas that stifle your creativity when thinking about your personal relationship with God. 6 x 9, 176 pp, Quality PB, 978-1-58023-452-8 **$16.99**

The God Upgrade: Finding Your 21st-Century Spirituality in Judaism's 5,000-Year-Old Tradition *By Rabbi Jamie Korngold; Foreword by Rabbi Harold M. Schulweis* A provocative look at how our changing God concepts have shaped every aspect of Judaism. 6 x 9, 176 pp, Quality PB, 978-1-58023-443-6 **$15.99**

The Seven Questions You're Asked in Heaven: Reviewing and Renewing Your Life on Earth *By Dr. Ron Wolfson* An intriguing and entertaining resource for living a life that matters. 6 x 9, 176 pp, Quality PB, 978-1-58023-407-8 **$16.99**

Happiness and the Human Spirit: The Spirituality of Becoming the Best You Can Be *By Rabbi Abraham J. Twerski, MD*
Shows you that true happiness is attainable once you stop looking outside yourself for the source. 6 x 9, 176 pp, Quality PB, 978-1-58023-404-7 **$16.99**; HC, 978-1-58023-343-9 **$19.99**

A Formula for Proper Living: Practical Lessons from Life and Torah
By Rabbi Abraham J. Twerski, MD 6 x 9, 144 pp, HC, 978-1-58023-402-3 **$19.99**

The Bridge to Forgiveness: Stories and Prayers for Finding God and Restoring Wholeness *By Rabbi Karyn D. Kedar* 6 x 9, 176 pp, Quality PB, 978-1-58023-451-1 **$16.99**

The Empty Chair: Finding Hope and Joy—Timeless Wisdom from a Hasidic Master, Rebbe Nachman of Breslov *Adapted by Moshe Mykoff and the Breslov Research Institute* 4 x 6, 128 pp, Deluxe PB w/ flaps, 978-1-879045-67-5 **$9.99**

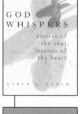

The Gentle Weapon: Prayers for Everyday and Not-So-Everyday Moments— Timeless Wisdom from the Teachings of the Hasidic Master, Rebbe Nachman of Breslov *Adapted by Moshe Mykoff and S. C. Mizrahi, together with the Breslov Research Institute* 4 x 6, 144 pp, Deluxe PB w/ flaps, 978-1-58023-022-3 **$9.99**

God Whispers: Stories of the Soul, Lessons of the Heart *By Rabbi Karyn D. Kedar* 6 x 9, 176 pp, Quality PB, 978-1-58023-088-9 **$15.95**

God's To-Do List: 103 Ways to Be an Angel and Do God's Work on Earth *By Dr. Ron Wolfson* 6 x 9, 144 pp, Quality PB, 978-1-58023-301-9 **$16.99**

Jewish Stories from Heaven and Earth: Inspiring Tales to Nourish the Heart and Soul *Edited by Rabbi Dov Peretz Elkins* 6 x 9, 304 pp, Quality PB, 978-1-58023-363-7 **$16.99**

Life's Daily Blessings: Inspiring Reflections on Gratitude and Joy for Every Day, Based on Jewish Wisdom *By Rabbi Kerry M. Olitzky* 4½ x 6½, 368 pp, Quality PB, 978-1-58023-396-5 **$16.99**

Restful Reflections: Nighttime Inspiration to Calm the Soul, Based on Jewish Wisdom *By Rabbi Kerry M. Olitzky and Rabbi Lori Forman-Jacobi* 5 x 8, 352 pp, Quality PB, 978-1-58023-091-9 **$16.99**

Sacred Intentions: Morning Inspiration to Strengthen the Spirit, Based on Jewish Wisdom *By Rabbi Kerry M. Olitzky and Rabbi Lori Forman-Jacobi* 4½ x 6½, 448 pp, Quality PB, 978-1-58023-061-2 **$16.99**

Kabbalah/Mysticism

Jewish Mysticism and the Spiritual Life: Classical Texts, Contemporary Reflections *Edited by Dr. Lawrence Fine, Dr. Eitan Fishbane and Rabbi Or N. Rose* Inspirational and thought-provoking materials for contemplation, discussion and action. 6 x 9, 256 pp, HC, 978-1-58023-434-4 **$24.99**

Ehyeh: A Kabbalah for Tomorrow
By Rabbi Arthur Green, PhD 6 x 9, 224 pp, Quality PB, 978-1-58023-213-5 **$18.99**

The Gift of Kabbalah: Discovering the Secrets of Heaven, Renewing Your Life on Earth
By Tamar Frankiel, PhD 6 x 9, 256 pp, Quality PB, 978-1-58023-141-1 **$16.95**

Seek My Face: A Jewish Mystical Theology *By Rabbi Arthur Green, PhD*
6 x 9, 304 pp, Quality PB, 978-1-58023-130-5 **$19.95**

Zohar: Annotated & Explained *Translation & Annotation by Dr. Daniel C. Matt; Foreword by Andrew Harvey* 5½ x 8½, 176 pp, Quality PB, 978-1-893361-51-5 **$15.99**
(A book from SkyLight Paths, Jewish Lights' sister imprint)

See also *The Way Into Jewish Mystical Tradition* in The Way Into... Series.

Spirituality

The Jewish Lights Spirituality Handbook: A Guide to Understanding, Exploring & Living a Spiritual Life *Edited by Stuart M. Matlins*
What exactly is "Jewish" about spirituality? How do I make it a part of my life? Fifty of today's foremost spiritual leaders share their ideas and experience with us.
6 x 9, 456 pp, Quality PB, 978-1-58023-093-3 **$19.99**

The Sabbath Soul: Mystical Reflections on the Transformative Power of Holy Time *Selection, Translation and Commentary by Eitan Fishbane, PhD*
Explores the writings of mystical masters of Hasidism. Provides translations and interpretations of a wide range of Hasidic sources previously unavailable in English that reflect the spiritual transformation that takes place on the seventh day.
6 x 9, 208 pp, Quality PB, 978-1-58023-459-7 **$18.99**

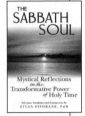

Repentance: The Meaning and Practice of *Teshuvah*
By Dr. Louis E. Newman; Foreword by Rabbi Harold M. Schulweis; Preface by Rabbi Karyn D. Kedar
Examines both the practical and philosophical dimensions of *teshuvah*, Judaism's core religious-moral teaching on repentance, and its value for us—Jews and non-Jews alike—today. 6 x 9, 256 pp, HC, 978-1-58023-426-9 **$24.99**

Aleph-Bet Yoga: Embodying the Hebrew Letters for Physical and Spiritual Well-Being
By Steven A. Rapp; Foreword by Tamar Frankiel, PhD, and Judy Greenfeld; Preface by Hart Lazer
7 x 10, 128 pp, b/w photos, Quality PB, Lay-flat binding, 978-1-58023-162-6 **$16.95**

A Book of Life: Embracing Judaism as a Spiritual Practice
By Rabbi Michael Strassfeld 6 x 9, 544 pp, Quality PB, 978-1-58023-247-0 **$19.99**

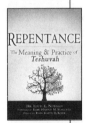

Bringing the Psalms to Life: How to Understand and Use the Book of Psalms
By Rabbi Daniel F. Polish, PhD 6 x 9, 208 pp, Quality PB, 978-1-58023-157-2 **$16.95**

Does the Soul Survive? A Jewish Journey to Belief in Afterlife, Past Lives & Living with Purpose *By Rabbi Elie Kaplan Spitz; Foreword by Brian L. Weiss, MD*
6 x 9, 288 pp, Quality PB, 978-1-58023-165-7 **$16.99**

Entering the Temple of Dreams: Jewish Prayers, Movements and Meditations for the End of the Day *By Tamar Frankiel, PhD, and Judy Greenfeld*
7 x 10, 192 pp, illus., Quality PB, 978-1-58023-079-7 **$16.95**

First Steps to a New Jewish Spirit: Reb Zalman's Guide to Recapturing the Intimacy & Ecstasy in Your Relationship with God *By Rabbi Zalman M. Schachter-Shalomi with Donald Gropman* 6 x 9, 144 pp, Quality PB, 978-1-58023-182-4 **$16.95**

Foundations of Sephardic Spirituality: The Inner Life of Jews of the Ottoman Empire
By Rabbi Marc D. Angel 6 x 9, 224 pp, Quality PB, 978-1-58023-341-5 **$18.99**

God & the Big Bang: Discovering Harmony between Science & Spirituality
By Dr. Daniel C. Matt 6 x 9, 216 pp, Quality PB, 978-1-879045-89-7 **$18.99**

God in Our Relationships: Spirituality between People from the Teachings of Martin Buber *By Rabbi Dennis S. Ross* 5½ x 8½, 160 pp, Quality PB, 978-1-58023-147-3 **$16.95**

Judaism, Physics and God: Searching for Sacred Metaphors in a Post-Einstein World
By Rabbi David W. Nelson 6 x 9, 352 pp, Quality PB, inc. reader's discussion guide,
978-1-58023-306-4 **$18.99**; HC, 352 pp, 978-1-58023-252-4 **$24.99**

Meaning & Mitzvah: Daily Practices for Reclaiming Judaism through Prayer, God, Torah, Hebrew, Mitzvot and Peoplehood *By Rabbi Goldie Milgram*
7 x 9, 336 pp, Quality PB, 978-1-58023-256-2 **$19.99**

Minding the Temple of the Soul: Balancing Body, Mind, and Spirit through Traditional Jewish Prayer, Movement, and Meditation *By Tamar Frankiel, PhD, and Judy Greenfeld*
7 x 10, 184 pp, Illus., Quality PB, 978-1-879045-64-4 **$18.99**

One God Clapping: The Spiritual Path of a Zen Rabbi *By Rabbi Alan Lew with Sherril Jaffe*
5½ x 8½, 336 pp, Quality PB, 978-1-58023-115-2 **$16.95**

The Soul of the Story: Meetings with Remarkable People
By Rabbi David Zeller 6 x 9, 288 pp, HC, 978-1-58023-272-2 **$21.99**

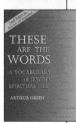

Tanya, **the Masterpiece of Hasidic Wisdom:** Selections Annotated & Explained
Translation & Annotation by Rabbi Rami Shapiro; Foreword by Rabbi Zalman M. Schachter-Shalomi
5½ x 8½, 240 pp, Quality PB, 978-1-59473-275-1 **$16.99**

These Are the Words, 2nd Edition: A Vocabulary of Jewish Spiritual Life
By Rabbi Arthur Green, PhD 6 x 9, 320 pp, Quality PB, 978-1-58023-494-8 **$19.99**

Spirituality/Prayer

Making Prayer Real: Leading Jewish Spiritual Voices on Why Prayer Is Difficult and What to Do about It *By Rabbi Mike Comins*
A new and different response to the challenges of Jewish prayer, with "best prayer practices" from Jewish spiritual leaders of all denominations.
6 x 9, 320 pp, Quality PB, 978-1-58023-417-7 **$18.99**

Witnesses to the One: The Spiritual History of the *Sh'ma*
By Rabbi Joseph B. Meszler; Foreword by Rabbi Elyse Goldstein
6 x 9, 176 pp, Quality PB, 978-1-58023-400-9 **$16.99**; HC, 978-1-58023-309-5 **$19.99**

My People's Prayer Book Series: Traditional Prayers, Modern Commentaries *Edited by Rabbi Lawrence A. Hoffman, PhD*
Provides diverse and exciting commentary to the traditional liturgy. Will help you find new wisdom in Jewish prayer, and bring liturgy into your life. Each book includes Hebrew text, modern translations and commentaries from all perspectives of the Jewish world.

Vol. 1—The *Sh'ma* and Its Blessings
   7 x 10, 168 pp, HC, 978-1-879045-79-8 **$29.99**
Vol. 2—The *Amidah* 7 x 10, 240 pp, HC, 978-1-879045-80-4 **$24.95**
Vol. 3—*P'sukei D'zimrah* (Morning Psalms)
   7 x 10, 240 pp, HC, 978-1-879045-81-1 **$29.99**
Vol. 4—*Seder K'riat Hatorah* (The Torah Service)
   7 x 10, 264 pp, HC, 978-1-879045-82-8 **$29.99**
Vol. 5—*Birkhot Hashachar* (Morning Blessings)
   7 x 10, 240 pp, HC, 978-1-879045-83-5 **$24.95**
Vol. 6—*Tachanun* and Concluding Prayers
   7 x 10, 240 pp, HC, 978-1-879045-84-2 **$24.95**
Vol. 7—Shabbat at Home 7 x 10, 240 pp, HC, 978-1-879045-85-9 **$24.95**
Vol. 8—*Kabbalat Shabbat* (Welcoming Shabbat in the Synagogue)
   7 x 10, 240 pp, HC, 978-1-58023-121-3 **$24.99**
Vol. 9—Welcoming the Night: *Minchah* and *Ma'ariv* (Afternoon and
   Evening Prayer) 7 x 10, 272 pp, HC, 978-1-58023-262-3 **$24.99**
Vol. 10—Shabbat Morning: *Shacharit* and *Musaf* (Morning and
   Additional Services) 7 x 10, 240 pp, HC, 978-1-58023-240-1 **$29.99**

Spirituality/Lawrence Kushner

I'm God; You're Not: Observations on Organized Religion & Other Disguises of the Ego
6 x 9, 256 pp, Quality PB, 978-1-58023-513-6 **$18.99**; HC, 978-1-58023-441-2 **$21.99**

The Book of Letters: A Mystical Hebrew Alphabet
Popular HC Edition, 6 x 9, 80 pp, 2-color text, 978-1-879045-00-2 **$24.95**
Collector's Limited Edition, 9 x 12, 80 pp, gold-foil-embossed pages, w/ limited-edition silkscreened print, 978-1-879045-04-0 **$349.00**

The Book of Miracles: A Young Person's Guide to Jewish Spiritual Awareness
6 x 9, 96 pp, 2-color illus., HC, 978-1-879045-78-1 **$16.95** *For ages 9–13*

The Book of Words: Talking Spiritual Life, Living Spiritual Talk
6 x 9, 160 pp, Quality PB, 978-1-58023-020-9 **$18.99**

Eyes Remade for Wonder: A Lawrence Kushner Reader *Introduction by Thomas Moore*
6 x 9, 240 pp, Quality PB, 978-1-58023-042-1 **$18.95**

God Was in This Place & I, i Did Not Know: Finding Self, Spirituality and Ultimate Meaning 6 x 9, 192 pp, Quality PB, 978-1-879045-33-0 **$16.95**

Honey from the Rock: An Introduction to Jewish Mysticism
6 x 9, 176 pp, Quality PB, 978-1-58023-073-5 **$16.95**

Invisible Lines of Connection: Sacred Stories of the Ordinary
5½ x 8½, 160 pp, Quality PB, 978-1-879045-98-9 **$15.95**

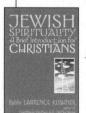

Jewish Spirituality: A Brief Introduction for Christians
5½ x 8½, 112 pp, Quality PB, 978-1-58023-150-3 **$12.95**

The River of Light: Jewish Mystical Awareness
6 x 9, 192 pp, Quality PB, 978-1-58023-096-4 **$16.95**

The Way Into Jewish Mystical Tradition
6 x 9, 224 pp, Quality PB, 978-1-58023-200-5 **$18.99**; HC, 978-1-58023-029-2 **$21.95**

Theology/Philosophy

From Defender to Critic: The Search for a New Jewish Self
By Dr. David Hartman
A daring self-examination of Hartman's goals, which were not to strip halakha of its authority but to create a space for questioning and critique that allows for the traditionally religious Jew to act out a moral life in tune with modern experience.
6 x 9, 336 pp, HC, 978-1-58023-515-0 **$35.00**

Our Religious Brains: What Cognitive Science Reveals about Belief, Morality, Community and Our Relationship with God
By Rabbi Ralph D. Mecklenburger; Foreword by Dr. Howard Kelfer; Preface by Dr. Neil Gillman
This is a groundbreaking, accessible look at the implications of cognitive science for religion and theology, intended for laypeople. 6 x 9, 224 pp, HC, 978-1-58023-508-2 **$24.99**

The Other Talmud—*The Yerushalmi*: Unlocking the Secrets of The Talmud of Israel for Judaism Today *By Rabbi Judith Z. Abrams, PhD*
A fascinating—and stimulating—look at "the other Talmud" and the possibilities for Jewish life reflected there. 6 x 9, 256 pp, HC, 978-1-58023-463-4 **$24.99**

The Way of Man: According to Hasidic Teaching
By Martin Buber; New Translation and Introduction by Rabbi Bernard H. Mehlman and Dr. Gabriel E. Padawer; Foreword by Paul Mendes-Flohr
An accessible and engaging new translation of Buber's classic work—available as an e-book only. E-book, 978-1-58023-601-0 Digital List Price **$14.99**

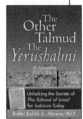

The Death of Death: Resurrection and Immortality in Jewish Thought
By Rabbi Neil Gillman, PhD 6 x 9, 336 pp, Quality PB, 978-1-58023-081-0 **$18.95**

Doing Jewish Theology: God, Torah & Israel in Modern Judaism *By Rabbi Neil Gillman, PhD*
6 x 9, 304 pp, Quality PB, 978-1-58023-439-9 **$18.99**; HC, 978-1-58023-322-4 **$24.99**

A Heart of Many Rooms: Celebrating the Many Voices within Judaism
By Dr. David Hartman 6 x 9, 352 pp, Quality PB, 978-1-58023-156-5 **$19.95**

The God Who Hates Lies: Confronting & Rethinking Jewish Tradition
By Dr. David Hartman with Charlie Buckholtz 6 x 9, 208 pp, HC, 978-1-58023-455-9 **$24.99**

Jewish Theology in Our Time: A New Generation Explores the Foundations and Future of Jewish Belief *Edited by Rabbi Elliot J. Cosgrove, PhD; Foreword by Rabbi David J. Wolpe; Preface by Rabbi Carole B. Balin, PhD* 6 x 9, 240 pp, HC, 978-1-58023-413-9 **$24.99**

Maimonides—Essential Teachings on Jewish Faith & Ethics: The Book of Knowledge & the Thirteen Principles of Faith—Annotated & Explained
Translation and Annotation by Rabbi Marc D. Angel, PhD
5½ x 8½, 224 pp, Quality PB Original, 978-1-59473-311-6 **$18.99***

Maimonides, Spinoza and Us: Toward an Intellectually Vibrant Judaism
By Rabbi Marc D. Angel, PhD 6 x 9, 224 pp, HC, 978-1-58023-411-5 **$24.99**

A Touch of the Sacred: A Theologian's Informal Guide to Jewish Belief
By Dr. Eugene B. Borowitz and Frances W. Schwartz
6 x 9, 256 pp, Quality PB, 978-1-58023-416-0 **$16.99**; HC, 978-1-58023-337-8 **$21.99**

Traces of God: Seeing God in Torah, History and Everyday Life *By Rabbi Neil Gillman, PhD*
6 x 9, 240 pp, Quality PB, 978-1-58023-369-9 **$16.99**

Your Word Is Fire: The Hasidic Masters on Contemplative Prayer
Edited and translated by Rabbi Arthur Green, PhD, and Barry W. Holtz
6 x 9, 160 pp, Quality PB, 978-1-879045-25-5 **$15.95**

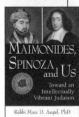

I Am Jewish
Personal Reflections Inspired by the Last Words of Daniel Pearl
Almost 150 Jews—both famous and not—from all walks of life, from all around the world, write about many aspects of their Judaism.
Edited by Judea and Ruth Pearl 6 x 9, 304 pp, Deluxe PB w/ flaps, 978-1-58023-259-3 **$18.99**
Download a free copy of the *I Am Jewish Teacher's Guide* at www.jewishlights.com.

Hannah Senesh: Her Life and Diary, The First Complete Edition
By Hannah Senesh; Foreword by Marge Piercy; Preface by Eitan Senesh; Afterword by Roberta Grossman
6 x 9, 368 pp, b/w photos, Quality PB, 978-1-58023-342-2 **$19.99**

*A book from SkyLight Paths, Jewish Lights' sister imprint

JEWISH LIGHTS BOOKS ARE AVAILABLE FROM BETTER BOOKSTORES. TRY YOUR BOOKSTORE FIRST.

About Jewish Lights

People of all faiths and backgrounds yearn for books that attract, engage, educate, and spiritually inspire.

Our principal goal is to stimulate thought and help all people learn about who the Jewish People are, where they come from, and what the future can be made to hold. While people of our diverse Jewish heritage are the primary audience, our books speak to people in the Christian world as well and will broaden their understanding of Judaism and the roots of their own faith.

We bring to you authors who are at the forefront of spiritual thought and experience. While each has something different to say, they all say it in a voice that you can hear.

Our books are designed to welcome you and then to engage, stimulate, and inspire. We judge our success not only by whether or not our books are beautiful and commercially successful, but by whether or not they make a difference in your life.

For your information and convenience, at the back of this book we have provided a list of other Jewish Lights books you might find interesting and useful. They cover all the categories of your life:

Bar/Bat Mitzvah	Life Cycle
Bible Study / Midrash	Meditation
Children's Books	Men's Interest
Congregation Resources	Parenting
Current Events / History	Prayer / Ritual / Sacred Practice
Ecology / Environment	Social Justice
Fiction: Mystery, Science Fiction	Spirituality
Grief / Healing	Theology / Philosophy
Holidays / Holy Days	Travel
Inspiration	Twelve Steps
Kabbalah / Mysticism / Enneagram	Women's Interest

Stuart M. Matlins, Publisher

Or phone, fax, mail or e-mail to: **JEWISH LIGHTS Publishing**
Sunset Farm Offices, Route 4 • P.O. Box 237 • Woodstock, Vermont 05091
Tel: (802) 457-4000 • Fax: (802) 457-4004 • www.jewishlights.com
Credit card orders: (800) 962-4544 (8:30AM–5:30PM EST Monday–Friday)
Generous discounts on quantity orders. SATISFACTION GUARANTEED. Prices subject to change.

For more information about each book, visit our website at www.jewishlights.com